324.973
Kaplan
FEB 0 7 2002

DATE

FEB 2 2 2002
APR 0 5 2002

APR 2 2 2002
4:26-02

MAY 0 4 2002
MAY 2 8 2002
JUN 2 4 2002

JUL 0 5 2002

GAYLORD No. 2333

WITHDRAWN

D1020267

PARK COUNTY LIBRARY
1057 SHERIDAN AVE.
CODY, WYOMING 82414

The Accidental President

Also by David A. Kaplan

THE SILICON BOYS

The Accidental President

HOW 413 LAWYERS, 9 SUPREME

COURT JUSTICES, AND 5,963,110

(GIVE OR TAKE A FEW)

FLORIDIANS LANDED

GEORGE W. BUSH IN THE WHITE HOUSE

David A. Kaplan

WILLIAM MORROW
An Imprint of HarperCollins*Publishers*

PARK COUNTY LIBRARY, CODY, WYOMING

THE ACCIDENTAL PRESIDENT. Copyright © 2001 by
David A. Kaplan. All rights reserved. Printed in the United States
of America. No part of this book may be used or reproduced in any
manner whatsoever without written permission except in the case
of brief quotations embodied in critical articles and reviews. For
information address HarperCollins Publishers Inc.,
10 East 53rd Street, New York, NY 10022.

HarperCollins books may be purchased for educational, business, or
sales promotional use. For information please write: Special Markets
Department, HarperCollins Publishers Inc., 10 East 53rd Street,
New York, NY 10022.

FIRST EDITION

Book design by Nicola Ferguson

Printed on acid-free paper

Library of Congress Cataloging-in-Publication Data
has been applied for.

ISBN 0-06-621283-9

01 02 03 04 05 RRD 10 9 8 7 6 5 4 3 2

For Joshua and Nathaniel

The Chapter of Accidents is the longest chapter in the book.

—Attributed to John Wilkes
by Robert Southey, *The Doctor* (1837–1847), chapter 118

contents

The Accidental President

37 Days

There's *bizarre, there's* weird, and then there's Florida. Where else could you have the Fisherman in the Closet and the Secretary of State with Those Eyelashes? Who else could *invent* these characters, Donato Dalrymple and Katherine Harris . . . in the same year? Inner tubes and dimpled chads entered the lexicon just because of Florida. In the good old days, Nixon used to vacation there.

Some years back, the state adopted a new tourism slogan—"Florida: The Rules Are Different Here!" Well, yes. The beaches, the palm trees, and the steamy sunshine. The Haitian refugees, the Jewish retirees, the native-born whites and blacks. Climate, topography, and demographics; hurricanes, wildfires, and man-eating alligators; and, of course, "Old Sparky," the only malfunctioning electric chair in the nation (but it was for convicted murderers, so-what-exactly-was-the-big-deal?). Such were the state's charms, and you couldn't find anything like them anywhere else in America—not in California or Texas and definitely not in Des Moines. The rules *were* different here! And perhaps the phrase would've stuck around longer, if only Florida hadn't become known everywhere not for Mickey, but as the one vacation destination where they yanked tourists out of their Avis cars and shot them in the head.

Still, the motto's perfect anyway. In the early part of 2000, we had the ridiculous saga of Elián Gonzalez, played as a pawn by Cuban-American extremists, Washington politicians, Fidel Castro, and the media, as well as by Dalrymple himself ("El Pescador," who saved Elián at sea and, later, from a closet in Elián's bedroom, watched the FBI raid). Cherubic little boys can't be rescued off the coast of Iowa, and even if they could, the show wouldn't be quite the same. When the curtain finally came down on week after week of Elián, who knew it would be merely the first bookend to the strangest year in a strange state's history?

And then came the other half of the circus—deciding the presidential election of 2000 between George W. Bush and Albert Gore Jr. The campaign leading up to Election Day may have been the dullest, most witless in ages. But it was nothing more than prelude. The real drama and consequence unfolded on the evening of November 7 and during the five weeks that followed.

Where were *you* on that surreal Election Night? How late did you stay up, how many times did the network chowderheads convince you they had it right when they had it wrong? Five and fifty years from now, your kids or grandchildren will ask, "Just what was it like back in 2000 when the nation couldn't seem to pick a president?"

There are few moments like it—when we share a consciousness of important events, often guided along, for better and for worse, by television. JFK's assassination, Nixon's resignation, the night John Lennon died, the explosion of the *Challenger*—they are the collective memories of a generation, snapshots of history we all clicked in our minds. (According to the *New York Times*, Manhattan psychiatrists found that the election ranked up there with JFK and *Challenger* for entering their patients' dreams.) But there's more to this moment than sentiment or surprise, or even enjoyment over the seriocomic proceedings, though the farce was delicious at times.

The improbability of the plots and the performers in Recount 2000 would have challenged Shakespeare—or Bill Murray in *Groundhog Day*. But it's one thing to relive the same day over and over with Andie MacDowell, quite another to listen to Jim Baker or Bill Daley each night disingenuously explaining that *he just wants the voice of the voter to be heard*. Gore scores victory! Bush strikes back! Hardball, Indecision 2000, History on Hold! The recounting in one county resumes, stops, resumes again! We've got the country's leading expert on pregnant chads on the satellite live from the courthouse steps—right after traffic-and-weather! Can you believe what Katherine Harris is wearing today? "The Grinch Who Stole the Election!" "Sore-Loserman!" An omnivorous MSNBC and CNN had all the details. Perhaps the only thing crazier would've been watching an electoral tie in New Mexico get broken. State law there provides for a poker game or coin toss to determine the winner. (That nasty British nanny on *The Weakest Link* could host it. "Good-bye!")

But apart from being unforgettable theater—the evening news hadn't been so riveting since the Watergate Summer of '73—the great recount battle of Florida represents an extraordinary instant in American political history. Rarely have essential constitutional, legal, and cultural issues been channeled into a single public controversy so compressed in time. What is a vote? Who decides? And who decides who decides? Are elections purely about winning, or does the process matter? How can we believe that "every vote counts" if all votes aren't counted? What's the proper delineation between federal and state power? Do racial considerations color how elections are conducted, just as they do in so many other areas of public policy? Are judges special actors in the system of government, obliged to follow certain neutral principles, including staying out of conflicts that nonetheless seem to cry out for intervention—or are the men-in-robes simply agents of realpolitik by any other name? Is the sacred precinct we call the U.S. Supreme Court merely a superlegislature of nine imperious partisans? For all the combatants, does the rule of law mean only trying to figure out a way *around* it? Have law and politics become so entangled in this country—Bill Clinton's presidential impeachment in 1998 represented their ultimate union—that we no longer can distinguish one from the other? Rarely do we get to look down these dark rabbit holes of democracy.

Surely these issues go to the heart of what we expect from imperfect elections and their various participants—candidates, vote counters, party operatives, the punditocracy. Politics is messy, but we've always imagined our elections to be pristine. Yet in a larger sense, the questions also ask what we demand of our political and judicial institutions—the promise of the nation rests not on who's president in any given four-year period, but on the vitality and legitimacy of the system in which he operates. What we got from the system in 2000, when we peered through the looking glass, was not inspiring.

Good stories often have heroes, and it's true that some of the characters in this melodrama behaved well. But like a large family on a small boat after a long cruise, no one came off looking particularly good. The only possible exceptions were David Letterman and Jay Leno, who reaped endless material and found themselves featured on C-SPAN—here was the final blurring of entertainment and news. Their TV running mates in the news divisions—the commentators, the prognosticators, and the analysts who evaluated legal opinions on the air live without having finished reading them—weren't as funny and sometimes had less to say.

Our institutions, too, were sullied. Though the Republic was never at risk—there wasn't rioting in the streets, nor did anyone have to call out the militia—the presidency, the Supreme Court, and the stand-on-the-sidelines Congress hardly earned any bonus points. Most of us were content to wait and see who won, but this wasn't so much because we trusted our institutions as it was because we probably didn't especially care one way or the other. If the stock of any group improved, it was the legal profession's: Most lawyers acted intelligently and civilly, a far cry from what people expected of them after O.J., though, as the late baseball commissioner Bart Giamatti liked to say, you could use a higher standard. (Simpson, of course, moved to Florida after his acquittal; he loves the golf.)

Good stories also have villains—the folks we can root against—but there weren't a lot of them either. Venality didn't win this battle for Bush, and stupidity didn't lose it for Gore. No, the outcome of Election 2000 had more to do with fortuity than anything else. This was an election gone bad, made worse by an almost inconceivable convergence of accidents, akin to a once-in-a-century perfect political storm: a vote that was basically a tie, both in the Electoral College and the actual number of ballots cast for each side; a state where the count was closer than any other—where the margin of victory was one-tenth of one-tenth of one-tenth of 1 percent of the one hundred million votes cast nationwide; TV coverage that got the results wrong *twice;* and a contest in which the eventual winner got the presidency because of an Electoral College majority despite losing the popular vote, the first president to do so since 1888, thereby earning the modern political equivalent of Roger Maris's infamous home-run asterisk. And there was more weirdness: Florida was a state that only a Jewish grandmother could love; a state that many foreign visitors equated with America unless they passed through Times Square or Knotts Berry Farm; a state that's managed to have enough conspiracies and mysteries to keep writers like Carl Hiaasen and Edna Buchanan busy for years, writing sentences longer than this one. A columnist for one Florida newspaper got it about right when he observed: "We were the heels, the electoral Bill Buckners, who let the easy grounder go between our legs, turning a routine task into a disaster."

A lucky tactical call here, a confusing ballot there, a state where it so happened that the Republican candidate's kid brother is governor, a state that permits absentee ballots from overseas to arrive up to ten days *past* Election Day so that unscrupulous types can vote after everybody else, a decisive Supreme Court justice who chose not to flip sides and turn a 5-to-4 decision into a 4-to-5 ruling the other way—these are the things that landed George W. Bush in the White House. A broken constitutional system, a broken electoral system, a broken kind of journalism—slightly different turns in the road might have cast destiny the other way. The various media-sponsored re-recounts showed as much. Some people ascend to the presidency because of a bullet to the previous president, others are war-decorated generals, a few have a pretty face and a velvet voice. Bush got there by a fluke, not by any plot.

He is our nation's first truly accidental president—just as Al Gore would've been if he'd managed to pull it out. Neither was the Dark Prince of Election Thievery, notwithstanding what *The New Republic* or *Wall Street Journal* editorialists might tell you. Nobody can seriously dispute that Gore lost out on thousands of votes in Palm Beach and Duval Counties due to flawed ballot design—the "butterfly ballot" and the "caterpillar." But it's also possible Bush never got hundreds in the Panhandle because would-be voters heard that Gore had been prematurely declared the winner and so they stayed home. Who knows? It's a parlor game that can be played without end. The margin of error was simply greater than either side's margin of victory or defeat; even if machines were 99.9 percent accurate, that would still leave 6,000 votes in doubt.

But the accident of his presidency doesn't mean Bush is illegitimate. He gets the keys to *Air Force One* just the same; no one proposes he receive only nineteen-gun salutes. Bush may prove deft in getting things done in a divided country and with a divided Congress; he may turn out to be a fine president, in the tradition of others whose margins of victory were marginal—Lincoln, the greatest of them all, got only 40 percent of the vote in 1860. Or Bush may prove his detractors right, and the world will little note nor long remember anything he does the next four years in the White House. But either way, few will soon forget the events after November 7 that got him there.

This is the story of those thirty-seven days and why they matter.

The Motorcade

It *was supposed* to be the end, not the beginning.

But it could just as well have been a funeral procession. The black limousines, the somber faces, the tears, the rain—this was Al Gore at 1:45 in the morning central time, on his way from the Loews Vanderbilt Plaza Hotel to the War Memorial in Nashville, Tennessee, to formally concede the presidential election of 2000 to George W. Bush. In a motorcade of thirty or so vehicles, Gore's was second in line behind a police cruiser. Just after him was the standard decoy limo (agents like to call it the "spare," as in case the other one gets a flat tire or is hit by a rocket mortar). Despite the apparent loss, Gore was still the vice president of the United States and traveled with the trappings of power—the bulletproof car; the platoon of Secret Service agents and armaments in the War Wagon, that ominous-looking Suburban near the VP's car; the military aide with the "football," the heavy leather briefcase containing the codes for nuclear war; and, most utilitarian of all, the best wireless communications hookups outside the Pentagon. Through a connection to the White House Signal Corps, Gore could reach anyone in the world and, if necessary, anyone could reach him. Nonetheless, one of the ironies of a vice presidential (or presidential) motorcade is that for all its communications firepower, in practice it's so insulated. Key aides are at least a car away; they can call the main limo, but they're loath to, preferring instead to route messages to the staffer riding in the decoy (along with a White House doctor).

In the sable darkness, early on Wednesday, November 8, Gore sat in the back of his car with his wife, Tipper. Secret Service agents rode in front and were struck by the silence of their passengers—so much so that they were still talking about it months later. Less than half an hour before, Gore had given up his race for the presidency after the TV networks proclaimed Bush, the governor of Texas, the winner in Florida and thereby the president-elect. Gore had called Bush in Austin to concede and then headed for the War Memorial stage, seven minutes away.

It had already been a long, strange Election Day.

Gore concluded his campaign with thirty-six straight hours of state-hopping, sound-bite-filling appearances. He hadn't slept much in four days, but managed to remain functional. Lying on a massage table for his back spasms at one point, he managed not only to stay awake, but to make calls to Democrats in New Mexico. Aware of the decisive role Florida could play in the election, Gore had made thirteen trips there during the campaign, and it was paying off, as Bush's lead in the polls had once been twenty points. Gore's last visit was in the early morning of Tuesday, November 7, hours before the polls opened—first a 1 A.M. rally in Miami's South Beach with the likes of Robert De Niro and Stevie Wonder (whose "Signed, Sealed, Delivered" would later be used at *Bush's* victory celebration); a 4 A.M. meeting in Tampa with nurses at a cancer center; and finally Cuban coffee with his running mate, Senator Joseph Lieberman, at the nearby Columbus Spanish Plaza. "Well, it's almost five-thirty Texas time," Gore goaded the crowd, "and George W. Bush is still asleep—and I'm still speaking to people here." (It was a nice bit, but who heard it at that hour? It would be too late as well for the morning papers, leading one Gore strategist to wonder if anybody was awake enough to be thinking clearly at this point.)

Gore was then off to Tennessee, to vote in Carthage, have a fried-chicken-and-mashed-potatoes lunch with his mother, do live satellite interviews with TV and radio stations in battleground states, and hunker down into his seventh- and ninth-floor suites at the hotel in Nashville.

Seven hundred and fifty miles away, at the governor's mansion in Austin, Bush was in fact still asleep before the first blush of dawn. He spent Monday in Arkansas and Tennessee, brazenly trolling for votes in the backyards of the incumbent president and vice president. Choosing to look calm and confident—a very different image from the itinerant Gore's—Bush opted to be in his own bed on Election Eve. Upon waking, he read from the Bible, fed the cats and dog, and served coffee to his wife, Laura, upstairs. He voted in a windbreaker at the Travis County Courthouse, made a few calls to encourage turnout, and went for his customary workout at the University of Texas.

Each side had its worries. Bush faced a prosperous economy in a time of peace. Gore, for eight years, had stood at the side of an ethically challenged president. Polling, both within the campaigns and by news organizations, showed a tight race since summer; "too close to call" and "within the margin of error" became stock lines in every piece of daily reportage in the country. States traditionally thought to be safe for either side were competitive this time and would be the electoral fulcrum for the presidency: Iowa, Michigan, New Mexico, Ohio, Pennsylvania, Washington, Wisconsin. The biggest jewel of all: Florida. Gore had invested much time and treasure there in the last month. At the Democratic National Convention in August, he took the unusual gesture of letting Florida, not his home state of Tennessee, put him over the top.

Bush's brother Jeb was Florida's governor and the state had gone Republican in the presidential election all but three times since 1948. Yet a rapidly growing population and changing demographics were realigning political assumptions; while the Elián spectacle had reminded Democrats that they were vulnerable to Cuban-American passions, they were convinced that other Hispanics, as well as the prominent Jewish vote in south Florida—electrified by Lieberman on the ticket—could give them the state. On the night before November 7, each side's internal tracking numbers showed the Sunshine State up for grabs: Bush's numbers had Bush up by five points, Gore's showed Gore ahead by three.

On Election Day, as exit polls came in and turnout in key states was gauged, both campaigns could see how close the election was nationally—and that Florida might be the tipping state. After six, Bush and his family left the mansion in Austin for dinner at the Shoreline Grill with his parents and siblings. (The *New York Times* said they had "parmesan-crusted chicken." The *Washington Post* said it was "crusted chicken with grilled shrimp." And people don't believe what they read in the newspapers—go figure.) There was a television off to the side and the governor couldn't resist keeping an eye on it. Before seven—and within a twelve-minute span—all the networks announced Gore the winner of Florida's twenty-five electoral votes. "If we say somebody's carried a state," chortled Dan Rather about CBS's super-duper, state-of-the-art predictions machine, "you can pretty much take that to the bank!"

In the restaurant, Jeb Bush, whose state had just deserted his big brother, was crestfallen. The subject of Florida had come up between them: George—"W." in family parlance—had teased him weeks earlier that it would be an unhappy family gathering indeed at the Bush Thanksgiving if Gore captured Florida. Now it was no joking matter. Jeb apologized, then left the table and put in a call to John Ellis, who ran the "decision desk" at the Fox News Channel. Jeb and W. made many calls to Ellis that evening, which would've been ordinary enough—except that Ellis also happened to be a Bush first cousin, a fact that didn't come out until the following week and was one more reason the networks lost credibility covering the election. Few accused them of bias. No, the problem was one of competence—making snap judgments based on polls and letting a candidate's cousin work inside the news operations didn't enhance one's institutional credibility. Back at the restaurant table, W. tried to console his two daughters, and his father—George "Poppy" Bush, the forty-first president—was ashen. Everybody could do the arithmetic: The trifecta of Florida, Michigan, and the soon-to-be-declared Pennsylvania made Gore the presumptive victor.

That put an end to dinner. W. went back to the mansion. Jeb told W. his political people in Florida assured him the networks had jumped the gun—W., they said, was really ahead. But Bush was privately skeptical—"reconciled to defeat," he later told the *Washington Post*—since he believed exit polls were reliable. He alternated his time between the TV and the phone. Over at Bush headquarters on Congress Avenue, Karl Rove, the governor's chief political strategist, kept studying the county-by-county spreadsheet he had prepared weeks earlier; it showed what Bush would need to win Florida, and that model seemed in line with the returns coming in. Rove was irate. He urged Bush to be optimistic and went on the networks to challenge their projections. "We think you're wrong," he complained to NBC's Tom Brokaw. Bush himself let a pool of reporters into his living quarters, hearth ablaze, and scolded, "The networks are calling this thing awfully early—the people counting the votes are coming in with a different perspective."

And soon the five networks came to agree. Two hours after awarding Florida to Gore, they took it back. This time, the pack took a full twenty-five minutes, with NBC last to eat its words.

Whence the error? The networks got their data for projections from the Voter News Service, a New York organization that conducted the national exit polls. VNS simply got sloppy—and unlucky. No mathematical model or historical pattern is perfect; they require human judgment. VNS's poll information was slightly off—particularly on absentee turnout, a vital part of the Florida vote that couldn't be figured into exit polls—and, in a close election, that was enough to poison an early call. VNS bungled actual votes, too. Preliminary returns from the Jacksonville area, according to VNS, showed Gore taking 98 percent of the vote—43,023 to 1,026; trouble was, the lead was 4,302 to 1,026, an embarrassing slip of the pen that VNS caught, but not before factoring the wrong numbers into Florida projections. In Nashville, Gore and his staff were deflated, yet knew from their own political operation that Florida had hardly been in the bag. With Iowa, New Mexico, and Wisconsin also near impasse, they settled in for a long night.

Bush did as well, but he viewed it as being back in the game—not that he ever had been out of it, except through the looking glass of TV. By midnight, as it became clear Florida would go down to the last precinct, he remarked to a *Newsweek* reporter, "I can't believe this is happening. This is like running for a city council seat." These were prescient thoughts from a man never given much credit for having them—and from someone who'd never run for a city council seat.

While George W. Bush never relinquished his Florida lead, the margin shown on the TV scoreboard kept dwindling—from a few hundred thousand down to 40,000 then 20,000 with enough uncounted votes out there in Democratic strongholds for Gore to overtake him. All of a sudden, the spread hiccuped to 50,000. The networks took notice: These were real numbers, so how could the arithmetic be off? You looked bad getting your projections wrong, but you also looked bad if you held back your trigger while the competition fired away. In the summer, NBC had gotten endless bragging mileage from announcing that Gore was choosing Lieberman, even though its correspondent, Claire Shipman, put out the scoop—leaked by Gore's spokesmen Mark Fabiani and Chris Lehane—only two minutes before the Associated Press and then everyone else. (Two of Shipman's fans were the Liebermans themselves. They found out he was the choice from watching her disclose it on the *Today* show—Gore hadn't told them yet.)

Given Bush's 50,000-vote margin, and aware that their four rivals presumably were seeing just what they saw, the networks made the call. First, Fox News, at 1:16 central time, trumpeted, "Bush wins!" with an American flag flapping and the other cheesy graphics that such a pronouncement required. Then NBC a minute later, CNN and CBS a minute after that (Dan Rather: "Sip it, savor it, cup it, photostat it, underline it in red, press it in a book, put it in an album, hang it on a wall! George W. Bush is the next president of the United States"). It took ABC all the way until 1:20 to get Peter Jennings to announce, "Unless there is a terrible calamity, George W. Bush, by our projections, is going to be the next president of the United States." Fair enough that he was cautious, but what terrible calamity did Jennings have in mind?

The networks weren't the only ones who were too eager. The chairman of the Democratic National Committee, Ed Rendell, couldn't wait to get on CNN to criticize Gore for misallocating advertising dollars and using Bill Clinton too timidly.

In Manhattan, the forty-second president and his wife were watching the election returns. When the networks projected Bush his successor, his expression turned hound-dog and he muttered, "Shit." (It was a common exclamation that night.) Like others, he thought Gore had locked it up with the earlier Florida projection—this was a numbing turnabout. In his mind's tallies, he'd correctly predicted every state other than Wisconsin. And now, Florida.

"Should I call Bush?" the president asked his chief of staff, John Podesta. "No, should I call Gore?" Podesta said he'd ring up Gore and Bill Daley, the chairman of the campaign.

"Maybe the Gores don't even want to talk to us," said Hillary Rodham Clinton, who then went to sleep believing Bush had won. "I'm so sad, I'm so sad." Later that night, the president and vice president talked about life's twists and turns, masking over what had become real antipathy at times since the Monica Lewinsky mess.

In the Gore suite at the Loews, TV delivered the bad news to the candidate's family, a reversal of fortune that was unimaginable at dinnertime. Even an hour earlier, Gore, Daley, and senior staffers had war-gamed the Florida scenario and believed it was most likely both sides would head to bed without the election resolved. At worst, Daley would go to the War Memorial and tell the faithful to go home. At best, Bush's lead would evaporate, he'd face political pressure because he'd lost the popular vote nationwide, and then he'd pack it in.

The networks had changed the script. Now Gore's daughters wept. When he discovered the networks' decision—furiously flipping from channel to channel to see if the news varied—Gore left the war games to comfort them. In nearby rooms, staffers who had been sharing champagne at 7 P.M. now reacted as if the floor had sunk beneath them; it was as if the campaign had been euthanized. These guys thought they had taken the prize and now, somehow, it was gone.

Gore attended to the details of defeat, finding David Morehouse, his trip director, down the hallway. "I want to leave in thirty minutes," Gore said. "I need to call Bush and get changed." Gore was still in flip-flops, blue jeans, and a rugby shirt hanging out over his pants. "Where's Eli?" He wanted to know if his speechwriter, Eli Attie, had prepared a concession. Minutes later, Attie was on the hallway floor making last-minute fixes before printing out a copy for the vice president; if you were the vice president's speechwriter, you knew he liked to change his speeches on the fly and you learned to carry the lightest portable printer.

Back in Texas, the Austin powers tried to absorb what had happened, how the pendulum of fate seemed to swing their way again. Presto! George W. Bush was the forty-third president, right there in the same room with the forty-first. "Jebby," clowned Bush's brother Marvin, "you can come in from the ledge now!" Right after the networks declared Bush the winner, Karl Rove took a phone call from the putative president-elect. Neither had any sense the regal title would be evanescent.

It fell upon Bill Daley to arrange the formal surrender. He called Don Evans, his alter ego in Austin, to let him know that Gore would soon be telephoning Bush. The two campaign leaders had been cordial to each other throughout—this time, Evans even put Daley through for a brief conversation with Bush—but Evans seemed irked that it was going to take Gore half an hour to make his concession public. Daley said it was only a matter of logistics and he meant it: Gore and his family had to make their way to the War Memorial. The interesting thing was that Evans's agitation stemmed in part from his awareness that the race was in fact too close to call.

Shortly thereafter, Gore spoke with Bush, congratulated his opponent, and wished him well. "You're a good man and I respect you," Bush offered back amiably, though efficiently. The Bush family prepared to leave the mansion for the stage and party at the granite capitol across the street.

Daley thought it was imperative that Gore reach Bush right after the TV proclamations—"so it didn't look like we were screwing around." "What you didn't want to happen is for Bush to run out and accept this and make Gore look small—like he wouldn't go out and was holding out for something," Daley explained later. "There was fear on my part they would do that."

Wouldn't that kind of preemptive strike have been tacky? "Tacky is in the eyes of the beholder," Daley says. Such was the level of enmity between the campaigns. In retrospect, he says, "I should not have allowed the vice president to make that call" to Bush.

Lieberman agreed. "I was surprised that Al decided so quickly," he recalled afterward.

By 1:40 A.M. in Nashville, at the loading dock of the hotel underground, the Gore-Lieberman campaign piled into the motorcade. As they departed, the last thing they saw was a big trash Dumpster.

Well back in the motorcade en route, Michael Feldman—Gore's thirty-two-year-old traveling chief of staff—was in a staff van trying to handle an electronic barrage: cell calls on the Nokia, e-mails on the BlackBerry, pages on his SkyTel. He wasn't in the mood to provide the "color" that journalists clamor for at moments like this, so he did his best just to look out for campaign-related messages. Three blocks from the War Memorial, the pager went off. The Signal Corps switchboard had the number and so did some friends and journalists, but people generally didn't use it unless there was an emergency. This message was from Michael Whouley, Gore's top political tactician, the grassroots guy who crunched the numbers and knew the wards and districts of the country better than anyone. It was his national organization of the get-out-the-vote effort that won Gore the popular vote and, in part, his pleas for more TV ads in Florida that made the state competitive. Twenty-four hours earlier, he had given his scorecard to a *Wall Street Journal* reporter of how the fifty states would go in the Electoral College, and he was on the money on them all; Florida would go to Gore, he had predicted.

"CALL SWTCHBD" read the message to Feldman. "CALL HOLDING WITH MIKE WHULEY ASAP."

Whouley was at Gore headquarters nearby, running the "Boiler Room." The appellation was apt: Here, far away from the rallies and oratory, cranked the mathematical apparatus of a campaign—telephones, computers, televisions, and sixty to seventy people to keep the machines happy. Off the Boiler Room on Election Night was "the Closet," which had been converted the day before from a janitor's storage room. Whouley secreted himself in the Closet with a TV, a cell phone, and a few staffers. What it lacked in charm it made up for in information about votes. Whouley couldn't understand why the networks had declared for Bush. Nor could he fathom why his candidate had telephoned Bush to concede—no one in the Gore brain trust had bothered to call the Boiler Room operation before deciding to give up and go to the War Memorial. "It didn't dawn on me that they *weren't* doing what we *were* doing," Whouley says.

Down in Florida, Whouley's ground troops were telling him the same thing. In Tallahassee, the capital, Gore's state campaign chief, Nick Baldick, was in contact with counties around the state, and the numbers plainly didn't support the TV projections of a Bush victory. Their models and working spreadsheet projected a 1,000-vote margin either way, though Baldick later preened that he got it down to 56 votes.

"Michael," beseeched Baldick, "I'm not wrong on these numbers. There's no way the networks can do this."

"I believe you," Whouley answered. "But they just did."

Even as the networks blathered on about President-elect Bush and unleashed colorful graphics they'd been waiting to use all night, Whouley could see from the numbers there on every computer screen in the Boiler Room that the race was approaching a stalemate. The Web page of Florida's secretary of state, who was in charge of elections, showed the margin between Gore and Bush shrinking from 50,000—the number that caused the networks to turn—to 18,000 to 10,000 to 6,000. As in a B movie, it was akin to watching a timer on a bomb tick, tick, tick down closer to zero, though in this case it was the explosion that Whouley was hoping for. For him, like so many other participants in both political camps, it was but one surreal moment in a night of supreme weirdness. Here he seemed to be in a dream not of his own making, screaming, yet nobody could hear him. "You're looking at all the networks and they're all saying that the other guy won Florida and you're saying, *'No, he didn't.'* Now that's surreal."

It wasn't as if Whouley possessed proprietary information. In the age of the Net, anybody with a modem and a PC—and the presence of mind to go to the Florida election-results page—could read the numbers and figure out the tale: Things weren't over at all. (Traffic on the Florida Web site eventually got so overloaded later that morning that it crashed for two days.) An AP reporter, Ron Fournier, saw the numbers when Whouley did and called Lehane, Gore's press secretary. AP's numbers were different from the networks', he told Lehane, and AP wasn't calling the race. But Lehane couldn't get through to anyone in the motorcade. There was too much wireless activity in the Nashville area right then; even in the digital universe there are traffic jams.

For their part, Bush's operatives were understandably disinclined to question the networks' call—they had a winner on their hands for the moment—but it wasn't just wishful thinking. Rove, as shrewd a political mind as either campaign had and someone who appreciated American political history, just couldn't comprehend the possibility that the networks had fouled up *again*. In Tallahassee, the GOP's main ground tactician, Randy Enwright, felt pitapatations in his gut. He was the one who had alerted Rove hours earlier, when the networks called Florida for Gore, to say they had it wrong. Now, he had the same uneasy feeling, though he didn't call Austin this time.

It was a premise born of habit—the assumption that the TV electoral machine was omniscient—that caused Gore and his high command never even to *consider* holding off from a concession. "I've been in lots of campaigns, from a few precincts in the city of Chicago to presidential runs," the fifty-two-year-old Daley says, "and no matter what, everyone runs to the goddamn TV because we think they spend more money and they're going to know." Another high-ranking staffer was more critical. "What did it say about our campaign that Michael Whouley was running the numbers for the country and they don't even check with him before conceding?"

But even Whouley was momentarily frozen by the TV. "When the networks flipped, we sat there stunned for ninety seconds," he says. "Nobody cried, nobody said a thing." To make sure they should believe their eyes, and not the news anchors, they then talked to Baldick in Tallahassee on the phone line they'd kept open the whole night. At that point, Whouley wanted to know where the vice president was. *"Where the fuck are these people?"* he shouted.

Gore may deserve credit for trying to do the right thing in folding. Even if he thought he'd lost, there was little political benefit in surrendering instantly. Appearing gracious, of course, never hurts, but one could hardly ascribe Machiavellian motives to Gore for merely wanting to get on with it. Election Night had passed into morning, the daily papers were long past deadline, and millions of Americans were awake in front of the tube wondering who'd be the forty-third president. At the War Memorial itself, the true believers, fairly conditioned to assume presidential races ended in time for Leno, had been standing in the rain for up to nine hours. Despite his past and future reputation as a ferocious politician who worked till he dropped—this was Marathoning Al the day before—Gore chose to move swiftly, gracefully, perhaps remembering his father's words that "no matter how hard the loss, defeat might serve as well as victory to shape the soul and let the glory out."

Yet Gore's decisiveness turned out to be a blunder. Had he waited a bit, had he checked with his own political operation, he would've avoided the appearance of being a sore loser later on. As it happened, Bush never tired of reminding the press that Gore was an Indian giver. Would that changed dynamic have mattered in the public-relations game that followed? Would the press have fixated more on Gore winning the popular vote nationally? Maybe not. But it surely would've avoided the preposterous chain of events in the wee hours.

In the back of a van on a miserable night, Feldman strained to read the message from the White House Signal Corps. He then called the switchboard operator, who connected him to Whouley. "It's down to 6,000 votes," Whouley said. "I'm looking at the secretary of state's page. Where are you?"

"I'm in the motorcade. Two blocks away."

Whouley knew that—by this point, others in the adjoining Boiler Room were waving at the TV screen, which was showing live shots of Gore's limousine nearing the War Memorial, bathed in light, and Whouley recognized that time was of the essence. What he wanted to know this second was where Feldman was relative to the vice president.

"It's down to 6,000?" Feldman asked incredulously. The last he'd heard it was 50,000.

"Are you with Daley?" Whouley knew it was vital to get him or someone else who could prevent Gore from taking the stage. Whouley was trying various cell and pager numbers.

Having reached Feldman, it was still utterly frustrating. Feldman was no more than a few hundred yards from Gore's limo, but in a parallel universe. He couldn't really jump out of his van and start chasing the limo down. Nor could he ask the van's driver—a Vanderbilt student recruited the day before for volunteer duty—to dart out of the motorcade; Secret Service rules frown on that sort of thing. Unless Feldman's universe connected with the Gore universe, the consequences were potentially dire. Feldman's cell has a three-way button, so he called Daley in a car ahead. Unfortunately, he got voice mail—the chairman had turned off his phone. Feldman next tried Daley's aide, Graham Street, who was in the car with him. Daley got on the phone and Feldman patched in Whouley, who gave Daley the news. "This thing's going to recount," Whouley told him.

"Oh, shit."

Daley turned to senior strategist Carter Eskew beside him and exhaled, "With ninety-nine percent of the vote counted, we're only 6,000 down—what do we do?" Their first instinct was simply to make sure Gore didn't use the word "concede" in his speech; Eskew and Attie, Gore's speechwriter, had been talking a few days before about how close the 1960 race between Richard Nixon and John F. Kennedy was, and how Nixon never used the C-word on Election Night. Not that a concession speech was a binding, irreversible proclamation, but shouldn't Gore similarly hedge his valedictory?

There wasn't time to work the thought through. Daley ordered Feldman, "Don't let him go out! Go to hold! Go to hold!" which was campaign vernacular for getting Gore into the War Memorial but then keeping him in the holding room until everybody could figure out how to proceed. Daley, however, didn't know that Feldman was even farther away from Gore than he was. It wasn't exactly an Abbott-and-Costello routine, but it was absurd that there was no easy way to stop Gore, who was in the very same motorcade. Daley, no political tenderfoot, tried to gain his moorings. "This is fucking unbelievable," Daley said to Streett. "Fuck!"

Feldman looked over at Vanessa Opperman, the fiancée of David Morehouse, the staffer designated as the logistics warrior. Morehouse was in the decoy limo. Unless there were security issues within the Secret Service's jurisdiction, he was the one who told the motorcade when to start and when to stop. When they arrived at the War Memorial, he would signal the Secret Service, which surrounded the car, when it was okay to open the door. The point was to let the vice president out only when all details were in place. "I don't have a radio in here!" Feldman said to Opperman. "How do I get ahold of Morehouse?"

Feldman was so panicked he forgot he could just use his phone. In virtually every other motorcade, he'd been in the "control" car near the front, which had direct radio contact with the decoy limo. Tonight, he was in a mere staff van, such was the rush to get out of the hotel. (Poor Mark Fabiani, the communications director, missed the motorcade altogether and had to commandeer a thirty-two-seat tour bus, which got stuck in traffic and never made it to the War Memorial. He didn't get to see Gore until five that morning, when Gore opened the door to his suite in his personally monogrammed hotel bathrobe.)

Opperman rang up Morehouse and gave her cell to Feldman. The motorcade was now at the War Memorial. "David," Feldman said, "whatever else happens, you have to make sure the vice president goes to hold and not to the stage!"

"Why?" Morehouse inquired.

"There are complications with the vote count. Daley needs to talk to him."

Morehouse had worked out a different plan en route. Gore would get no introduction onstage, there would be no music, there would be no rope line to shake hands. There wouldn't be a "hold" for the vice president to gather his thoughts or talk to family. This was a concession speech, intended to happen quickly. But Feldman's message changed the plan. Morehouse wanted more details about the emerging Florida mess, but there was no time. Gore was supposed to wait in his limo until a Secret Service agent opened the armor-plated door at Morehouse's signal. It always went that way—it was the basic protocol Morehouse had followed in his fifteen months with Gore. On this night, though—on this night, *of course*—Gore had other ideas. He opened the door himself, got out, and began to walk hurriedly with Tipper to the War Memorial. "This is the one time he decides he doesn't need Morehouse!" Morehouse thought. He tried to stop Gore and tell him the electoral landscape had shifted. How do you corral the vice president of the United States who's hell-bent on getting the hardest speech of his political life over and done with?

Morehouse, forty and in reasonably good shape, normally would have had no trouble running after the vice president. But he'd hurt his knee earlier and could barely keep up. Meanwhile, Gore seemed to be striding faster than usual and other people were getting in between Morehouse and Gore. *How could this be happening?* Two steps before Gore reached the stairs to the stage, Morehouse got to him. "We need to go to hold, sir."

"I'm not going to hold," Gore replied resolutely. "I'm going straight out to give this speech."

"Daley needs to talk to you for five minutes."

"No. I told the governor I was going to do this thing, and he's waiting in Austin to give his own speech until after I give mine." Gore was irritated.

Morehouse swung around in front of him and stepped in Gore's way. "You *need* to go to hold." Gore was now clearly annoyed, but did relent. Daley caught up and they all walked to the holding room in the basement of the War Memorial. Only inside did Gore learn of his latest reversal of fortune, such as it was. With Whouley talking in his ear, Daley put his arm around Gore's back and whispered the numbers to him. Gore looked half shocked, half rapturous. He turned to Tipper and gave her the news, and she seemed to be in disbelief. Gore then briefly took a seat in a small, incommodious anteroom, leaning back with his arms behind his head and putting up on a desk his favorite resoled cowboy boots, the ones that his uncle Frank had given him long ago.

Others from the motorcade made their way into the holding area— Gore's daughters and son; his running mate Joe Lieberman and Lieberman's wife, Hadassah; his brother-in-law, confidant, and cowboy-boot maven, Frank Hunger; and more than a dozen aides. There was an informational domino effect, as everyone got the new numbers. People who had been in shock that had been converted to grief were now sent back into shock. The rooms and hallways filled with the noise of chatter, vibrating pagers, and bedlam. Communications with the outside world, however, were difficult. Most cell phones didn't work here underground, there was no cable TV (just one with an antenna and a fuzzy connection to the local NBC affiliate), and only a few hard telephone lines were set up. More information trickled in from Florida and there were reports of widespread voting irregularities in Palm Beach County—something about a confusing ballot and accusations that many blacks had been turned away from the polls. There were also a few outstanding precincts in the southern part of the state where Gore could yet narrow the gap. Gore's press people weren't there, so Daley, Feldman, and others spoke to network executives or at least e-mailed them on BlackBerries: Were they seeing the new numbers? Would they withdraw their declarations of a Bush win?

The networks wanted to know why Gore wasn't at the podium, which already bore the vice presidential seal. If he wasn't going to concede, what was he going to do? What *was* Gore to do? Daley wondered. There was great risk in pulling back a concession. "We'd look really stupid if this was just some Internet mix-up," Daley thought. "We'd look like *schmucks*."

Bush's margin out of nearly six million votes cast in Florida had moved to nine hundred, then six hundred, then *two hundred*, according to some of the reports coming in. Whouley, in the Boiler Room Closet back at headquarters and never a Pollyanna, had it at one thousand. Bob Butterworth, the Democratic attorney general of Florida and state co-chair of the Gore campaign, confirmed by phone that Florida law required an automatic recount in an election this close—where the margin was less than one half of 1 percent of the total votes cast. "Recount"—despite the polls that all along showed Gore and Bush neck and neck, this was the first time the word came up.

Out on the stage, Gore's concession speech was being taken off the TelePrompTer screens in front of the podium. Eli Attie had drafted five versions for the evening: one for winning; one for losing; and the rest for taking the Electoral College while losing the popular vote, winning but losing Gore's home state of Tennessee, and the improbable event of a 269–269 tie in the Electoral College, which early exit polling suggested was possible. "The people of our country have spoken," Gore was to have begun. "And I accept their judgment. Just moments ago, I called Governor George W. Bush, and congratulated him on his election as the forty-third president of the United States." Gore spoke of "a hard-fought campaign" and his twenty-four years in the national government, and quoted Lincoln, the Beatles, and finally, as he had done throughout the campaign, Bachman-Turner Overdrive. "Even in this hard hour, my heart is full. And that is because of you . . . This I know in my heart, you ain't seen nothing yet."

Shortly before 2 A.M. central time—roughly forty-five minutes beyond when Gore was to have given his farewell and departed the stage—Daley decided to call Evans, the Bush campaign chairman. But nobody had the cell number. The Secret Service found it through their comrades on the Bush detail. When Daley got through, he said, "Don, don't let your guy go out. We've got a problem here."

"What's the problem?"

"I'll get back to you. Where is the governor? Because the vice president may need to talk to him."

"About what?" Evans pressed, though he and others in Austin knew full well what it was about. Rove could add and subtract, and Bush's lead was vanishing. In Tallahassee, Randy Enwright had left Bush's campaign office to go over to the GOP celebration at the Doubletree, but his great expectations were no match for the tally on the secretary of state's Web page. The folks in Austin eventually called him for whatever encouragement he could offer, but the numbers couldn't be spun, particularly with those remaining precincts in south Florida. "After you had been on the roller coaster for seven hours," Enwright recalled later, "you just couldn't jump up and down and go nuts anymore."

Daley knew Evans knew, but nothing could be gained by getting into it. Answering Evans's question, he said only, "Don, I'll get back to you."

With a difference of just two hundred votes between the candidates, and with a recount mandated by Florida law, Gore and Daley and the rest of the team knew any concession had to be pulled off the table. The only issue was how to orchestrate the move—the un-concession, surely the most unbelievable moment on an already implausible night.

"I'll just call him," Gore told Daley. Gore felt strongly that since he had "called the guy and conceded" in the first place, he had to undo it directly. Doing it staff-to-staff—Daley to Evans—wouldn't be right.

While Attie prepared new remarks for the crowd, Daley placed another call to Austin, on the secure phone line the White House Signal Corps had rigged up previously.

At the white-pillared governor's mansion, George W. Bush and his family gathered in front of a TV to watch Gore concede. A few minutes after 2 A.M. central time, Bush and his father walked upstairs. That's where the call from Nashville came in.

"Circumstances have changed dramatically since I first called you," Vice President Gore said to Governor Bush, trying to be cordial. Gore had one foot on the floor, one on a desk. He took a breath, attempting to keep his composure, peeved as he was that he could be in this predicament. "The state of Florida is too close to call," he told Bush.

The latter was an unremarkable observation, given the numbers. Yet the uttering of the words, the actual making of this call, had an undeniable impact on those dozen or so on Gore's side who overheard it, not to mention Bush himself. In the world of modern American campaigns—with the presidency the No. 1 prize—politics and honor are rarely used in the same sentence anymore. Whatever the numbers, in Bush's mind, what Gore was doing was astonishing. "Are you saying what I think you're saying?" Bush abruptly asked. "Let me make sure I understand, Mr. Vice President. You are calling back to retract your concession?"

"You don't have to be snippy about it!" Gore parried back, in a line that became instant political lore. The Revolution produced "Give me liberty or give me death." The Civil War gave us "A house divided against itself cannot stand." The presidential election of 2000? Two boys in the schoolyard. "Did not!" "Did too!"

"Let me explain," Gore tried to explain. If Bush positively was the winner, if the recount proved it, then Gore would be fully behind him. "But I don't think we should be going out making statements with Florida still in the balance."

Bush countered that his brother Jeb—the governor of Florida, after all—was right there with him in Austin and had guaranteed him he had won the state.

"Well," Gore noted sarcastically, even snippily, "your younger brother is not the ultimate authority on this."

"Mr. Vice President, do what you have to do."

There may have been a muted "thanks" and "you're welcome" somewhere in there (nobody remembers), but both men then hung up— it'll never be clear who got to do it first. There was frost on both phones. The call lasted ninety seconds.

Bush told his family and friends downstairs what had just happened. He asked Jeb to monitor Florida, and Evans to address the crowd outside. And then he went to bed.

In Nashville, Gore was jubilant, exhilarated—"almost smug," one person near him later called it. He did a little jig, then let loose a smile and a grin that creeped from one ear to the other. He had just experienced a resurrection. He pumped his right fist. The room exploded. Aides cried and hugged, and clapped like seals.

"It was like being in Game Seven of a basketball championship and one team wins by a point," Feldman recalls. "The final buzzer goes off and the winning team celebrates as the losers witness the celebration. And they're thinking, we're better than them, we could've beaten them, we should've beaten them, and that last play was sort of suspicious. But you accept the buzzer, okay? And then the ref puts four seconds back on the clock and suddenly the momentum and the emotions shift." Feldman said Gore had gotten those four seconds back.

One man wasn't reveling. In a corner of the holding room, Bill Daley put his hands over his face. The scion of one of America's great political families, experienced in the ways of recounts and political ground warfare and all the mischief attached thereto, knew better than to celebrate. He was already playing things out in his mind, to the extent anyone could even conceive of the next act: The waters ahead were uncharted, as the cliché went, and his boat was less seaworthy than the opponent's. The race was close, but Gore was behind, and you never want to be behind in a recount. All the leader had to do in a recount is stand still; it was the trailer who had to have everything go right in order to pass by. "It is very tough to turn an election around if you don't do it in the first twenty-four hours, and if you don't do it by literally finding ballots that someone accidentally took home or just forgot to count," he explained later. "Part of the problem in these situations is that ninety-nine percent of the rumors and the stories and the allegations turn out to be totally wrong. And if you base your decisions upon them, you generally get embarrassed in the end."

To the consternation of other, less experienced hands in the campaign, Daley couldn't dispel this pessimism—realism by another name—over the next five weeks. As the rest of the room hooted it up, Daley tried to catch his breath. "Oh, is this going to be tough," he murmured.

What to do with the crowd outside and the TV audience? "I don't think *you* should go out there," Eskew said to Gore.

"No, I should. They want me and Joe."

"If you go out," interjected Attie, "it'll seem like you're resisting the outcome." That rapidly became the consensus—and underscored the strategic goof in conceding earlier. Had Gore not done so, there wouldn't have been a second call to Bush. Nor would anyone have to take the stage now. While he still would've been behind by hundreds of votes—and he couldn't erase the TV networks' initial declaration of a Bush victory—he wouldn't have looked like he was yanking back what he chose to give away. It's one thing to be a few yards back in the marathon and tenaciously press on, quite another to tell your opponent he's won, stop running, and then change your mind a mile later and attempt to pass him as he takes a breather.

Daley would be the one to go out with a brief statement. Attie, with Daley, Eskew, and Gore's eldest daughter, Karenna, hovering, banged out a few sentences on his Dell laptop. For all the versions of a speech he'd compulsively planned for the evening, Attie hadn't thought of the need for this one. Daley had barely a minute to look over his statement—his son Billy made him read it aloud for practice. Someone joked that Daley better not pass out—a reference to when he fainted at the 1996 presidential press conference when his nomination as commerce secretary was announced.

Daley turned to Graham Streett and observed, "Can you *believe* this?" Into the rain he went, as if in a state of suspended animation. "I have some news to share with you tonight," Daley said, as some in the crowd of several thousand, who sensed what was coming, shouted, "Fuzzy math!" "And let me say: I've been in politics for a long time. But there's never been a night like this one. . . . This race is simply too close to call and, until the recount is concluded and the results in Florida become official, our campaign continues." Election Day was but another step in the campaign—the campaign *continues*. Before Daley even finished talking onstage after 3 A.M., Gore was back in the motor-cade to the Loews.

As Daley left the stage, he saw his son, looked him right in the eyes, and offered wanly, "What am I doing here?" Reflecting on the events of the evening and what he had just done, Daley two months later said there was only one word: "crazy."

In Tallahassee, Katherine Harris, the Florida secretary of state who would soon become the GOP diva of the post-election period, had made it home by now from the Doubletree. The phone rang. It was Jeb Bush. *"What is going on?"* he asked.

The television networks were beside themselves. They had messed up once that evening—when early on they put Florida in the *Gore* column. As the slogan went: Florida, the rules were different here! But how do you screw up a state twice in the same election? The earlier blown call on Florida wasn't monumental: It did have the effect of wrongly presaging a Gore triumph, because along with Michigan and Pennsylvania, it gave him an electoral majority. And it might have discouraged some voters in the Florida Panhandle from voting; because those counties were in the central time zone, rather than the eastern, their polls were still open when the networks gave their projections, which was contrary to the networks' policies. (Apparently, the networks forgot that northwestern Florida wasn't in Alabama.) Later, the GOP continued to claim that thousands of Panhandlers didn't vote because of the networks. While there's no way to prove it either way, the claim seemed unlikely. It's hard to believe that many residents of this rural area—who often lived a distance from polling places—were planning to vote, watching TV at the appointed hour, and then decided *not* to go vote based on what they heard.

But the mistake—the cardinal sin of TV political analysis—only took on significance when the networks made it again six and a half hours later. It was another catastrophic failure of the quadrennial predictions system the networks spent the prior four years boasting of. And this time the networks called Florida for Bush, handing him the front-door keys to the White House. It wasn't as if they had to do it, or that all media outlets did. The Associated Press, to its great credit, refused to call the state. And so, too, did the Voter News Service. VNS was funded by ABC, CBS, NBC, CNN, Fox, and AP; each got the same data but made its own judgments based on them.

This time, the problem seemed to be Volusia County, where software gremlins were astir around midnight. Gore's electronic vote totals included a –16,000 entry. A *negative* number? That couldn't be—except *tonight*. The error was soon deleted by Volusia officials. But the correction wasn't picked up for hours by VNS or the networks—their Bush-Gore scorecard was off by 16,000, a huge amount on this night. The Gore counters knew it sooner only because they had a regional Democratic organizer, Deborah Tannenbaum, in the offices of the Volusia election board. Her boss in Tallahassee, Nick Baldick, was initially skeptical about Tannenbaum's startling story and asked four times if she were certain. She said she was, and Volusia County's own Web page corroborated the information. Without Tannenbaum, Whouley wouldn't have gotten the confirmation from Baldick that the networks had bad numbers.

Now, with Florida a virtual dead heat according to actual returns (not just projections), the networks had to figure out how to recant again. It was sort of like asking a firing squad to take back its fusillade. They tried, each pulling back their projections and returning Florida to the "Undecided" column. The big jigsaw piece in the lower right corner of their TV maps turned back to white, surrounded by the blues and reds of the states already decided. "We don't have egg on our face," cringed Tom Brokaw on NBC. "We have an omelette." Over at CBS, Dan Rather confessed to his viewers, "If you're disgusted with us, frankly I don't blame you." And that was six hours earlier, when CBS had to disavow its *first* blown call on Florida.

Many newspapers around the country, too, trusted the tube too much. The *Boston Globe, USA Today, New York Post, San Francisco Chronicle, Philadelphia Inquirer, Washington Times, Sacramento Bee, St. Louis Post-Dispatch, Austin (Texas) American-Statesman*, and at least three Florida papers, the *Miami Herald, Orlando Sentinel*, and *Tallahassee Democrat*—all these reported Bush was the next president. Such was the power TV news had, not because any legislature had bestowed it upon them, but because no one among the newspaper overlords demanded better. In a near-vacuum of journalistic responsibility—in the competitive rush to be first—caution and accuracy were the bridesmaids. The *New York Times* ran off more than a hundred thousand copies of an edition announcing "Bush Appears to Defeat Gore" before having to redo the front page; they really did "stop the presses." The next morning, papers with "Bush Wins!" headlines were going for up to twenty-five dollars on eBay.

Foreign countries followed the TV returns, and a few had hair triggers. England, China, Germany, and South Africa wired congratulatory messages to Bush early Wednesday, then had to take them back. The puckish foreign minister of Cuba, so often lectured on American democracy, offered to send observers to Florida to assist in any recount.

And then there was the jinxed Ted Koppel of ABC's *Nightline*. He was all set to go profile the winner Tuesday night. He flew from Washington to Atlanta to await word whether to fly to Nashville or Austin. When Michigan and Pennsylvania went for Gore, Koppel chose Nashville. Arriving near midnight, he saw a crowd at a CNN monitor in the airport terminal. Florida was not in the Gore column anymore, but he didn't know that, having been out of touch with the ABC election desk.

"What do we do now?" Koppel asked his executive producer. They decided to head for the Loews, where they learned that Florida had been awarded to Bush. Once at the hotel, Koppel tried to hop a ride to the War Memorial in a staff van but, once in the door, was politely asked by the disconsolate staff to get off. Koppel then chartered a Learjet for Austin, arriving after 5 A.M. On the drive in from the airport, Koppel remembers, the radio was lit up with the "bitching and moaning about the stupid-ass networks." That's how he and his crew found out the election was still undecided and their chase had been for naught. Koppel had been a victim of bad timing all night, which finally ended in Austin at Katz's Never Kloses Deli.

Bill and Hillary Clinton had voted near their suburban home outside Manhattan, but the first couple was in the city that night waiting to see if she'd become the new U.S. senator from New York. All the numbers soon showed she would—apart from the question from television pundits of whether the president and first lady would embrace onstage, the tension of the evening was in the Gore-Bush race.

On the thirty-fourth floor of the Grand Hyatt in Midtown, the president spent much of his time in the room set up for him to monitor election returns on TVs and PCs—the "POTUS War Room" (as in "president of the United States"), aides called it. Hillary and Chelsea came in at times, but otherwise stayed in their suite. As it became clear Florida would be the difference, Clinton became frantic for more information. He thrived on data and could process chunks of it in his head as well as anyone. "Why is it so fucking close?" he said to the handful of people in the room. "What counties aren't in yet? See what's going on down there." The moment represented a culmination, or one of many, for Clinton in his ambivalent relationship with Gore during the campaign. Gore had the impossible task of linking himself to the economic prosperity of the Clinton administration while at the same time distancing himself from the president's personal transgressions. How to be the protégé of a policy genius and moral miscreant? Clinton wasn't especially sympathetic to that view and, in any event, saw Gore's class-based politics during the campaign as antithetical to what he had worked for in the Democratic party the past eight years. He'd ridicule the professionals around Gore as "Washington consulting populist crap." The fact that Gore was on the verge of losing the election was proof to Clinton that Gore's campaign strategy had been flawed. For the moment, he just wanted to know what was happening "on the ground."

"I'll call Nick Baldick," volunteered Jonathan Prince, a former speechwriter for the president who visited the War Room that night for old times' sake. Prince had been best man at Baldick's wedding and assumed that Baldick in Tallahassee would have the most current information. Baldick had been Gore's New Hampshire state campaign director during the pivotal primary against Bill Bradley; at thirty-two, he was regarded in the campaign as a masterly political operator in the tradition of Michael Whouley—"almost as mean and a little more bald," according to a colleague.

Prince dialed Baldick's cell and found him in the midst of pandemonium. At 514 East College Avenue in downtown Tallahassee, in the dilapidated, ant-infested house the campaign was using as a nerve center, the phones had been ringing continuously most of the night. It was now around 1:40 A.M. in Nashville and the Gore motorcade was on its way to the War Memorial. As Prince's call came in, Baldick was talking to Whouley in Nashville, desperately trying to get information to the inner circle that the concession might be premature. "The numbers are wrong! The numbers are wrong!" he was telling Whouley. Baldick couldn't pick up his cell—so his mother did.

Jackie Baldick liked to be with her son for the final week of all elections. She'd come down from her home in the Washington area to enjoy the scene and "as Nicky took care of the numbers," she'd "take care of Nick." "Only Nick's mom could do it," she said. "I could shoo others away—and make sure Nick was eating." "Mumishka," they called her around 514 East College Avenue.

When Prince's call came in, Nick Baldick recognized his friend's number on Caller ID and knew as well that Prince was with Clinton in New York. He flipped his cell phone to his mother and pleaded, "Take care of this!"

"Hello?" she said, and paused. "Yes, Nick's busy. He can't talk to the president right now." There was a longer pause.

"I have the president *right here*. Really."

"You know Nicky loves you," Mumishka Baldick continued, "but he can't talk to you or the president now." The others in the house couldn't help but overhear this byplay and roared with laughter. Bill Clinton never did get through.

The Gore motorcade on the way *back* from the War Memorial was rather jolly. On the way there, in the big green van carrying the Gore children and other relatives, the only words came from Drew Schiff, husband of Karenna. "Can someone turn the heat down?" he demanded. On the return trip, after Gore came back from the dead, his daughters mocked the conversation between their father and Bush. "Well, you don't have to be snippy about it!" one would say. "Well, *you* don't have to be snippy about it!" was the comeback. And on it would go. Partly from lack of sleep, partly in disbelief, they were understandably giddy.

The margin in Florida between Gore and Bush was now around 1,700 votes—awaiting the recount, as well as the overseas absentee ballots.

The Gore campaign had always been about methodical planning—scouting the audience, testing the field, gaming the other guy's moves. But there was no playbook anymore and no time to build one. An hour after the un-concession, Chairman Daley gathered advisers in the campaign headquarters bunker they called the Kitchen to improvise legal and political strategy: How to handle the automatic recount and the irregularities in Palm Beach? How to maximize mileage from Gore's unexpectedly winning the national popular vote? They would need a boatload of lawyers and observers in Florida and they would need two

PARK COUNTY LIBRARY, CODY, WYOMING

key bodies—a legal general to map the battles and an éminence grise to defend the war.

Ron Klain was ideal for the first role. Only thirty-nine, he was the archetypal blend of skilled lawyer and political savant. In less than twenty years, he had starred at the Harvard Law School, clerked for a justice of the U.S. Supreme Court, been named by *Time* as one of the fifty most promising young leaders in America, and served as chief counsel to the Senate Judiciary Committee, associate counsel to President Clinton, and chief of staff to Vice President Gore. If anyone could navigate the crosscurrents of law and politics, Klain could. He might have run Gore's drive for the White House, but was elbowed aside in August 1999 by Tony Coelho, the former congressman; Klain left government for the stability and partner's draw at a snazzy Washington law firm, O'Melveny & Myers. When Coelho departed the following summer—replaced by Daley—Klain was brought back to Nashville, where he remained for the entire autumn, into Election Night. Still, though part of Gore's Kitchen cabinet, Klain was hardly driving the campaign train. The looming conflict in Florida gave him the chance of a lifetime—hours *after* the campaign was supposed to end. " 'Recount' wasn't in my vocabulary before this point," Klain says now.

Klain could manage the troops and implements of combat, but his O'Melveny partner, Warren Christopher, offered gravitas. He was one of the party's wise men—he was a former secretary of state under Clinton and a former law clerk to Justice William O. Douglas; he had vetted Gore and Lieberman as running mates and chaired the Rodney King commission in Los Angeles; he'd negotiated the Iranian hostage crisis under Jimmy Carter. If you could deal with the ayatollah, how hard could it be resolving a presidential recount? "A man of impeccable credentials"—that's how Gore spokesmen Fabiani and Lehane described the seventy-five-year-old Christopher while he conducted the running-mate hunt; they delightedly competed with each other to see who could use the phrase more, which, in turn, might get others to adopt it. Despite his slight, thin frame and a face that at times looked shriveled, Christopher had stature across the political spectrum. Everyone but the ayatollah referred to him as "Chris"; his more revered nickname, because of his portfolio and demeanor, was "the cardinal."

Klain was easy to locate. When he found out about the automatic recount, he left his Loews room for headquarters and Daley tapped him there. Christopher, however, was asleep at his home in West Los Angeles. His wife, Marie, picked up when Daley called at 4 A.M. central time. A dazed and groggy Christopher, pin-striped as always, was on a plane within three hours and arrived at Gore's hotel suite in Nashville after lunch Wednesday—around the same time Al Gore woke up. The vice president had finally crashed near dawn.

In Austin, the Bush campaign needed a countermove, and the obvious choice was James Baker III, who had been Poppy's secretary of state and was a less dour figure than Christopher. Baker guzzled Dr Pepper; Christopher savored a fine Chardonnay. Now seventy and a senior law partner at the venerable Baker & Botts in Houston, "Jimmy" was mentioned by Evans, Rove, communications director Karen Hughes, and others, but it was Dick Cheney, Bush's vice presidential candidate, who selected him. Baker, said Bush, was "a man of impeccable credentials"—not realizing the words were already popular. Fabiani and Lehane shared a guffaw.

While Baker had run five Republican presidential campaigns between 1976 and 1992, he'd had virtually nothing to do with Bush's. This wasn't about any chilliness between the two; Bush was worried about image—he didn't want it to look like he was about nothing more than his father's Restoration. For his part, Baker had led a full life since leaving presidential politics. It sure didn't hurt, though, that here he was being asked to lead the cavalry. Who would play the Republican version of Klain? Baker would work that out in the next day or two.

So, just hours after the networks had mistakenly declared Bush the forty-third president, each side had chosen its new commanders. Bush and Gore would stay above the fray—the governor in Austin, the vice president back in Washington—but there would be one more fight between them. Now the terms of engagement had to be decided—for a confrontation that few could have imagined, at least no one still living.

One hundred and twenty-four years earlier—to the day—the United States had found itself deadlocked in a presidential election. Samuel Tilden, the Democrat, had narrowly won the popular vote, but twenty-two electoral votes were in dispute, including, of all places, in Florida. Sixteen weeks of drama followed before an electoral commission created by Congress gave the presidency to Rutherford B. Hayes, the Republican, ever after "Rutherfraud B. Hayes" to his detractors. (In return, the Democrats won the removal of federal troops from the South, which marked the end of Reconstruction.) In this centennial year of the Republic, eleven years after Appomattox, the election of 1876 gripped and divided the nation. State officials were accused of rank partisanship, newspapers were attacked for their projections, the army brought four artillery companies to Washington to keep order. If nothing else, the protagonists of the election of 1876 could agree that they had been through a sensational event and one that could never, ever happen again. Not only did it, but this time it would be on TV—no need to wait for the newspaper to come out tomorrow or next week. Give Tilden and Hayes credit: They may have survived the country's first prolonged electoral standoff, but they didn't have round-faced Tim Russert or cute-as-a-button Ashleigh Banfield hosting it live.

two

The Gathering Storm

The day before the election, Benjamin Ginsberg, the chief lawyer for the Bush campaign, was having lunch in Austin. Another attorney asked about the possibility of recounts. Ginsberg thought it was a funny question—recounts in a national election of one hundred million votes? "It'd be a lawyer's nightmare," he answered. "We agreed it would never happen."

That night, the Florida division of elections got an e-mail from a student at Manatee Community College. Crissy Howell wanted to know what would happen if the popular vote in Florida ended in a tie. An employee routed the message to Clay Roberts, the director of the division, which is part of the office of the secretary of state, Katherine Harris. "I assume," wrote the employee to Roberts, that " 'Don't worry about the math, everybody would sue everybody, and the courts would have to figure it out' is not the correct answer."

"That's the answer," replied Roberts the next morning, as 5,963,110 Floridians, give or take a few, were going to the polls.

Little did he know how much he knew.

■ ■ ■

Outside his Tallahassee home the day after the election, Major Harding ran into one of his neighbors in the driveway. Harding was a justice of the Florida Supreme Court, its second most senior member and perhaps known best for his bow ties and courtly manner. The neighbor had been following the TV coverage and newspaper headlines about the contested presidential election and how it all came down to a few hundred votes in Florida. There was talk of recounts and deadlines, but little so far about the election coming down to a court ruling. Nonetheless, the neighbor had a question—and in the small-town, easygoing atmosphere of Tallahassee, it couldn't hurt at least to ask. "How does it feel to be one of the people who'll be picking the next president?" the neighbor inquired.

Harding laughed. "That's silly—a story no one would believe," he said.

In New York City around the same time, at a luncheon at the Columbia University School of Law, a reporter was sitting next to Jane Ginsburg, a professor there. "Can you imagine being a justice of the U.S. Supreme Court these days and wondering if this storm is headed your way?" the reporter asked another teacher at the table.

Professor Ginsburg heard the question, cleared her throat, and smiled. "Yes, actually," she said. "I can." Her mother was Ruth Bader Ginsburg, one of the nine justices of the highest court in the land.

At the Court itself, Chief Justice William Rehnquist was preternaturally prescient. Right after Election Day, he sent out a memo to employees admonishing against betting pools on who would win the presidency. Court staffers found the memo hilarious because there were so many other office pools around the building—for the NCAA basketball tournament, for the football playoffs, for which ruling would be the last each term and on what date it would be decided. A round of betting on Bush-Gore? "Let me in!" one employee joked, out of earshot of the chief justice. Too bad Rehnquist cut off the fun. If there had been a pool for *when* there would be a decision on the presidency, or *who* would make it, the chief might have made a bundle.

Before sunup that Wednesday morning, the Gore recount offensive was under way. In Nashville, when Bill Daley and Ron Klain came back to the headquarters after the drama at the War Memorial, they found that campaign attorneys weeks before had assembled legal materials to be used in a close race. No one ever needs to look at this kind of stuff in presidential elections—they're never that close—but you prepare them anyway, like writing rules and regulations for life after a thermonuclear exchange. In the Bush-Gore race, attorneys had concentrated on roughly twenty states where recounts seemed in the realm of possibility—and Florida was one of them. Before Daley and Klain arrived in the Kitchen—the campaign's war room, where day-to-day communications and "action response" were organized—Michael Whouley had begun going over the recount materials with Joe Sandler and Jack Young.

Sandler was counsel to the Democratic National Committee. Young was a Washington-area lawyer and a virtuoso on recounts; six years earlier, he had co-written the book on them with Chris Sautter and Tim Downs. *The Recount Primer* was a self-published manual complete with sample worksheets, forms, and goofy cartoons. "Recounts have played a decisive role in countless elections over the years, some even changing the course of history," the manual begins. "Lyndon Johnson secured his 87-vote win in the controversial 1948 Texas Senate race as much on the strength of his *post-election strategy* as by his aggressive election campaign." An accompanying illustration showed Joe Candidate seated with a fortune-teller. She looks into the crystal ball and says, "You lose the election, but there's a recount. You lose the recount, but I see another recount, which you *win!*"

The Recount Primer was the Bible to Democratic recount litigators; for the Gore campaign, having Young in the room was akin to having Moses at your Passover seder. The primer contained basic commandments. The first, always, was to have enough information. Without it, you wouldn't know which commandments to heed. Not all commandments could be obeyed; actually, some were mutually exclusive. Your commandment depended on your candidate.

"If a candidate is ahead," says one commandment, "the scope of the recount should be as narrow as possible." That means "duplicat[ing] the procedures of election night"—nothing more. But "if a candidate is behind," reads another commandment, "the scope should be as broad as possible." *Keep the counts going.* This made sense: Whatever happened on election night, by definition, didn't work. So you have to try something else, and then something else again. This is more challenging: The odds favor the guy in the lead. Still, as any statistician would tell you—and they repeatedly did on TV in those interludes of information that had to occupy round-the-clock coverage—every recount will yield a different number, so why not keep trying until you find the right one?

To obey either commandment, you have to have the troops—the larger the jurisdiction, the greater number of precincts to cover, the more people you need in the trenches, fighting for one vote at a time. On the book's opening page, there's a sketch depicting Election Night in a nip-and-tuck contest between Smith and Jones. "We squeaked a win—now we need a recount attorney!" exhorts Smith's manager, grasping *The Recount Primer*. "We barely lost—now we need a recount attorney," says Jones's guy. (Somebody is going to lose in the end, but it isn't the attorneys.) In Gore's case, this demanded armies on the ground fanning out to sixty-seven separate counties for the automatic recount that Florida law mandated. And because Gore was behind, he had to follow the second, more arduous, commandment.

Before an automatic recount was even technically triggered, state officials would first conduct a "canvass." This was merely an arithmetic "retabulation": Did any vote-counter transpose two digits or write in "100" when it was supposed to be "10"? If the canvass showed a gap between Bush and Gore of less than half of 1 percent, then Florida law ordered the recount. But even that process was mostly mechanical and not based on human judgment: Ballots, whether of the punch-card or optical-scan variety, would be put through the machines that counted them the first time. While the process could yield different numbers—maybe a machine malfunctioned or didn't register a ballot the first time around, or additional ballots were located—they probably would be insufficient to change the outcome. Daley recognized this early that Wednesday morning. The whole thing was subject to the law of probabilities, the classic flip of a coin: *Each* side would gain and lose votes in the recount, but why was either side more likely to come out any better than where it went in? "It's going to be a crapshoot," he told Klain, Whouley, and the others.

To get beyond the statistical likelihood of the same result, you have to change the data. "If a candidate is behind," said *The Recount Primer*, "the scope should be *as broad as possible*." That means harvesting *new* votes—ballots that haven't been counted before. That dictates a recount done not by a cold-blooded machine but by a friendly hand—subjectivity over neutrality, art over science, the human eye over a microchip. There were three categories of votes from which to pluck: the "undervotes," the "overvotes," and the absentees:

- Undervotes are those ballots that a machine determined cast no vote. This might occur because voters really cast no vote (the familiar "none of the above"), or it might be because they didn't punch in the hole on the ballot correctly, or fill in the little circle with enough pencil mark,* or whatever. In any case, determining what the voter intended requires examining each ballot by hand.
- Overvotes are ballots that a machine determined cast more than one vote for a candidate. This typically happened on confusing ballots or in the case of voters who were nitwits. (Voting for *two* presidential candidates sort of defeats the purpose.) The problem with overvotes was that manual inspection wasn't likely to accomplish much, unless voters clearly indicated what they intended— say, by writing on the ballot that they made a mistake voting for Smith and Jones, and really preferred Jones.
- In most states, absentee ballots have to be in by Election Day. In Florida, though—because primaries are held so late in the campaign season, and it takes time to print up absentee ballots for the general election—absentee ballots from *overseas* are given ten more days to come in legally. (This is because federal law requires that Americans abroad be given a minimum number of weeks to return their absentee ballots.) Florida's unusual arrangement—and the fact that so many absentee ballots come in to Florida, because of military bases there and the advantage of declaring Florida residency (no income tax)—means that these ballots are ripe for picking by an aggressive candidate in a close election. Unless, of course, the candidate thought those ballots might weigh against him, in which case the candidate would aggressively look not to harvest them, but to declare them spoiled.

---

*This raised the sticky question of why, then, all paper ballots shouldn't be manually inspected. Suppose a ballot had *two* pencil markings, but the machine read only one and therefore counted the ballot as legal. Under the logic of recording all marks by voters as evidence of intent, such a ballot should be invalidated.

One other rule for either side in a recount situation: Get good lawyers. If you didn't manufacture the right numbers in the precincts— if the local election boards used the wrong standards or failed to meet deadlines or didn't release adequate information—you'd have to go to court. As they arrived in Florida, the Democrats went about finding the lawyers they'd need from around the state and the country. Though they'd soon find two of the best—David Boies, the lionized litigator who beat Microsoft at trial and was defending Napster, and Professor Larry Tribe of Harvard, the preeminent American constitutionalist— the Democrats had early hassles putting together their legal lineup. The source of their woes was Jeb Bush.

Governors are powerful folks in any state's legal community. They hand out jobs, including judgeships; they hire law firms and authorize millions in legal fees; they control the regulation of industries and corporations. If you're a lawyer, it pays to be pals of the governor or, at the very least, not to be his blood enemy. It didn't take Clarence Darrow to figure out that representing the opponent of Jeb's brother wasn't the way to win Jeb's heart or patronage.

The most significant manifestation of the legal establishment's skittishness toward Gore was Holland & Knight, the biggest firm in the state, with branches in Tallahassee, West Palm Beach, Miami, and eight other cities. It had a long tradition of public service. It offered prestige and credibility, and would have obviated the need, as Klain put it, "to build our own law firm from scratch." And while Holland & Knight did have some ties to Jeb, it also had well-known Democrats like Martha Barnett and Chesterfield Smith on its partnership roster. She currently headed the American Bar Association. He was a past president of the organization and, at eighty-three, was the dean of the Florida bar; twenty-five years before, *Time* magazine had suggested him as a candidate for the White House should Americans be willing to look outside conventional politics. "This seemed like our only real chance at a major Florida firm," Klain says now. He tried to land Holland & Knight immediately.

At 1 P.M. on that first Wednesday, Barnett and Smith met with Joe Sandler and Jack Young in a sedan outside Democratic Party headquarters on Calhoun Street in Tallahassee. Sandler thought it was like something out of a John Grisham novel. (The car thing should've been a tip-off—Barnett and Smith didn't want to be seen in the building.) They worked out what Sandler believed was a retainer agreement, even discussing an hourly billing rate. (Yes, billing rate. No pro bono. While most would agree that working on the recount was a matter in the public interest, a client who had raised millions in campaign funds couldn't convincingly claim he'd be unable to pay legal fees.) Barnett and Smith arranged to meet again at five, with Klain, for a conference call with other lawyers around the state. Holland & Knight would then be given lead oar on the day-to-day legal wrangling.

But 5 P. M. came and there was no Martha Barnett and no Chesterfield Smith—nor was anyone answering at their offices. Inexplicably (and rather rudely for a firm whose mission statement promises "to cherish and nurture our relationships with clients by providing prompt, personal service"), Barnett and Smith had "stiffed us, absolutely stiffed us," Klain says. The conference call got under way at five-thirty without them. It was only an hour and a half later that they got in touch with Sandler and announced that they had concluded that the conflict-of-interest rules governing lawyers didn't allow them to represent Gore.

Were they correct? The conflict they cited was the firm's ongoing representation of the Seminole County canvassing board. As it turned out, that board subsequently did become involved in important litigation in the presidential race, and Holland & Knight represented the board. But on the Wednesday that Holland & Knight begged off, the firm had no conflict. All it had was the potential for one—and there's a big difference. Existing clients don't have veto power over new clients. Potential conflicts can be worked out. For example, Holland & Knight could've proposed that it represent Gore, as long as Gore knew it would have nothing to do with any lawsuit against the Seminole board. Could Holland & Knight have said it preferred not to represent Gore? Of course. A law firm that represents Coke is always free to say it would never defend Pepsi; it's even free to be evasive and vague when Pepsi pleads for the representation. But that's a different response than "We have a conflict of interest," which tells the prospective client the firm is ethically forbidden to take the case, when that is just not so. Holland & Knight's brief minuet with Gore simply shows the quagmire that Florida law firms found themselves in. They chose not to represent Bush either.

In his Wednesday-night monologue on CBS, David Letterman declared he had a solution to the crisis: "George W. Bush is not president of the United States. Al Gore Jr. is not president of the United States. What do you say we just leave it that way?"

The forty-three-page Recount Primer, as well as common sense, cast Gore and Bush in different combat roles: Gore would be the attacker, Bush would try to hold his ground. Either way, both sides needed to get troops in. If you were Gore and had superior talent on the ground, you had the chance of mining the best data—the arithmetic error or hidden vote, as well as the greenhorn county elections official who could be swayed in debatable cases. "You weren't on some random hunt," according to Klain. You were on a very specific hunt. Even if you were Bush, if you had the right personnel, you might go after certain types of remaining votes—say, military absentee ballots from overseas—but mostly you could fend off the Democratic incursions.

To amass the requisite armies, overnight, it was time to scramble the jets. Joe Lieberman was supposed to fly home to Connecticut on Wednesday for a rally celebrating his reelection to the U.S. Senate; state law had allowed him to run for that consolation prize at the same time as the vice presidency. Instead, his campaign plane would be used to transport volunteers from Nashville to Tallahassee. Seventy staffers, besides Klain and Sandler, early Wednesday boarded what had been Lieberman's charter, a Spirit Airlines DC-9, now rechristened *Recount One.* Those who lived near campaign headquarters went home to pack their dirty laundry. The rest went to the airport with only their BlackBerries. On board the plane, they got a crash course in recount warfare, direct from the pages of *The Recount Primer.* The staffers were given a one-page summary. "We decided it would not be a good idea to give the whole book to a bunch of twenty-year-olds who hadn't slept for days," says Nick Baldick, the Florida ground operative.

"I told my wife I'd be home by Saturday," Klain recalls. "How long could a recount take? How long could the nation go without having a president?"

When they landed in Tallahassee at 10:30—barely six hours after they thought they were done for, in what they believed was an impressive logistical turnaround—the Gore folks found company. Right next to them on the tarmac was a small private jet just in from Texas. Klain and the others watched out the right windows as a passenger deplaned, noticed the DC-9, and looked quizzically at his companions, as if to say, "That plane's got 'Gore-Lieberman' emblazoned on its side." The passenger from the private jet was Governor Jeb Bush. Life is timing: He and Klain realized at about the same time that they had just happened to fly in simultaneously. Jim Baker followed later in the day on a flight from Houston.

Jeb Bush's return to Florida had symbolic value, and he would work behind the scenes to mobilize his political infrastructure and legal connections within the state. Doing the latter would not only reap talent but keep it away from the Democrats. From Austin, the critical player brought in was Ben Ginsberg—the campaign counsel and D.C. superlawyer who, the day before, was certain a recount "would never happen," a prognostication he would never live down. Despite his amiability—the press loved his wit and probably the fact that he had once been a reporter, for the *Berkshire (Mass.) Eagle* and lesser papers—Ginsberg was a warrior.

Earlier in his career, Ginsberg was counsel to the Republican National Committee, and had served as a lawyer for various governors, senators, congressmen, and state legislators. And he had been involved in no less than two dozen recounts, the most notorious of them back in 1984, when he was just thirty-four. That recount was in Indiana's eighth congressional district, in the southern part of the state, between Democrat Frank McCloskey and Republican Richard McIntyre; the district was celebrated for its close races, picking five different congressmen in the six elections between 1972 and 1982. Though McCloskey was ahead by 39 votes (out of 233,000) when the polls closed, McIntyre was later certified the winner. But Congress—then under Democratic control—chose to seat McCloskey. In between were a string of recounts over six months. Ginsberg wasn't the only veteran of that conflict. Jack Young and Chris Sautter, later the creators of *The Recount Primer,* had represented the Democrat.

The slugfest became known in the lore as the "Bloody Eighth." The irony of it was that Democrats, going into the recount with a lead, had little interest in further vote counting and stalled the Republicans at every chance. Ginsberg, on the other hand, thought recounts were altogether dandy. If anybody had any illusions that the Florida recount of 2000 was going to be about something other than realpolitik—if some Pollyanna was going to argue there was any principle involved, be it Gore's "Count all the votes" incantation or Bush's "How many recounts are enough?"—the Bloody Eighth proved otherwise. The legal position you take depends on your candidate. If today's political mantra is 180 degrees opposite from yesterday's, well, such is politics. "Election officials are concerned with accuracy, not outcome," taught *The Recount Primer.* "Candidates are concerned with outcome. Election officials may (and should) conduct a recount innocent of the effect of their procedures and operational decisions. *Not so partisan representatives.*" Michael Whouley, the cut-the-crap pol from the Gore high command, was at least honest about it. "The point of a recount is to win," he liked to say. "All the rest is talk."

After Ginsberg consulted election-law specialists Wednesday morning, he, too, caught a flight into Tallahassee. GOP field staff and canvassing observers, from Austin and around the United States, made their way around to the sixty-seven counties in Florida, roughly matching their Gore counterparts. Operatives from congressional staffs and the Republican National Committee also arrived from Washington; Representative Tom DeLay, the House majority whip and a leader of the effort to impeach President Clinton in 1998, set up his office as a clearinghouse for volunteers. Neither side would gain the upper hand in bodies. The general election campaign over the prior four months had been too brutal for anyone to risk losing at this stage because of logistical ineptitude.

While Baker was going to run the show and Ginsberg would be part of the legal team, additional guns were needed. Baker signed up his old adjutants from Washington days, Margaret Tutwiler and Bob "the Human Adding Machine" Zoellick, to help with media and strategy. From Austin came Joe Allbaugh, the campaign manager, who would track all the moving parts, office space, and meal carts. Top advisers Karl Rove and Karen Hughes would stay close by Bush; Don Evans would log time both in Austin and Tallahassee; and Josh Bolten, the policy czar but also a Stanford-trained lawyer and Goldman Sachs investment banker, would remain in Austin as a liaison and, hopefully, to begin a presidential transition.

And what about more lawyers for the Republicans? They were like mosquitoes in a Florida swamp, as Dan Rather might've said. Baker, Evans, and Ginsberg rounded them up from all jurisdictions, including George Terwilliger III in Washington, who was a deputy attorney general in Poppy Bush's administration; partners from Baker's Houston firm; and a range of talent from Tallahassee and other points in Florida. Terwilliger, for one, got a call from Evans in Austin while he was on the air with Fox News in D.C. and had forgotten to turn off his cell phone. Most important, by Thursday afternoon, the GOP recruited Ted Olson from D.C., the top conservative appellate specialist in America, who had frequently litigated before the U.S. Supreme Court.

There was one other name that came up early on in the Bush camp—someone who combined politico-legal smarts and moral rectitude. Why not the former "Boy Scout of the U.S. Senate"?

Two days after Election Night, Jack Danforth and his wife, Sally, were on their way to a Caribbean vacation. A former three-term senator from Missouri and state attorney general, as well as a Yale-educated attorney and minister, the sixty-four-year-old Danforth was now in private law practice in St. Louis. Despite having been a mentor to Clarence Thomas and championing him for the U.S. Supreme Court during volcanic Senate confirmation hearings back in 1991—and being vilified for it—Danforth remained a nationally respected political figure, as well as chairman of the three-hundred-million-dollar Danforth family foundation. When President Clinton needed an outsider to serve as the administration's investigator of the Waco incident, he chose Danforth. Earlier in the summer of 2000, Danforth had been interviewed by George W. Bush for the vice presidential spot. Earnest, reflective, independent, occasionally sanctimonious—this was gray-haired John Claggett Danforth.

On this Thursday, the Danforths arrived in Cancún and checked into La Maroma resort. Enjoying margaritas by the turquoise sea, they expected to have the week to themselves, far from the electoral struggle of friends at home. But before they finished a second drink, a hostess walked over to Danforth and told him he had a phone call. It was his secretary, who informed him that Don Evans was trying to reach him.

Danforth left his wife there and returned to their room to call Evans, the Bush campaign chairman, who got right to the point. "We want you to represent us in a federal challenge to the constitutionality of the manual recount in Florida," Evans said. It wasn't clear to Danforth what Evans meant by "represent." Did Evans want Danforth to be the in-the-courtroom lawyer or the public face of the litigation who might spend most of his time on television? Resolving this wasn't paramount at this moment—Danforth had more immediate concerns about a legal strategy that revolved around federal court, a venue that Republicans had been sniping about for decades.

It was federal judges, they complained, who constantly meddled in matters better left to legislators and state courts. Federal judges were imperial activists hell-bent on "making" law rather than "interpreting" it, as the old saw went. Once nominated by the president and confirmed by the Senate, they served for life (the only thing rarer than impeaching a federal judge was a pennant for the Red Sox). American politicians going back to the time of Jefferson and Jackson had their gripes about federal judges. When the French historian Alexis de Tocqueville in 1835 made his prophetic remark that "scarcely any political question arises in the United States which is not resolved, sooner or later, into a judicial question," he never dreamed what American society would become.

The gist of the Republican complaint essentially dated to the 1950s and '60s, when the federal judiciary turned more activist. Landmark decisions about school desegregation, public accommodations, travel freedoms, and voting and marriage rights came from the federal courts. They, too, were in the vanguard of rulings limiting school prayer, abolishing capital punishment, expanding the rights of criminal defendants, protecting the press from libel suits, and creating new constitutional rights under the rubric of "privacy" that included the right to contraception and abortion. The Supreme Court provided most of the legal loot bag, but the lower federal courts often came to the party.

Federal judges, in short, were the darlings of the political left: What you couldn't get by winning elections and forging legislative majorities you got by hiring gifted lawyers and going to federal court. Damn the ballot, get me a subpoena! Why try convincing thousands or millions of citizens to adopt a position when all it took was the right decision by a federal judge or, at worst, five of nine Supreme Court justices? When demonstrators periodically convened outside the Court building, they surely missed the irony that they'd marched right past Congress across the street. From racial justice to equality for women, from environmental reform to product regulation (think tobacco lawsuits, not surgeon general warnings), the courtroom was the place to get results in government. It was a wonder that elections, too, weren't just fodder for litigation. Indeed, the only great social or political question that the Supreme Court hadn't seized in the past forty years had been the conduct of the Vietnam War.

For close to two generations, the legal system had hijacked the political system—and it drove most Republicans and conservatives nuts. They could win presidential elections, they could parry some legislative thrusts by Democrats, but there were always those federal judges waiting in the wings to smuggle politics into the law. Richard Nixon ran part of his 1968 campaign for the White House railing against the Supreme Court—and he followed through in his presidency by giving the nation William Rehnquist in 1971, who lasted the next thirty years and became chief justice halfway into his Court tenure.

From 1981 to 1989, Ronald Reagan aimed to make a conservative reformation of the federal judiciary a key part of his legacy. In addition to filling the lower federal courts with the most conservative judges in history, he put three justices on the Supreme Court. Reagan's successor, George Bush, added another two, though the first of them—David Souter—proved to be far more liberal than Bush anticipated and endures as the poster boy for how even the best-laid plans can go awry on the federal bench. Souter was an object lesson. And, in any event, bad memories don't fade so readily. Even with the Supreme Court and the lower federal judiciary full of conservatives, Republicans remained distrustful of the federal courts. The sea may look inviting now, but you always remember the terrible storm. Fool me once, but not again. People like Danforth had institutional recall and never liked the idea of trusting the federal courts to get anything right. It wasn't some philosophical inconsistency that worried him—that somehow his party would be seeking political salvation from the one branch of government it had learned to despise. No, he was afraid of losing and being made a fool of.

"Don, I have three questions for you to think about," Danforth told Evans. "Is this a frivolous lawsuit—is there a legitimate chance of us prevailing? If not, what will this do to the reputation of Governor Bush permanently? And what about logistics if I go to Florida? I don't even have a coat and tie down here." Danforth returned to his wife and they had dinner. He was concerned with Bush's reputation, all right—and his own. So weak did he consider any federal claim that any lawyer who filed it was jeopardizing his long-term credibility. You didn't want to look dumb with the whole nation watching.

The next morning, Evans called back and said, "We've thought about it and we want you do this." Danforth talked to others in the Bush camp, including Ben Ginsberg, the campaign's counsel, and got no indication there was any ambivalence about bringing him aboard. If there were apparent misgivings, they belonged to Danforth. As much as he might have liked the notion of reentering the political game—he'd been out of the Senate for six years and he'd been intrigued months earlier by the possibility of being Bush's running mate—he just couldn't imagine how a manual recount could be per se unconstitutional. "It didn't seem to violate due process or equal protection by itself, which is a different question from whether a recount *as executed* might not be okay," he recalls. This latter infirmity, however, wasn't something any of the Bush advisers had raised at this point. In fact, there was no discussion whatsoever of what specific claims to bring in court. The consensus only was that federal judicial intervention was needed, for two reasons: to rein in any recount and to get the legal ball *out* of the Florida court system, in which the Republicans had no faith. While "states' rights" were all well and good on the conservative lecture circuit, they had no place in this battle in this state.

Danforth spoke to his secretary, who went to his St. Louis home to procure business clothes. The Bush campaign arranged to send a private plane to Cancún to take Danforth to Tallahassee. Danforth checked out of the hotel, though he remained uneasy about the assignment he'd accepted. "Sitting around waiting to leave," he said, "I decided that if I was really going to be their lawyer, I should talk to Governor Bush himself and discuss my reservations with him." In his next call with Evans—this time, with Jim Baker on the line as well—Danforth said so.

"Well, you're the lawyer," Baker agreed.

"Well, I'd like to speak to the client."

Danforth assumed they'd put him through momentarily. The phone rang a few minutes later, but it was Evans. "Jack," he said, "it sounds like your heart's not in this. So, maybe it's best for you not to do it. Have a nice vacation."

At a lectern at his Nashville hotel, before a backdrop of seventeen American flags, Gore sought to reassure the nation. "No matter what the outcome," he said, "America will make the transition to a new administration with dignity, with full respect for the freely expressed will of the people, and with pride in the democracy we are privileged to share."

In a courtyard of the governor's mansion back in Austin, Bush also sought to reassure the nation. He and his running mate "will do everything in our power to unite the nation, to call upon the best, to bring people together after one of the most exciting elections in our nation's history," Bush said.

Flag count: Gore 17, Bush 0. The imbalance wouldn't happen again. Patriotic Bush would match patriotic Gore.

Tallahassee is a peculiar place—a mixture of old, genteel ways and a modern company town no different from any other state capital. It was the seat of Florida government not because of resources or size, but for reasons of history and geography. When Andrew Jackson took possession of Florida from Spain in 1821, there were two distinct provinces, West and East Florida, governed, respectively, from Pensacola and St. Augustine. When the provinces were merged, the little Indian village midway between the towns became the new capital. Its name was Tallahassee.

Old versus new runs deep. Some locals like to sport the bumper sticker "Tallahassee: Florida, with a Southern Accent," which is a dig at south Florida and its transplanted Northeasterners. The return gibe was that "with an accent" meant "south Georgia"—not twenty miles away—and it wasn't anybody's idea of a compliment. The one thing they all could agree on is that an invasion of media and traffic and out-of-towners had but one positive by-product: revenue.

The town of Spanish moss, gentle hills, and bureaucrats in short sleeves turned into "Ballot Land," as an ABC news producer, Eric Avram, later put it in *Talk* magazine. Central Tallahassee became an electoral theme park. If Disney World down the Florida Turnpike had Frontierland and Tomorrowland next door to each other, then it made perfect sense for everybody in the Florida Follies—election officials, judges, lawyers, as well as satellite trucks, hotels, bars, and party headquarters—to be packed in together. It sure made covering the show easier. The makeshift TV stages on public plazas often had twenty spots airing against the same Tallahassee backdrop. At one point, George Terwilliger and Ron Klain were five feet apart, simultaneously giving live interviews on the same subject, from diametrically opposite positions. It was like the old *Saturday Night Live* "Point-Counterpoint" skit, wherein Dan Aykroyd answered a Jane Curtin news commentary with the refrain "Jane, you ignorant slut"—except Terwilliger and Klain were talking at the same time and to different audiences.

In the middle of five square blocks of Tallahassee was the ghastly New State Capitol Building—a twenty-two-story fortress built in the 1970s by Governor Reubin Askew. If you approach it from Apalachee Parkway to the east, you see the tower rising up between two small, round domes atop structures that house the two branches of the state legislature. Because of that unfortunate configuration, architecture wags called the new capitol "Reubin's Erection." In the lobby was Governor Jeb Bush's office; twenty yards down the corridor, opposite each other, were the suites of Attorney General Bob Butterworth and Secretary of State Katherine Harris. Across South Duval Street, and down a clay slope, was the Florida Supreme Court, and across South Monroe were the Leon County circuit courts that would initially hear many of the election disputes. In Tallahassee during those thirty-seven days, you could meet all the participants simply by standing in one place and watching them bump into each other.

As Recount One taxied to the terminal at the Tallahassee airport, Klain believed that Al Gore was behind by a few hundred votes and that, under state procedures for the canvass and resulting automatic recount, he had three days to make up the shortfall. He was wrong. Circumstances had changed again. Katherine Harris announced that the official canvass had been completed and the vote totals formally submitted to her office. She was accelerating the process, proceeding to a recount immediately. The recount, she said, might be done by Thursday—the next day. To the extent a machine recount in Bush's favor would be a public-relations defeat for Gore, she had made his job that much tougher. It was *Recount Primer* tactics right back at you; what's sauce for the Democrat goose was sauce for the Republican gander.

Still, to Klain, it was the first odor of partisanship from the secretary of state—"bringing down the gavel on us as quickly as she could," he said later. Harris meekly tried to proffer a less sinister explanation. She had hundreds of reporters in her lobby, spilling out into the capitol rotunda, camped out on the Great Seal of Florida. She was eager to have them leave, and the only way to do that was to finish up the process as soon as possible. Her credibility wasn't helped by the fact that in the recount that followed, eighteen counties actually didn't. They only rechecked their numerical totals and whether their computer software was functioning properly, thereby ignoring a 1999 directive from her predecessor stating that ballots had to be put back through a machine. In Recountland, even "recount" was subjective, meaning different things to different canvassing boards. As much as the GOP would later argue that every ballot in the state had been counted and recounted and counted yet again, in fact, in eighteen counties they were counted only once.

As a result, more than 1.5 million ballots—25 percent of the state total—were never recounted at all. While it's true that Clay Roberts, the director of the election division under Harris, did try to get Volusia County (which surrounds Daytona Beach in northeast Florida) to obey the directive, Volusia was only one county and, anyway, a phone call from him didn't have the imprimatur of, say, a certified letter from Harris. A big deal? Hardly. But if Harris wanted to go out of her way to be fair, or appear like she had no institutional preference for a candidate—and, after all, she had been an honorary state co-chair of the 2000 Bush campaign—this was a particularly unskilled attempt. A political stage manager she was not.

Similarly, it may have been perfectly innocuous for Harris to be carrying on correspondence with Bush supporters during the post-election period. But when William Perry, who was advising the Bush team on Latin America, e-mailed her, "My heartiest congratulations for having won this triumph on Jeb's home ground," perhaps discretion might have led her to say nothing. Instead, she sent back: "What a night!!! Let's catch up next week." At the least, someone claiming to be nonpartisan ought to write—in what she knew was publicly available e-mail—that she thought it best to proceed cautiously and fairly.

In the two hours that the Gore plane was en route from Nashville, something else had changed. The magic number was now 1,784 votes, as the last precinct totals filtered in from Dixie and Lake Counties. That might not seem like a substantial number among the six million votes cast in Florida; however, in a contest where a dozen votes here or there could be the difference, it was significant. But there was another possibility—a repository of votes in the thousands if Gore could undo the Election Day meltdown in Palm Beach County, forever a Democratic bastion.

Sprawled along the Atlantic Ocean, Palm Beach County is Florida's "Gold Coast," so named historically for the booty recovered from Spanish galleons that sank offshore. The name also fit because of all the Old Money that has wintered there since the 1890s. (New Money likes it, too; Jim Clark, co-founder of Netscape, escaped from Silicon Valley and California's income tax.) The streets of Palm Beach are lined with pampered gardens and houses so large they deserve a gift shop. Yet the wealth is misleading; across the Intracoastal Waterway is the bulk of the huge county's population, a mix of agricultural poverty and the condominiumized middle class. In the presidential race of 2000, Republicans hoped for no more than 40 percent of the vote and, according to the *Palm Beach Post*, assigned no resources to the county.

Al Gore's hurdle wasn't George W. Bush, but the ballots in the 531 precincts of Palm Beach. A 1998 change in the state constitution liberalized access to the ballot for third parties; in 2000, Gore and Bush were only two of ten candidates listed. That numerical fact—plus, critically, the large elderly retiree population in the county—presented the elections supervisor, Theresa LePore, with a design challenge: How do you fit all those candidate names on a punch-card ballot without making it unwieldy? If the names were too small, voters might not be able to read them; if the ballot had more than one page, voters might not persevere to the bottom. Ballot architecture isn't supposed to be the stuff of great political theater, but in the Florida Follies, such little details—accidents in the electoral process rather than anything one could anticipate—became decisive. Her solution: the infamous butterfly ballot.

Like so many of the actors in the drama, the forty-five-year-old LePore—who herself happened to run unopposed for reelection that day as supervisor—was more of a chance bystander than a purposeful participant. She wasn't driving the freight train—it just happened to run her over. She presided over a snafu, not a cabal. How in anybody's wildest dreams could a poorly (or LePorely) designed ballot in *one* county of *3,141* in the United States affect the outcome of a presidential election? Editorial cartoonists had a field day with LePore. In one of them she was portrayed by Don Wright as a toddler doodling with her Crayolas. "Who could have known that little Theresa LePore would grow up to become elections supervisor of Palm Beach County and go down in history for putting the wrong man in the White House?" That kind of dig found its mark. "You want my blood?" she said months afterward to the *St. Petersburg Times*. "Here—take it." Bryant Gumbel sent her flowers.

LePore's punch-card butterfly ballot—though never actually called that until after Election Day—alternated the ten presidential candidates between a left column and a right column on two pages that faced each other. (The two pages were the "wings"; the punch holes down the center of the pages were the "spine" of the "butterfly.") This way, instead of the more intuitive alignment of all names being top to bottom on a single side, more names fit on the spread. The candidates were supposed to be listed according to how the political parties finished in the last gubernatorial election. Thus, Bush got the first spot up on the left and below his name was Gore's, and so on down to the bottom. But in between Bush and Gore, *on the right side* of the ballot, was Patrick Buchanan, the Reform Party candidate. Even though the Reform Party was entitled to only the sixth-best position, it effectively had been given the second spot.

The problem with all this was that the punch holes—where you registered your vote with a stylus—ran down the middle, so an inattentive voter might get confused. Since punch-card ballots traditionally contained only choices lined up on the left—and since Gore's name appeared second on the left—somebody might punch the second hole down the center. But that hole was for the second candidate on the ballot, whose name appeared on the right. That was *Buchanan*. He was the arch-conservative in the race who once wrote that Hitler wasn't such a bad guy in 1940. There probably weren't a lot of residents in the heavily Jewish Palm Beach County who were going to be big fans, all the more so with Lieberman on Gore's ticket. Buchanan spent no radio or TV money there, directing his Florida efforts at the Panhandle. (Opening his *Late Night* show on NBC, Conan O'Brien suggested the voters in Palm Beach were so old that they thought they were voting for *James* Buchanan, who was the fifteenth president, right before Abraham Lincoln.)

Had a Democrat won the Florida governor's race in 1998, Bush's and Gore's names would've been flipped—so Pat Buchanan would have siphoned off votes from Bush and the dead heat would never have happened. Gore would've won the presidency. The '98 race was just another fortuity that crashed into Gore.

Days after the election, a twenty-six-year-old animator in upstate New York, Mike Collins, inspired by LePore's handiwork, created the "Official Florida Presidential Ballot." It showed a straight line from "Bush" to a dot. But below was a spaghettiesque maze of squiggles and arrows amid the names "Buchanan," "Gore," and "Nader" that no mortal could follow. Collins mailed his gag to thirty friends. Twenty-four hours later, his Web site had thirty-four thousand hits and was on countless joke lists. In the electronic echo chamber of the Internet, his mock ballot eventually circulated to millions worldwide.

Voting for Gore, in the five-minute period permitted under the rules, demanded care. Picking Bush, by contrast, was easy: He was listed first and the little hole for him was first as well. Scores of Gore supporters in Palm Beach expressed fear on Election Day that they'd punched the hole for Buchanan. At seven in the morning, the very first voter at the Gleneagles Country Club in Delray Beach—a county commissioner— was confused enough that he hollered from inside the voting booth to his wife, "Sheila! Take a real careful look—it's tricky." Poll workers often were of no help, and there were stories of some of them directing voters who wanted Gore to punch the second hole on the ballot nonetheless. Back in Nashville, Gore's political staff was advised as early as 7:40 A.M. on Election Day that funny things were happening in Palm Beach, and election lawyers were researching remedies on the butterfly long before they were thinking about an automatic recount. When Butterworth, the attorney general, first heard the Palm Beach returns, he was incredulous. "There's no way four thousand Jews in Palm Beach County voted for Pat Buchanan," he told a Democratic staffer in Nashville the day after the election.

Buchanan wound up getting 3,407 votes—barely a fraction of the 270,000 Gore received, but still nearly 20 percent of his Florida total. (Palm Beach County has about 7 percent of the state's population.) Was it genuinely plausible that Buchanan could have done so well there? Even if not, if a ballot was punched for Buchanan rather than Gore, it surely would be shameless to claim it was a vote for Gore. On their face, the 3,407 Buchanan ballots were legal, even if Buchanan himself went on the *Today* show to acknowledge that most of the 3,407 probably intended to vote for Gore.

The more suspect class of Palm Beach electromechanical ballots was the 19,000 that constituted "overvotes"—those with at least two candidates punched for president, which in many, many cases meant Gore and Buchanan, especially, as it turned out, in precincts that went overwhelmingly for Gore. How could *that* be? Voters might have realized the butterfly trap and, wrongly thinking they had retrieved their Buchanan vote, then selected Gore; or they may have been fooled by ballot instructions that seemed to suggest they had to vote for both Gore *and* Lieberman, with the latter being the beloved candidate of Palm Beachers. Trying to decipher what voters intended in an overvote, of course, is a game of forensics and suppositions. But Gore could well argue that the circumstantial evidence made it far more likely that a Gore-Buchanan double-punch represented a vote for Gore than for Buchanan or just an irrational act. Still, quite apart from what could be done legally about the overvotes, Gore faced the commonsense question: Most Palm Beachers who wanted him—270,000 of them—apparently didn't have any trouble with the ballot. Were they truly that smart—or were the 3,000 and 19,000 just not? And whatever the flaws of the butterfly, it had been shown to the campaigns and local party chairmen in October—and nobody had peeped.

These were the kinds of things Ron Klain had to consider as he searched for a political and legal strategy in the first twenty-four hours after the election. If nothing else, he knew he shouldn't be the only member of the Gore inner circle in Tallahassee. So, Daley and Christopher caught a charter from Nashville.

For a short time, as cane-carrying protesters in Palm Beach began to organize and agitate for some remedy on the Buchanan screwup, the butterfly issue consumed the Gore campaign—much more so than the automatic recount. If it went their way, the butterfly would conclusively eliminate Bush's lead. But how could Gore operatives efficiently collect tales of voting problems in a short time? To litigate the butterfly ballot, they needed a critical mass of horror stories sufficient for a judge to hold that the ballot interfered with enough people casting their votes and that it would have made a difference to the outcome. If this purely logistical challenge—quite apart from whether it was relevant *legally* and whether there was any way to undo the damage—couldn't be solved, the rest didn't matter.

At twelve-thirty in the morning on Friday, November 10, the phone rang in Ron Klain's room at the Governors Inn in Tallahassee. It was Al Gore, back in his official residence at the Naval Observatory in Washington. He'd not only been thinking about the problem, but he'd done something about it. Forget enlisting the help of the AFL-CIO and its manpower reserves—an earlier idea, for which Gore offered to call John Sweeney, president of the AFL-CIO. No, Gore had called Erin Brockovich. Not Julia Roberts, who played Erin Brockovich in the movie about a small town's legal fight with a polluter—but the *real Erin Brockovich*. The vice president thought "she should come to Florida and lead our efforts to collect affidavits in Palm Beach County." Gore had figured it all out. "What Erin Brockovich is good at is going to real people and getting them to tell their stories in a way that they're useful in a legal proceeding," he told Klain. "That's her specialty."

Klain was tired, "really tired." But you can't exactly put off the vice president of the United States. "Sounds fine to me, it's great," Klain said to Gore.

"Well, Michael Whouley thinks that Erin Brockovich is a really bad idea. What do you think?"

"I don't know. This really isn't my part of it. Michael's down there running the political operation, collecting these affidavits and gathering the teams of people. If Michael thinks it, I'm sure it's right. I'm up here trying to deal, like, with Tallahassee."

"Well, I think Erin Brockovich would be great."

The call ended. Klain rolled over and tried to go back to sleep, bemused by the conversation. Barely two days into this Florida morass, oozing with legal mysteries, and the vice president of the United States was trying to recruit somebody to the cause who he'd heard about in a movie. "Bring in a camel with three heads," Klain said afterward. "It just seemed like the whole thing's a huge menagerie at this point. Erin Brockovich—of course!"

Twenty minutes later, the phone rang. It was Gore again. "I tried to call Bill [Daley], but his phone's off the hook and his cell phone's turned off," Gore said.

"Silly me," thought Klain. "I'd kept mine on."

"I've just decided I really want to go forward with this Erin Brockovich thing. Tell Bill in the morning we're going to do Erin Brockovich."

It was the last Klain heard of it. Brockovich was not spotted in Florida at any time during the thirty-seven days.

three

"Pennies Behind the Sofa Cushion"

on Klain's most pressing need was to familiarize himself with the situation in Palm Beach. When he first heard from a junior political staffer about the 19,000 overvotes there, his response was, "What's an overvote?" It didn't take long to recognize the potential mother lode. "We'd been gypped out of some subset of the 3,000 Buchanan votes, but now there were 19,000 more," he recalls. In the numbers game of an election stalemate, the more numbers in doubt, the better. But Klain was also affronted by what Theresa LePore's incompetence had indirectly wrought. That outrage helped persuade him that the Florida cause was not just politically tenable, but morally right. When he and Al Gore spoke by phone, he told the candidate so, and Gore was eager to get on with the war. Once Klain documented the Palm Beach numbers that afternoon, he passed the information along to the *New York Times*, which ran a front-page story the next day.

In the emerging political and legal war, spinning the media was essential. Gore was already behind and the Gore campaign had compounded the deficit by initially conceding to George W. Bush and then unconceding. Klain and others believed they had a small window of time to put Gore ahead before support among Democratic party leaders—and the public—waned. Gore never publicly, or privately, examined why there might be so little patience for the Florida process—Inauguration Day was still more than two months away—but he assumed it was so. Maybe he was correct; in any case, there's no way to test it. Certainly the media kept raising the patience issue and congressional Democrats repeatedly broached it. But even if spin did matter, Gore's obsession with it didn't make him look particularly good. It wasn't that Bush was unconcerned with image. Gore's problem was that his entire campaign—from his changing sartorial preferences to his newfound populism at the convention to his occasional tall tales of inventing the Internet—seemed like an exercise in spin. For the candidate behind in the vote count, that track record made his task a more formidable balancing act. If he didn't press, he might not get the public-relations benefits of, say, a front-page story in the *New York Times*; if he pressed too much, he'd look like a sore loser.

Gore's operation set up temporary shop in an un-air-conditioned strip mall in a run-down part of Tallahassee, right across from Sonny's Bar-B-Q. Even though it was late autumn, it was still hot, muggy Florida. When Bill Daley and Warren Christopher showed up in their suits and ties, they were soaked and spent; if the scene wasn't quite poignant, it was at least ridiculous. These two men of the world discovered the battlefield was different now.

Similar absurd scenes played out for the GOP, at their three-story state headquarters over at 420 East Jefferson Street; Joe Allbaugh called the place "Stalag 17," after the 1953 satire about American POWs in Germany during World War II. A former U.S. secretary of state, Jim Baker, may have had world-class lawyers in tow, but that didn't mean it was a world-class organization. Overmatched volunteers answered an overwhelmed phone system. George Bush, the ex-president, was unceremoniously disconnected every few days. A secretary who'd never typed a legal document in her life had to ask, "What's a footnote?" Hygiene was a luxury. Baker himself was spotted one day cleaning up hand towels that missed the trash can in the men's room. A garden became so full of Margaret Tutwiler's True butts (along with others) that it was nicknamed the Cigarette Graveyard.

And there was the story of Brody Enwright, the nine-year-old son of Randy Enwright, a key Republican consultant. One Saturday, Brody came with his father to headquarters. Dad had to attend a big meeting in the conference room with Baker, Don Evans, Ben Ginsberg, and the rest of the team. Brody stayed at his father's desk, playing GameBoy. The phone rang. It was someone from the Palm Beach recount festivities. It was urgent.

"I'll get my dad," Brody told the caller. He put the phone down, took his GameBoy and went in search of his father. Half an hour later, Tutwiler saw Brody in the hall. He mentioned something about a call. They went back to Enwright's office. A voice was bellowing out of the receiver, "I need an adult!"

Said Randy Enwright: "That was this whole five-week period in a nutshell—we needed an adult."

Back at the Democrats' shop, two top aides were sent to Palm Beach. Chris Lehane, Gore's press secretary, was supposed to grease the media machine—"pabulum with flair," he termed it—but he was deemed too partisan for what Gore hoped would be a more low-key press contact carried out by lesser-known staffers. Lehane said he was hounded by reporters and news crews, including one that followed him to an airport urinal and pleaded for a radio interview. Early on, he called Mark Fabiani, the campaign communications director back in Washington, and asked if he could be set free from Florida. "You need to airlift me out of here," Lehane told him. "It's like being on the roof of the embassy in Saigon."

Michael Whouley, the Gore campaign's chief political tactician who had run the Boiler Room in Nashville, was also dispatched to Palm Beach. He would coordinate fact-gathering efforts there. Within a week, he was supervising, behind the scenes, hundreds of Democratic observers at the recount tables. For the thirty-seven days of gridlock, when Gore wanted to know what was happening on the ground in Florida, he called Whouley's always-humming cell phone. As Klain and the vice president talked almost daily about legal matters, Whouley and Gore went over the vote-counting minutiae. The joke around Whouley's work space in Palm Beach was that if you wanted to speak to the vice president, all you had to do was pick up Whouley's ringing cell; on a few occasions, staffers did.

Whouley had stayed in Nashville on Wednesday and Thursday to close down the political operation. After Election Night and his heroic effort to corral the Gore motorcade, he actually found time for a few

Heinekens, a smoke, and two hours of sleep. Except perhaps for Daley—son of legendary Mayor Richard J. Daley, the old "King Richard" of the Democratic machine in Chicago—Whouley was the toughest pol Gore had. The fact that the campaign wanted him and his lieutenants in Palm Beach underscored how important Gore initially thought the butterfly was.

At forty-one, Whouley was already a character in the Democratic Party. Insiders each had a favorite story—like the one about Whouley and the Iowa caucuses in early 2000. Near its end, Gore's supporters were on edge in this first test of his base. Angelique Pirozzi was field director and had been in Iowa for months. Whouley had been there five weeks. One afternoon, Pirozzi was sick to her stomach with a fever and the flu. "I'm going to throw up," she told Whouley.

"Okay," he answered, "go out to the alley, throw up, and then come back and get to work."

She did and she did.

Such were Whouley's charms that the story made him seem sweet rather than mean.

Despite the tailored Brioni suits and well-organized if thinning hair, his thick Boston accent and tart tongue bespoke his roots in the blue-collar wards of Irish Dorchester. His political mentor, Bobby White, remembers him knowing more about the neighborhood at twenty than he did. When White needed a few hundred people to show up at city hall to sing "Happy Birthday" to the mayor, Boss Whouley brought them in. His admirers called him a street-smart Patton; Al Gore called him "the brain," for his knowledge of demographics, polling data, and elections gone by. Whouley scoffed at the cerebral tag. "Put me in a black leather jacket walking down the street and I'd look like I came out of *Miller's Crossing*."

One of Whouley's partners in private consulting, Charlie Baker, said figuring out which prospective voters to target is 85 percent science, 15 percent art. You don't win on the science. "It's the difference between getting a thirty percent return on your money and a three percent return." Whouley, according to Democratic Party wisdom, yielded a 30 percent return. He did, after all, correctly call forty-nine states on November 7 and had been the one to push Florida as a battleground state in the general election. "I wish we had more guys like Whouley," says Ben Ginsberg, counsel to the Bush campaign. "Smart guys are a dime a dozen, but there are few mechanics like him."

A day after he arrived in Tallahassee, Jim Baker began maneuvering. He took to the TV cameras to say Warren Christopher wasn't returning calls for a meeting, which was possibly true to the extent that Christopher had spent much of the prior twenty-four hours getting up in the middle of the night to go from L.A. to Nashville to Tallahassee. Baker and Christopher did meet that Thursday afternoon, in a conference room at the Governors Inn, which had become the Democratic hotel of choice, just across from the capitol. "You know we're going to disagree, but we need to disagree agreeably," Baker told Christopher. "The nation needs to see a civil tone." The two former secretaries of state went through the "rituals," as Daley later put it, but resolved nothing. It was the only time the two sides met formally during the thirty-seven days. Klain later said it surprised him that there wasn't more discussion of a negotiated settlement out of the mess, or of a process for getting there. His thinking was that the race was dead even at this point—a margin of votes in the hundreds or very low thousands (depending on the machine recount), with the Palm Beach 19,000-plus-3,000 looming.

The chances for a peaceable solution were further smothered by dueling press conferences Baker and Daley gave that day in Tallahassee, covered live by the networks. "The purpose of our national election is to establish a constitutional government, not unending legal wrangling," Baker said, waving his finger. "We will therefore vigorously oppose the Gore campaign's efforts to keep recounting, over and over, until it likes the result. For the good of the country, and for the sake of our standing in the world, the campaigning should end and the business of an orderly transition should begin." Anything else, Baker cautioned, would "destroy, in my opinion, the traditional process for selecting our presidents in this country," thereby "imperil[ing] how Americans govern themselves." He hinted that recounts opened a Pandora's ballot box; if Florida, why not Iowa or New Mexico or Oregon or Wisconsin, where Gore's margins of victory were slight? Bush hadn't asked for recounts in those states—yet.

Daley joined the game and raised the stakes. "What we are seeing here is democracy in action, a careful and lawful effort to ensure that the will of the people is done," Daley fired back. "I believe that [the Bush campaign's] actions to try to presumptively crown themselves the victors, to try to put in place a transition, run the risk of dividing the American people and creating a sense of confusion. Let the legal system run its course."

For two measured men, who had spent careers dealing with hot-headed politicians as well as lunatic lawyers, these were strong words. Good-of-the-Country versus Will-of-the-People! What would each have said if they'd been playing with opposite hands—Gore in front, Bush demanding a recount? No doubt the same things—this was an apocalyptic clash of good versus evil, light against darkness—only in reverse. It just depended on whether it was your Gore being oxed.*

Consider what their comrades were insisting just two years earlier in a different political and legal context—the attempt to remove Bill Clinton from office. Those who maintained that the lengthy impeachment proceedings were necessary, even if they entailed the disruption of all three branches of government, were now claiming that allowing the system to "run its course" endangered "how Americans govern themselves." And those who maintained that impeachment threatened our national institutions—even though little in the land changed other than daytime TV schedules—were now saying, well, who needs a president-elect before Christmas? The notion that Florida was about anything other than realpolitik—that this was a contest of ideas—was disingenuous.

When asked months after Florida if they would've been happy reversing roles, Baker and Daley each demurred. Then they each smiled, reflecting on the accident into which both had driven.

The Baker and Daley statements established the dynamics of the remaining thirty-five days—though neither at the time remotely believed it would go on for that long. The Bush side cried for finality and no more counting; Gore pleaded for patience and lots more counting—both in the name of legitimacy. Each side was convinced it had the better argument.

---

*Frank Michelman of the Harvard Law School has used this play in his writing. I consider myself another lucky monkey at the keyboard.

In 1876, the Democrats had won the end of Reconstruction in return for giving up their claim to the White House. What could they possibly bargain for this time—a few bills in Congress or parity in the cabinet or a promise not to utter the words "Bill Clinton" for four years? No, there wouldn't be compromise, neither in momentous constitutional litigation before the U.S. Supreme Court nor in the tedium of counting individual ballots in one precinct. Each side would sharpen its rhetoric and play to its constituencies, which wasn't hard to do in a country divided. With the center forsaken, it meant an ugly path ahead.

Al Gore's top dogs wanted a meeting with Katherine Harris. The time was right: Their Palm Beach strategy was still unclear and the results of the automatic recount would most likely be announced soon. "We were concerned," Klain says, "that once the machine count was completed," the popular conclusion was going to be 'Counting is done, Gore lost, and, well, that's it.' We needed to put a marker down that this wasn't over." He, Christopher, Daley, and another lawyer met Thursday with Harris, but got no more than what Baker had previously offered. They asked her not to certify any total until there was more information on Palm Beach, and they wanted an investigation of Volusia irregularities, for starters.

"I'll take it into consideration," Harris said. "Thank you for coming by."

That Thursday night, Christopher, Daley, and Klain went to Cypress, a restaurant recommended by their hotel. Who was having dinner at a nearby table? Harris, along with her husband; her chief of staff, Ben McKay; and, curiously, Mac Stipanovich, the top GOP strategist-lobbyist in Tallahassee and former chief of staff to Governor Bob Martinez. It turned out that Harris's first cousin owned the restaurant. She came over to the Christopher table, and while she had nothing more to say about the election, she did have half an hour to talk about her efforts in promoting Florida trade around the world, and how much she enjoyed talking shop with a former U.S. secretary of state and secretary of commerce; by golly, she'd even gotten an award from the Commerce Department. After calling out the chef from the kitchen to meet her friends, Harris just pulled up a chair and sat right down with these "two other secretaries."

"It was totally surreal," Klain says. Daley was less charitable: "She kept playing with my cell phone. Finally, she walked away. I had to ask her, 'Can I have my phone back?'"

First thing on Friday, Harris called her new friends at their hotel. She wanted a meeting at 8:30 A.M. sharp. "It felt very much like a setup," Klain says. They got to her office in the capitol just in time to see Baker and his retinue departing. In thirty minutes, Harris told Christopher, Daley, and Klain, she was going to announce a final total from the automatic recount. "I appreciate your interest in looking into various things," she said, "but this is my view of Florida law." She said there was a process for factoring in overseas absentee ballots a week later, but that she had no discretion to keep the totals pending any longer. There was no point in debating her. The Gore command, Klain said later, concluded the meeting was "all-baked and all-done," and that any attempt to dignify it by engaging in argumentation would be a farce. When they left her office at five minutes before nine, they saw that Harris had already printed up the press releases for her announcement. The meeting had been purely for show.

The day would go badly for so many reasons. Daley was excoriated in the press—most significantly the *Washington Post*, which had endorsed Gore—for remarks Daley had made the day before. "It appears that more than 20,000 voters in Palm Beach County, who in all likelihood thought they were voting for Al Gore, had their votes counted for Pat Buchanan or not counted at all," he had begun, with Christopher standing next to him. "Because this disenfranchisement of these Floridians is so much larger than the reported gap between Governor Bush and Vice President Gore, we believe this requires the full attention of the courts in Florida and concerned citizens all around our country.

"More than one hundred million Americans voted on Tuesday and more voted for Al Gore than Governor Bush," Daley continued. "Here in Florida it also seems very likely that more voters went to the polls believing that they were voting for Al Gore than for George Bush. . . . Technicalities should not determine the presidency of the United

States—the *will of the people* should." And then the finisher: "If the *will of the people* is to prevail, Al Gore should be *awarded* a victory in Florida and be our next president." Commenting later, Daley alluded to Palm Beach, its effect on the election, and "what may be an injustice unparalleled in our history" that demanded court intervention.

What did Daley mean by "will of the people," a phrase he repeated four times in his brief statement and that was used again by Christopher in case their listeners hadn't picked up on the day's "talking point"? Was it that Gore was the victor, regardless of any vote count? Did *he* know the "will of the people" better than the ballot box, however flawed, had tallied it? Was a judicial remedy for Palm Beach County really that clear? Absent blatant fraud, was involving the courts such a good idea to begin with? "For the second time in my lifetime," cracked Senator Bob Bennett, a Utah Republican, "a Chicago politician named Daley is try-ing to steal a presidential election."

On Friday morning, a *Post* editorial called Daley's line "a poisonous thing to say in these extraordinary and unsettling circumstances, and Mr. Gore makes a huge mistake if he fails promptly to disown it." Daley's remark seemed to be saying that "a Bush victory would mean the White House had been stolen," the *Post* wrote. Daley was being "reckless" and so, too, was his boss. The odd and ultimately ironic thing about the editorial was its implicit condemnation of the courts. To be sure, Daley's tone had been arrogant, but the substance of what he said was only that it might take the judicial branch to unravel the Palm Beach mess. Courts did this all the time in other realms: in school and in the workplace, boardroom and bedroom. Was it so unusual to expect them to insinuate themselves into an electoral jam?

Piling on with the *Post*, the *Wall Street Journal* editorial page said if the vote tally didn't give Gore the White House, "the Gore campaign will try to find a judge to do it instead. In your ordinary banana repub-lic, this would be recognized as a coup d'état." The *New York Times* held off just a bit, and admonished both sides to avoid a "scorched-earth legal strategy."

The Gore camp felt the heat of the *Post* editorial, read as it was by everybody who mattered in Washington. "We got whacked," as Klain put it.

Almost drowned out in Daley's statement was his announcement that

Gore would be requesting hand counts of ballots in four Florida counties: Broward, Miami-Dade, and Volusia along with Palm Beach. This represented nearly 1.8 million votes, roughly 30 percent of those cast in the state; out of the 1.8 million, there were about 30,000 undervotes, which, unlike overvotes, might yield actual votes for either candidate.

Along with the butterfly ballot, Gore now had two lifelines. The machine recount under way showed Bush's margin waning. From 1,784, it was on its way down to a slender 327 or thereabouts, depending on which total you believed at a given instant; all that remained to be counted were overseas absentee ballots due in late the following week. Pinellas County, containing St. Petersburg, yielded 417 more votes for Gore and 61 fewer for Bush—a net gain for Gore of 478, a third of his overall pickup. How could one county do this? Although different elections officials gave somewhat different explanations—some punch cards were counted twice and some not at all—nobody was alleging any conspiracies. It illustrated how fallible the vote-counting process could be, even without the subjectivity of manual counts.

The fact was, a mere machine recount, which presumably should have benefited neither side, was reaping a windfall for Gore. But statistical theory has little to do with it when the margin is naught—1.04 inches on a hundred-yard football field, as a Jacksonville newspaper neatly described it. The pickup was a fluke. Gore had reasons to hope just the same.

The notion of a manual recount came relatively late in those early days after Election Night. One of the attorneys Klain brought in to create his own legal Dream Team was Kendall Coffey from south Florida. "When Coffey raised the issue of hand recounts," Klain says, "it was the first time I'd heard of it."

Coffey was formerly the top federal prosecutor in the region and Klain knew him from his days as chief of staff for Attorney General Janet Reno. Coffey also happened to be pure Florida. He had been forced to resign after allegedly biting the arm of a topless dancer at the Lipstik Adult Entertainment Club in Miami. No strange behavior in Florida goes punished forever, and Coffey got back his professional moorings in private practice. Earlier in 2000, he had participated in

Florida's other sideshow—the matter of Elián. Coffey represented the Miami relatives of the little boy in the inner tube, who were trying to block his return to his father in Cuba. Coffey also knew something about election law, having led the voter-fraud suit that overturned the 1997 mayoral race in Miami.

Coffey explained to Klain that Florida law permitted a manual recount once the machine recount was done. Each side normally had seventy-two hours in which to make the request—and the last day of the window was a holiday, Veterans Day. The devilish part of the law was that it laid out no procedure for a statewide recount; the last statewide challenge to an election had been in 1919—long before the current statute was enacted. "There was no one to apply to, no one to call," according to Klain. The law seemed to contemplate only the local sheriff's race, where determining standards for evaluating ballots would be manageable. But how to do that across the sixty-seven counties of the state in an election where six million ballots had been cast? Unless Gore could somehow convince an enterprising court to order a statewide recount with a snap of a juridical finger, there simply was no *single* mechanism for it. The statute seemed to have been drafted by Lewis Carroll.

The only way under the statute was to request each three-member county canvassing board for a manual recount. Apart from the issue of standards, this presented a logistics horror. It required, in effect, filing sixty-seven mini-lawsuits and persuading local bureaucrats to do something they had no obligation to do—all within seventy-two hours. Moreover, what happened if there were a statewide recount but the Republicans became obstructionist only in Democratic counties? With Gore tactically unable to go tit-for-tat in GOP counties, the result would be net gains for Bush, without Bush ever having to ask for recounts himself, something he never could've done without undermining his stance against manual recounts.

So, Gore chose two counties—Palm Beach and Volusia—then added on two more, Miami-Dade and Broward (which encompasses Fort Lauderdale). Why just four counties and not all sixty-seven? Was it solely about logistics? Or was it that the Democrats were desperately attempting to cherry-pick additional votes in populous counties that went for Gore? Was it a political calculation that going after the entire state would look worse, since that would look like a fishing expedition? ("Cherry-picking"? "Fishing expedition"? The metaphors and clichés flew fast and furious.)

In the eventual postmortems, four-versus-sixty-seven became the central question about the early Gore strategy. Chris Sautter, a co-author of *The Recount Primer*, would later claim that he had urged Gore to seek a statewide hand count—all six million votes—but he said his advice "was pretty much rejected out of hand." Daley was especially dubious that Democratic leaders or the public would have much forbearance for a time-consuming recount, even if it presented the best chance for mining more votes. That view seemed to give little credit to the public, about whom politicians were quick to judge. The interesting question is whether one craving to be president might have tried to *lead* rather than follow perceived public sentiment. Ginsberg says Bush would've fought a statewide recount, but "it would have put us on the defensive. Though we worried that their decision to go after only four counties was based on a view they'd have enough votes there to swing the election, we were still pleased they didn't pursue the statewide recount."

Admittedly, Gore was in a box. As with so many hurried decisions Gore had to make at the edge of exhaustion—and, worse, having to do so from the disadvantaged position in a standoff—Gore never had a choice among pleasant alternatives. If he went after a few counties where there had been irregularities, he'd be called a cynic who professed wanting to "count all the votes," but then only picked those likely to ring up on his side. "We thought we were pretty cute hitting the big four counties," Daley acknowledged later. "Of course we went to the counties where we thought we'd pick up the most votes," Whouley says. "Recounts have rules. Socrates didn't write them. They're not necessarily about truth and justice. It's about what the election laws are by jurisdiction."

Yet that reeked of craven manipulation—stuffing ballots, not counting them—the kind of sanctimoniousness that gives politicians in general and Gore in particular a bad name. Since Gore believed he had the moral high ground after Election Day—he'd won the national popular vote, and here he was struggling to let people's electoral voices be heard, whereas his opponent was trying to mute the will of the people—anything Gore did that made it seem like he was forfeiting that high ground in order to win would expose him as a phony. Protestations about the absence of a mechanism for a statewide recount, however legitimate, were still realpolitik analysis in the end. You can't argue principles, then cite the practicalities; "counting all the votes" ain't the same as "counting some of the votes." The apparent hypocrisy in Gore's position hurt him later in court, when he was trying to invoke the kinds of lofty, vague constitutional clauses that invite judges to read between the lines and decide which litigant ought to get the equitable break.

What was the alternative? Gore could rightly have believed he was damned either way under Florida's ill-devised law that exalted local autonomy over consistency. If he opted for the so-called statewide recount, he'd first merely have to get it done and then fight off Bush's charges that he had no principle of selection—that he just wanted to keep the clock running. Without Bush also demanding a sixty-seven-county recount—and, one week later, Bush unsurprisingly turned down Gore's belated, televised proposal for one—it wasn't likely to occur, and Gore would still suffer the political consequences for having asked. "I remember being in a conversation with a couple of our people about that," says George Terwilliger, a senior Bush lawyer. "Well, gee, should we ask for a statewide recount? Why the hell would we agree to a recount? We *won*."

Finally, not that anybody recognized it at the moment, a statewide recount engineered by Gore would have highlighted at the outset the lack of standards in the Florida statute: What *counted* as a vote? On an optical-scan ballot (which looked like an SAT exam), a vote was relatively easy to decipher. Except for those ballots that didn't have a fully penciled-in oval, machines worked fine. But for those that had incomplete marks, should an "X" or an "O" or an underlined name count, and how much of a marking did there need to be? It was a subjective judgment, for which the Florida statute offered no guidance.

Punch-card ballots, like they used in Palm Beach and twenty-four other counties, were the most unreliable kind of voting system—up to eight times more likely in the presidential race to register no vote than optical-scan ballots. When voters poked their styluses into the punch holes on the ballot page, in theory they would push through to a perforated, confetti-sized paper rectangle that fell out. The remaining hole could then be "read" by a counting machine. These rectangular flecks, though, were a stubborn, idiosyncratic bunch. These were the notorious "chads," soon to be as infamous as Katherine Harris's eyelashes or Warren Christopher's brow. (The *St. Petersburg Times* on Wednesday won the prize for first mentioning the word "chad," hitherto known only as a country and half of a 1960s pop duo.)

Chads were a minefield in Recountland. What if the chad wasn't fully knocked out ("clean-punched," in the trade)? Or if the chad was "dimpled" or "pregnant" (meaning it was indented, but with no corners detached and no light passing through); or "pinpricked" (no corners detached, but with light passing through either a pinhole or around the edges); or "hanging" by one, two, or three corners (some called two corners detached a "swinging" chad and three a "tri"); or even marked with a pen or pencil, with no indentation? What about the "sunshine rule," which seemed a close cousin of the "pinprick"—any light shining through? Should a decision whether to count these ballots be based on the condition of *other* chads on the ballot, which would take into account a voter's consistency? And another wrinkle: Could too much handling of ballots actually knock some attached chads out? (Republicans fixated on this physical deterioration, even raising it at the U.S. Supreme Court. But it made little sense. Any chad knocked out was presumably well on its way. Or, if any chads could be knocked out by manual contact, then it stood to reason that the distribution of knockouts would be random, which would mean the odds of just the Gore chad being removed—and thereby being mistakenly counted as a Gore vote—were statistically infinitesimal.)

How to evaluate this medley? As with the optical-scan ballots, Florida law said nothing about how to judge punch cards. Canvassing boards in sixty-seven counties could have sixty-seven different rules; that sure didn't sound like equal treatment for the voters of the respective counties.

Other states—like George Bush's Texas—had established specific statutory standards. The Lone Star State said that manual recounts were in fact preferable to machine recounts in tight races. A 1997 law, signed by Bush himself, directed that even dimpled chads be counted if the indentation "indicates a clearly ascertainable intent of the voter to vote." That language elevated subjectivity over objectivity. It created a liberal standard, but more important, it created *a* standard. Florida had none. One former U.S. attorney from the Panhandle, a Republican named Kenneth Sukhia, watched in disgust as a canvassing board tried to invent a standard. "This," he said, "is not the way you run an election for the leader of the free world." It was hyperbole. Virtually all elections incorporated some manual counting—at least of absentee ballots—and there was always going to be some interpretation. The question that would reign over Florida was whether manual counts were worth it, or whether the alternative—eliminating human judgment and, by and large, trusting machines—was worse. And, as important as that predicament was, so was who got to resolve the question.

On the sprawling grounds of his residence, the turreted Naval Observatory in Washington, Gore staged a game of touch football with Tipper and their children. Sporting regular-guy athletic wear, like a black cable-knit turtleneck sweater, the vice president made clear to the invited cameras that all was well with the Republic. Asked about the recount, Gore quipped, "I think we're going to win this game. We're ahead six to nothing, so I'm very optimistic. I'm talking about the football game." This one lasted fifteen minutes—just enough time for TV footage.

In the grand parlor of the governor's mansion in Austin, Bush and Dick Cheney met with their "potential administration"—including a chief of staff, national security adviser, communications director, and economics expert. The topic was transition planning for the presidency. And, wouldn't you know it, photographers were invited in, too, to record a scene that practically squealed "Oval Office!"

The Washington and Austin news events, in which the media were perfectly happy to be complicit, were more studies in spin than any substantive moment. The campaigns intended them that way; the politics were about conveying images, not information. Today's winner in the Looking Presidential Sweepstakes: Gore by default. He may have appeared positively daffy in his football apparel—nobody mistook him for Bobby Kennedy at Hyannisport—but Bush was undone by The Boil. On his right cheek, Bush was wearing a large bandage, which aides informed the press was covering a boil. Was it an infection, an ingrown hair, a product of the stress of recent days, or merely, as Karen Hughes explained, "not a pleasing sight"? It wasn't like he'd had a heart attack or anything—that would be his running mate two weeks later—but whatever the diagnosis, the boil became the day's message.

The four counties Gore selected were fairly obvious. All but Volusia used punch-card ballots, with demonstrable anomalies. Palm Beach had the butterfly—who could know what confused folks might've written down on ballots or otherwise attempted to show their intent? Volusia on Election Night had briefly lost 16,000 Gore votes because of a computer glitch. It also had registered 9,888 votes for the Socialist Workers Party, but a later count indicated only eight; what happened to the other 9,880? There, too, were press reports out of Volusia about ballots being taken away from voting sites in "mysterious black satchels," and yellow crime-scene tape blocking the election supervisor's office for nine hours. Initially, those two counties were it for Christopher, Daley, and Klain. But Coffey and others urged inclusion of south Florida's neighboring Miami-Dade and Broward Counties, with their trove of undervotes. He might've been thinking of the illustration in *The Recount Manual* of a huge mound of ballots, on top of which stood a smiling prospector displaying his lucky strike. There were stories out of both Miami-Dade and Broward of black voters being intimidated. Between them, the two counties had seen almost 1.2 million voters go to the polls on Election Day, the majority of whom picked Gore. These were good places indeed to troll for a few hundred more.

But Gore's failure to go after other counties left him open to the inevitable second guess. In heavily Democratic Gadsden County, in the Panhandle to the west of Tallahassee, the canvassing board on Wednesday had decided to look over more than 2,000 ballots rejected on Election Night. The board did this as part of the automatic recount mandated by state law, even though manual inspections aren't part of the process. The result: Gore picked up 170 more votes, Bush only 17.

How so? Gadsden was rural and poor, and had many first-time voters. They marked ballots incompletely, or put their marks next to circles but not in them, or in some cases wrote in "Gore." It so happened that Gadsden used optical-scan ballots rather than punch cards. If Gore had seen the potential for gains in some optical-scan counties and requested hand counts in them, the story line of the recount might have changed spectacularly: Media counts later showed him with a net gain of several hundred votes in all forty-one optical-scan counties. If Gore had selected the right counties among them—after all, it was a smorgasbord as long as Bush refused a statewide recount—he could very well have reaped enough votes to roll the tumblers and put himself ahead. If that had happened at *any* instant during the recount, the psychology and public relations would've changed. If the Republicans were going to attack Gore for going after Democratic strongholds in Florida, at the least they'd have to admit he was pretty slipshod about it.

Manual recounts surely could pick up real votes, especially under-votes—"pennies behind the sofa cushion," in Klain's words—but they also offered a tactical benefit for any butterfly litigation. That, for the moment, remained the centerpiece of Gore's master plan. Recounts would buy time, as well as give Gore lawyers a chance to see actual Palm Beach ballots.

Residents of Palm Beach had already started going to court, unencumbered by Gore's strategic machinations. As affidavits accumulated by the thousands, three voters—a county commissioner, a chiropractor, and a housewife—on Wednesday filed a lawsuit seeking a new election. By Thursday, half a dozen more individual cases had been brought. The operative relief sought was a revote. Some wanted it open to anyone registered, others wanted it limited to those who voted November 7. Theresa LePore was in hiding and the canvassing board faced requests to submit no official totals to Katherine Harris's office until the legal questions were resolved. In short, there was litigational bedlam—the opening lawsuits in what would total some 58 around the state, involving 413 lawyers, before the presidency was decided. The main courthouse over in West Palm Beach, where the carnival accompanying the William Kennedy Smith rape trial had come to town nine years earlier, turned into a second locus of media frenzy.

The first was the county's Emergency Operations Center, a window-less, hurricane-proof building to which the county canvassing board had retreated. Here, amid the palm trees, were the microphones and cameras, the spinmeisters from both campaigns who could tell viewers with certainty why the other side was sending the nation to hell in a handbasket, and the protesters with "Free the Palm Beach 19,000!" and "Honk for Re-vote" signs. Some did. Bush loyalists paraded their own signs: "If you can read this, you must be Republican." The guy selling ten-dollar "In-Decision 2000" T-shirts made a killing. Some of the demonstrations were spontaneous, others were performed. Jesse Jackson showed up at noon and told the crowd of more than two thousand that the butterfly constituted a denial of voting rights. "In Selma, it was about the right to vote," he bellowed. "Today, it's about making votes count." (Jackson's fire-breathing appearance in Florida concerned Gore enough that he told Daley to tell the minister to dial it down; an unlucky Jackson later would keep using the word "illegitimate" to describe the Bush victory.)

It used to be that "news cycle" meant every twenty-four hours, with the newsmagazines adding a weekly perspective. Now, with CNN and MSNBC and the Internet, the news cycle never ended. If you cared about public relations—and each side did—you sought constant control of the cycle, even though at the very minute you mastered it, another one was beginning.

The Bush campaign moved aggressively to try to counter the furor over Palm Beach, which, given the show, became the focal point for TV. In Austin, Bush's spokesman, Ari Fleischer, boldly claimed that "Palm Beach County is a Pat Buchanan stronghold" (an assertion that Buchanan's own campaign manager, his sister Bay, called "ridiculous"). Karl Rove, the political strategist, was next. He said that Palm Beach's apparent support of Buchanan was altogether credible and that nearly 17,000 locals were enrolled members of the Independent Party, American Reform Party, or Reform Party. (The problem with those numbers, though, was that out of the 17,000, only 336 were in Buchanan's Reform Party; and the Independent Party had endorsed Bush.) At the same press conference, Don Evans, the Bush campaign chairman, accused Gore of "politicizing" Florida. Talk of a new election was dangerous.

"Our democratic process calls for a vote on Election Day," he said. "It does not call for us to continue voting until someone likes the outcome." Others did their best to rationalize the Buchanan numbers. A local Republican congressman, Mark Foley, cited voters who showed up at polling places in trucks flaunting Confederate flags. Theresa LePore herself initially pointed to the thousands of votes Buchanan received in 1996, but failed to note that was in a primary. And there was Congressman John Boehner, Republican of Ohio: "The people of Rome never thought their government would ever collapse. The Greeks never thought they'd lose it. Americans, being the great Pollyannaists of the world—I don't think they realize the great threat."

Among them all, Evans's rhetoric was the soundest. No matter how confusing the butterfly ballot had been, it was technically legal, it had been approved beforehand, and it was not designed to benefit any candidate. It was only a hapless mistake.

The same was true with Duval County's "caterpillar" ballot. Instead of cramming the names of all ten presidential candidates on two facing pages, elections officials put them on two sequential pages. There were five names on page 1 and five names on page 2. You snaked through to see the choices. Unfortunately, the instructions told the voters to make sure they picked a candidate on every page. That meant they'd wind up voting for two in the presidential race, which was listed on two pages. Duval, in the northeast corner of the state that included Jacksonville, had many first-time voters, many of whom were black. In the end, 20 percent of the votes in Duval's black precincts were thrown out—triple the percentages in white precincts. More than 22,000 overvotes were excluded in Duval, including 9,000 from black precincts that Gore took nearly ten to one. In some ways, given the history of black disenfranchisement in the South, Duval offered a more compelling case for relief than Palm Beach. Yet there was little clamor for litigation there. One lawsuit was filed and quickly dismissed.

Besides, what could be done to remedy either county after the election? As Daley soon explained it to Gore, "People get screwed all the time, and they have no remedy, you know. A lot of black people get screwed every day and they don't have a remedy. It's not fair, it's not right, but it happens, and that's just the way it is." A do-over was fine on the schoolyard playground; mulligans were a golf tradition, as any

Palm Beacher knew. But a revote—or even a statistical apportionment of the questionable votes—in a U.S. presidential election? That seemed unworkable; they were rare in any election, since it was impossible to re-create the conditions of Election Day.*

The judge who was assigned the butterfly cases saw as much—what precedent was there for a revote in this election? "Find a case in the continental United States since 1776," deadpanned Jorge Labarga in one of the first hearings. "That's my homework for you lawyers." For his part, Jim Baker concluded this early on. He said afterward that he had pretty much "ruled out" the possibility of butterfly litigation going Gore's way and thereby reversing Bush's lead.

Despite his boundless reservoir of political will, Gore recognized this soon enough about Palm Beach. Having closed down the Nashville operation, he was back in familiar surroundings at the Naval Observatory in northwest Washington—the staff acronymically dubbed it "NAVOBS" (which was less pretentious than "the Residence"). It was from this white-brick Queen Anne mansion, rather than his office in the West Wing of the White House, that he would monitor Florida—where neither he nor Bush set foot during the thirty-seven days. NAVOBS was comfortable and secure and might have enabled Gore to seem above the fray, except for the protesters, satellite encampments, and media stakeout crews just outside the gates, for whom Tipper Gore periodically sent out doughnuts and black coffee.

Backstage, Gore's party wasn't thrilled generally with the prospect of the vice president challenging the election results in court. His former opponent Bill Bradley, as well as various party elders, privately worried that, whatever the outcome of this race, protracted litigation could backfire on the party and set bad precedent in future races with squeaker margins. "My personal view is that when the votes are counted, that should

---

*There was support in the legal journals for a revote. The seminal article appeared in the *New York University Law Review* in December 1974. It argued that decisive intervention by courts in questionable elections was particularly appropriate "when serious violations occur and the election is close." The author was Ken Starr.

be it," Bradley told the *Washington Post.* "It is a perilous course to try to delay in the expectation that things will be turned around by lawyers." Perhaps, the argument went, Gore should accept the results of any recounts, await the last of the overseas absentee ballots, and then concede if he hadn't pulled ahead. Klain was defiantly taking the opposite position, saying no winner need be declared until December 18, when members of the Electoral College met and voted—what was the big rush? (Actually, the December 18 date was set only by federal law, not the Constitution itself. As such, Congress could theoretically change that, and delay even into January the casting of electoral votes. Inauguration Day wasn't until January 20. As long as Bush led, a GOP Congress wasn't going to do this—but, out of fairness, it could have.)

On Saturday, November 11, Gore gathered his war council at the Naval Observatory to discuss Palm Beach. Daley and Christopher flew up from Tallahassee for the weekend. Joe Lieberman attended, even though it was the Sabbath and, as an Orthodox Jew, he ordinarily wasn't supposed to work. Still, he followed the proscription against driving, and had to walk the two miles from his Georgetown neighborhood to Gore's house; as he walked along Wisconsin Avenue, escorted by five cars of the Secret Service, strangers honked and yelled, "Go, Joe, go!"

The meeting lasted all afternoon, as they discussed how hard to press the butterfly ballot and whether to formally join the lawsuits already filed by Palm Beach residents. The position in favor was the classic lawyer's argument—if the case isn't frivolous, why not make it? Lieberman agreed with that view. "You use the justice system to achieve justice," he remembered telling them. "How can that be too aggressive?" Lieberman was a former Connecticut attorney general and had a litigator's temperament, but he was also mindful of the politics—Florida loved Joe, the first Jew ever on a national ticket, and he wanted to be loyal to the constituency. But the politics cut both ways, as Christopher and Daley warned. Litigating a loser case paid no dividends, and would only further portray Gore as a man bent on blocking the rightful winner from taking office. Moreover, there were other options on the table— the hand recounts in Democratic counties. Gore understood the liabilities of the butterfly—the ballot had indeed been consented to ahead of time and any remedy now was impracticable—and began the process of letting the issue go emotionally. In deference to the impassioned voters in Palm Beach, he wouldn't forcefully disavow court action, though by his actions it amounted to the same thing. In a confidential legal memorandum of options that went to Gore and Lieberman two days later, the butterfly remained an item, but it had faded in importance. Four days later, in a revised memo, it receded some more.

For Daley, the debate typified what happens when law and politics collide. "A lot of the legal geniuses were saying we could get this and get that—a special election or a reallocation of votes," he recalls. "Get real here. These are not legal cases, these are political cases. And there's a big difference. What drives them is politics, not law books. There's no such thing as an election-law case that's not driven by the politics. No way some judge is going to name a guy president of the United States. It's not going to happen."

When the Gore campaign first called for a four-county hand recount, the Palm Beach and Volusia canvassing boards immediately agreed. That was Thursday. The next day, Broward decided by a 2-to-1 vote to conduct recounts of three sample precincts come Monday; depending on the results, it would then determine whether to proceed with a full recount. On Saturday, Palm Beach went forward with its own sample—1 percent of the votes—finishing the next day with Gore coming out with a net gain of 19 (this did not include the ballots that were double-punched for Gore and Buchanan—there were 80 such overvotes, out of 144 disqualified ballots in the sample). At 3 A.M. Sunday, Palm Beach reiterated it would then do a full recount, though there was yet another complication. The chairman of the canvassing board, Judge Charles Burton, wanted an advisory opinion from the secretary of state about the propriety of a full recount. A lawyer for the secretary of state, who was present, told the board that a full count was warranted only if there was evidence the machines malfunctioned. This interpretation appeared to be at odds with the statute, which said no such thing.

"Call the vote! Call the vote!" cried Carol Roberts, the outspoken sixty-four-year-old Democrat on the canvassing board, who would become to Republicans what Theresa LePore was to the Democrats: the village electoral idiot. Both received enough threatening messages that they were given police protection.

Following her motion, an exhausted Palm Beach board voted 2–1 in favor of a full recount—Roberts and LePore in favor, Burton against. Two days later, the board members would go through the same debate and would suspend the Palm Beach recount for several days because of both a legal opinion from the secretary of state's office telling them to stop and their unfounded fear that disregarding that directive could subject them to criminal sanctions. The lost time didn't seem critical at that moment, but it would come back to haunt the county.

All the while, the board wrangled over what standard should govern votes—dimples, pregnancies, or rays of sunshine. And what about the occasional deviant ballot, like the one LePore found that had a thin layer of chad removed but still left a gossamer of paper? Palm Beach's endless haggling over standards, and the actual counting, at which partisan observers weren't allowed to touch ballots, but were entitled to make objections and generally mouth off, raised the question of whether too much public access was a good thing. TV cameras were unobtrusive—they didn't directly affect the proceeding, though they did seem to exaggerate the amount of squinting and microscopic dimple inspection going on. But why was it so obvious that observers should be able to make ongoing, contemporaneous challenges to the decisions of the canvassing board—especially when some of the GOP objections were obstructionist, designed only to stall the counts? When a judge makes an evidentiary ruling in court, lawyers speak only when the judge permits it. When a judge announces a decision in court, there is silence. When a judge weighs a ruling in chambers, nobody's there except the law clerks. Was a canvassing board's resolution of disputed ballots so different from a judicial proceeding, such that the political interference that ensued was worth it?

On Sunday, Volusia, too, began to count—a day behind schedule. The delay had been caused by quarrels over what color pens the observers could use, who could pass notes to whom, and how long any recesses would be. It sounded a bit like third grade, except that smoking was allowed in the hallway. Volusia would include all precincts. Working in teams of two, fourteen hours a day, counters would be going through 184,000 optical-scan ballots. Typically, counters weren't regular election employees, but firefighters, sheriff's deputies, and other volunteers. Observers were volunteers, too, who also served as protesters when the parties asked.

Votes for Bush, Gore, and "others" would be separated out and the remainder of unresolved ballots would be put in piles of twenty for the canvassing board to resolve. If everything went apace, Volusia would be completed by Tuesday at 5 P.M., the statutory deadline for vote totals that the secretary of state had announced she'd enforce. Later on, Volusia's ability to count like mad and meet the cutoff would stand in marked contrast to the other three counties.

On Monday afternoon, Broward's sample recount—done behind glass windows and with open microphones, for the benefit of partisan observers—netted Gore only four votes, so elections officials abandoned any further counting. Their decision turned on the same issue Judge Burton had raised in Palm Beach County: What criteria determined if counts should go forward? The Broward board believed a full manual count could be done only if the machines were defective. The genesis of that legal view had a back story in the political maneuvering at the capitol in Tallahassee.

Even after Palm Beach had decided early Sunday to do a full recount, Burton sought a formal opinion from the secretary of state's office. The brief advisory opinion came Monday from Clay Roberts, the young director of the office's elections division. The only basis for a full hand recount was machine error resulting from "*properly* punched" ballots, he said. Roberts offered no explanation for his conclusion—no statutory citation, no court cases that interpreted the recount statute, no analysis of the Florida election law generally or analogy to the law in other states that used recounts. It was more in the nature of a summary edict, like something he'd have written during his West Point days. And, contrary to the normal procedure in her office and unreported by the media, his boss, Katherine Harris, reviewed the opinion before it went out. The subtext, according to subordinates in her office, was that she wouldn't approve a different interpretation. This special interest in an opinion letter could only substantiate suspicions about her neutrality. Maybe she didn't need to be Caesar's wife, but looking like Brutus would confer on her no legitimacy.

The odder thing about the opinion letter is that another version of it had gone out to Al Cardenas, the chairman of the Florida Republican Party. The day before, he had asked for a state opinion and in the response he received, Roberts explicitly rejected "improperly punched" ballots as grounds to recount. Why Cardenas got the more specific statement isn't clear, though at best, in hindsight, it made Roberts appear to be egging Cardenas on. The bigger question, though, is why Roberts was responding to a political party at all, when it was the canvassing boards that had to figure out how to proceed. Political parties were entitled to advisory opinions only when they were conducting primaries or fulfilling duties specific to them. While Roberts did not violate any explicit prohibition by responding, it only aggravated the secretary of state's appearance of bias. The opinion letter to Cardenas made its way to the Broward canvassing board, and it was decisive in its 2-to-1 vote against further recounting—even though opinion letters are advisory and can't be enforced against a canvassing board or anybody else.

The Florida attorney general, Bob Butterworth, a Democrat, did think Roberts was out of line advising Cardenas. But more important, Butterworth thought Roberts was dead wrong, and that his letter "smelled" bad. Butterworth had his own appearance problems as state chair of Gore's campaign; he had resigned the post once the recount began, but that was rather like bombing the enemy for four years and then professing neutrality. Butterworth enjoyed the publicity. On Election Night, he had been on TV from his home at 4 A.M. giving interviews on the stalemate. And on occasion, Butterworth could forget to pull the rhetorical ripcord: in 1997, after a botched execution caused enough flames in the death chamber that a corrections official had to open a window to let the smoke out, Butterworth warned would-be murderers that "they better not do it in the state of Florida because we may have a problem with our electric chair."

Butterworth called in his own staff to draft a rebuttal to the Roberts letter. In a formal opinion the next day to the canvassing boards, Butterworth attacked them as "clearly at variance with the existing Florida statutes and case law." He cited long-standing statutory provisions calling for a canvassing board to look at ballots "to determine the voter's intent"—even in the age of mechanical vote tabulation.

Though it wasn't entirely clear that an advisory from the attorney general trumped one from the secretary of state, who was a constitutional officer in her own right—and the AG by his own policy stayed out of election matters altogether—Butterworth's five-page opinion was better argued than either of Roberts's opinion letters, which contained no argument at all. But Broward County didn't have the Butterworth opinion on Monday when it decided against a full recount; the Palm Beach board members did have it, but suspended their count anyway because two state officers were giving conflicting advice. Nonetheless, the Butterworth opinion didn't have any more neutral imprimatur than the one issued just across the hall from the secretary of state. He was as much a partisan for Gore as Katherine Harris was for Bush. There's no expectation anywhere that elected politicians won't declare allegiances in a presidential election—after all, politicians engage in politics—but the risks that come with those declarations were never clearer than in Florida in November 2000.

Butterworth's advisory opinion was notable for one other reason. He made a prophetic observation in his cover letter. The multicounty mess in Florida, he wrote, was about to create a "two-tier system" for recounts, based on "differing behavior by official canvassing boards." This "would have the effect of treating voters differently, depending on what county they lived in. A voter in a county where a manual count was conducted would benefit from having a better chance of having his or her vote actually counted than a voter in a county where a hand count was halted." Butterworth knew that Volusia was going to finish by the Tuesday afternoon deadline. He knew, as well, that the other counties would not. The consequence of the "two-tier system," he warned, was "legal jeopardy, under both the U.S. and state constitutions." Bob Butterworth, to his subsequent horror, was presaging the "equal protection" problem that the U.S. Supreme Court would find conclusive a month later.

Volusia, Palm Beach, and Broward were certainly busy since Gore asked for full recounts in those counties. But what of Miami-Dade? Even by now, Miami-Dade hadn't decided what to do, despite being asked to do so four days earlier and despite the looming deadline.

How hard could this really be? As the *Los Angeles Times* delightedly reported: "From China, incidentally, came reports that its fifth census of modern times had been completed. It took 10 days to count 1.3 billion people." Ari Fleischer, the Bush campaign spokesman, mocked the Florida process; at the current rate, there wouldn't be a president-elect for weeks, he said, neglecting to acknowledge that most of the road-blocks to resolution were being put up by Bush representatives.

For both Bush and Gore, keeping track of the goings-on in the four counties was like being in Las Vegas during the NCAA's "March Madness" and trying to watch all the TV screens at the casino. How many basketball games can a mere mortal keep straight? How many recount proceedings—which often included not counting but debates on whether to count, and if so, which precincts and when, and do-we-need-to-talk-to-our-lawyers?—could you follow, either on the tube or by phone with your ground operatives? Cable television did the best job, with its running stock-market-like ticker across the bottom of the screen. If there had been sixty-seven counties, surely someone in either campaign would've gone mad at the spectacle. All the chaos suggested the dilemma posed by hand recounts. Since an election was an imperfect process and some votes were susceptible to interpretation, didn't it pay in a close election to give individualized attention to any questionable ballots? But was it humanly possible to have such a process and make it fair? Manual recounts seemed both necessary and problematic.

For his part, Bush understandably didn't ask for any of his own hand counts. But he thought about it. Just before the Friday cutoff for filing requests for manual recounts, the Republican legal hierarchy went over the issue at length at GOP state headquarters in Tallahassee, and presented the pros and cons to the one man in Florida besides Jim Baker whose advice counted most to George W. Bush. Brother Jeb had come over from the capitol for the discussion. He was firmly against pursuing any Republican recount, be it partial or statewide, and that view prevailed in Austin. Recounts meant peril for Bush. They had to be stopped before Gore had a chance to pull ahead.

■ ■ ■

Ted Olson had gone to bed early on Election Night. As a Bush partisan—and one who stood to get a plum legal job in a GOP administration, perhaps as solicitor general (the person responsible for arguing appeals before the U.S. Supreme Court) or even a seat on the Court someday—Olson didn't like the sound of things when Gore had taken Michigan and Pennsylvania, and Florida at best was too close to call. "I wasn't enjoying myself watching it," he says, "and I sort of can go to bed in the seventh inning and find out what the score was the next morning." Apparently so, because not even his high-profile, firebreathing wife, Barbara—a lobbyist, lawyer, and very blond pundit on the talk shows—woke him to tell him he might have Bush work to do sooner than he thought. The next day, several senior campaign lawyers in Austin called to ask him if he'd pitch in should the Florida recount become litigious. One of those lawyers was a former clerk to Chief Justice William Rehnquist. It may have been the first time after the election that anyone in the Bush camp even conjured the notion that the U.S. Supreme Court would become relevant.

Of course he'd pitch in, Olson said. But there were no more calls, and on Thursday he got on a transcontinental flight from Washington to Los Angeles for management meetings of his law firm.

Olson, known best for his sonorous, baritone voice and his standing within the Republican establishment, was a partner in the Washington office of Gibson, Dunn & Crutcher, one of the largest law firms in the country. Now sixty, he was a protégé of William French Smith, the first attorney general for Ronald Reagan in the 1980s; he and another lawyer, Ken Starr, were considered two of the prime young intellects of that conservative administration. Olson personally defended Reagan, as former president, during Iran-contra and had the peculiar distinction of being a party in a case that reached the Supreme Court—*Morrison v. Olson*, which upheld the constitutionality of the independent-counsel law over Olson's objections. Olson was mixed up in the suit to begin with because Democrats had accused him of lying to Congress about Reagan's cleanup of toxic-waste sites. A special prosecutor investigated him for two years, but concluded that while Olson's congressional testimony had been "less than forthcoming," he shouldn't be indicted.

Later on, during the Clinton presidency, Olson and his much younger wife became Washington's most renowned right-wing power couple. She worked for congressional Republicans during Clinton's impeachment and wrote a 344-page screed against Hillary Rodham Clinton just in time for her Senate campaign. He was on the board of the *American Spectator*, the magazine that helped make Paula Jones a household name; he was a darling of the Federalist Society, an influential network of lawyers, judges, and law students, in self-styled opposition to the "orthodox liberal ideology" that "strongly dominates" American law; and he was socially friendly with several Supreme Court justices, including the ultraconservatives Antonin Scalia and Clarence Thomas. During the Monica Lewinsky affair, ABC retained him to convince his friend Starr, the independent counsel, to lift his gag rule against Lewinsky so Barbara Walters could interview her in prime time. In between those activities, he managed to find time to represent core conservative causes before the High Court and elsewhere, like the Virginia Military Institute's appeal to remain all-male and the case against the University of Texas's race-based admissions policy.

But whatever anyone thought of his outspoken partisan preferences, he was—like Harvard Law School's Larry Tribe on the left—regarded as one of the nation's premier appellate advocates.

On his Thursday trip to L.A., Olson worried the Bush campaign might be looking for him. Every few states, he used the American Airlines in-flight phone to check his voice mail. Over Indiana, he got the word: Get thyself to Tallahassee. "God, let me at it!" Olson thought to himself. He made a series of calls to clear his calendar and begin rounding up his own crew of appellate specialists, many of them former Supreme Court law clerks, who knew justices and their judicial predilections best. His only problem, apart from being on a plane heading west when he needed to go east, was that making confidential phone calls on a plane is tough enough, even when Larry King *isn't* sitting a few seats behind you. Olson and King knew each other from Washington, and they'd run into each other at the Admirals Club lounge at Dulles. King saw Olson on the plane, but had no sense Olson was on the horn making arrangements to be the lead lawyer for the man about to become president. Oh, well. "The whole thing was surreal," Olson says.

When Olson arrived on the West Coast, he turned around and returned to Washington—on the same plane. Next morning, he caught a dawn flight to Florida. He had assumed he'd be running all the litigation. What he didn't know was on how many different fronts the fight would be waged—state court, federal court, canvassing boards, press conferences, even on Larry King. It became obvious to him immediately that he'd be both the "manager" and "performer" of "the federal litigation side of this thing."

Federal litigation? The step Jack Danforth believed was such a bad idea—a view that got him fired before he was hired? Yes, federal court was going to be the GOP path to the White House.

Customarily, federal courts stayed out of state affairs. This was conservative gospel, the mantle of "states' rights" that dated to the nineteenth century and was a central ideological line of demarcation between Republicans and Democrats. But because Republicans had controlled the White House for all but four years between 1969 and 1993, the top federal court—the U.S. Supreme Court—was dominated by GOP appointees and could usually be counted on to deliver at least 5-to-4 rulings for Republican interests. It wasn't pretty to think about ostensibly neutral judges in those realpolitik terms, but such was the way it was, especially with a Court that had become so politicized. If Bush was going to prevail by way of the judiciary, the U.S. Supreme Court could be his best chance.

Olson contemplated federal judicial intervention specifically because of an obscure series of cases that came out of Alabama in 1995. There had been an extremely close statewide election for chief justice of the state supreme court, among other offices. Several thousand absentee ballots weren't included in the tally because they had not been correctly notarized or signed by two witnesses. Litigation ensued in the state courts and then in the federal system, where the constitutional question became this: Did the state judicial rulings, which liberalized the authentication rules for absentee ballots, constitute an unfair change in state procedure and, if so, did that amount to a violation of "due process of law" or "equal protection of the laws" under the Fourteenth Amendment? What is the *federal* interest in an election for *state* office, no matter how outrageous the change in state processes might be and even if some votes wound up being "diluted"? What's the federal interest particularly when there's been no allegation of fraud or partisanship to manipulate results? Federal judges—the least democratic of all officials by virtue of being unelected and serving for life—are given their independence to insulate them from politics. But they're not supposed to be monarchs, roving the jurisprudential landscape in search of doctrinal foolishness and legal results they happen to disagree with.

The federal appeals court—the 11th U.S. Circuit Court of Appeals, headquartered in Atlanta—ruled the state courts had been wrong to include the absentee ballots, and this error triggered federal intervention. (The U.S. Supreme Court never heard the case.) So, Ted Olson figured, if there was a federal interest in ensuring fairness in a state election for state office, would there not be a greater interest in a state election for national office? It was true that the rules for those elections were set by states and localities, but, Olson thought, in the case of the presidency, surely those rules should be subject to review by a higher authority. In his mind, it was more a matter of "due process," which was constitutional longhand for "fairness," than "equal protection," which usually pertained to racial or other invidious classifications. At this stage of the recount, the problem was going to be the manual recounting of some ballots but not others—rather than the varying standards that different counties might use in those counts. But in any event, the two constitutional clauses were often used in tandem in election challenges, and choosing among them wasn't important. The real hurdle was getting the federal judiciary involved in the first place.

Olson was wise enough to realize that the institutional dance between state and federal courts had many steps. He understood that a federal lawsuit challenging manual recounts in Florida could well fail. But given the alternative—subjecting Bush to the interpretative mercies of the Florida judiciary, which was presided over by a state supreme court full of Democrats—it was the better road. As George Terwilliger, another lawyer working for Bush, put it: "The first thing they teach in law school is 'Give me the court, and I'll give you the ruling.'" Terwilliger considered the Florida Supreme Court to be "result-oriented, philosophically liberal, and politically Democratic"—as opposed, he might have added, to the U.S. Supreme Court, which Gore lawyers said was result-oriented, philosophically conservative, and politically Republican.

Courts, of course, weren't the only way to go. There was another, political route—the Florida legislature or, as a last resort, the U.S. Congress. The former was responsible constitutionally for picking presidential electors for the Electoral College; the latter selected the president if the Electoral College were deadlocked, either because of a tie or competing electoral slates. While Bush wouldn't rule out these political options, litigation seemed more predictable by comparison. Any action by the Florida legislature or U.S. Congress would occur weeks or even two months down the road, and in the world of politics that was an eternity, all the more so when Gore led in the national popular vote and might be able to use that as political leverage.

As the Danforth subplot had foretold, going to federal court was going to be controversial within Bush's circle. Not only would he be first to cross the judicial Rubicon—which, given appeals, would further delay a resolution and shore up the resolve of both sides—Bush would be doing it in a way that was antithetical to Republican principles. Terwilliger agreed with Olson. On his flight down to Tallahassee Wednesday night, Terwilliger had sketched out a list of questions to ponder, strategies to pursue. Number one on the list: "How do we get into federal court?" As a defense lawyer for corporate America—after the Justice Department, he went to the behemoth White & Case, fourth-largest law firm in the country—Terwilliger had readily availed himself of federal court because of the "feeling you get a more intellectually honest approach there than you do in state courts generally." The contrary conventional wisdom drove him crazy. "The only time I came close to losing my temper in all the media appearances I did was with Paula Zahn [of Fox News]," he recalls. "She must have been using Klain's talking points. 'How is this a federal question?' she asked. I mean, what does Paula Zahn know about the law? And I said, 'Look, this is about who's going to be president of the United States. It's the ultimate federal question.'"

Yet others lawyers weren't so sure. Terwilliger's partner, Tim Flani-

gan, and Michael Carvin, another Washington lawyer, argued that manufacturing a federal question out of state election law could be a
"stretch"—and they were hearing catcalls to that effect from others
versed in constitutional law. "Are you guys nuts?" one lawyer asked
Terwilliger. The one thing they didn't want was to take the federal
plunge and then drown. That would accomplish nothing and embarrass
Bush. It was fine to do that in commonplace constitutional litigation—
clients paid their bills anyway—but politics and public relations had
created a different kind of game. Terwilliger, along with Olson and the
campaign counsel, Ben Ginsberg, acknowledged Flanigan's and Carvin's
worries, but they were unbowed. They didn't have complete faith in the
political options and Terwilliger didn't want to "leave our fate in the
hands of the Florida courts." "Our job is not to find reasons we can't get
into federal court," he told them, "but to figure out how we can. What's
the best theory of a case we can cobble together?"

On Saturday morning, the Bush campaign cast the first legal stone
between the candidates. Its PR rhetoric would now be backed up by the
firepower of law. Attorneys would be running the show. The lawsuit
didn't guarantee that the presidential election of 2000 would ultimately
be settled in court by judges. But it set in motion that denouement.
Once again, the legal process was on its way to swallowing up the political process. "Rule of law" meant "ruled by lawyers" in search of law
that would give them political victory.

On behalf of Bush and Cheney, and the voters of Florida, Olson
went to federal court in Miami for an injunction against manual
recounts. The defendants were various elections officials and canvassing boards. "Though perhaps carried out with the best intentions,"
Bush's eighteen-page complaint stated, "the manual counts would not
be more accurate than the automated counts. . . . Human error and
subjectivity would replace precision machinery in tabulating millions
of small marks and fragile hole punches." Certainly there would be
"irreparable harm" in allowing those inaccurate tallies to happen and
then have the TV networks announce them as they happened, Bush
argued (without noting the irony of precisely that having taken place
on Election Night). And not only were manual recounts unfair in gen-

eral, utilizing them in some counties but not in others is a violation of "equal protection."

The last point was not without its intellectual flaws. After all, Bush had been afforded an equal *opportunity* under Florida law to ask for one, two, or sixty-seven manual recounts. Furthermore, carried to its extreme, the equal-protection argument would apply to, and seemingly invalidate, the very system of American national elections, which consists of 3,141 counties, each conceivably with its own voting and tabulation and recount systems. But Olson wanted to be sure to assert the equal-protection point along with the due-process claim. In that way, he could have it both ways: If selective hand counts were declared unfair, the remedy could be *more* counts. No votes would then be diluted because they hadn't been "recounted." But *more* counts raised the problem of standards—could a dimpled or hanging chad mean different things to different counters? It was a neat little conceit by Olson, creating a constitutional hall of mirrors for Gore.

Baker took to the capitol steps to announce and defend the lawsuit. Had the Democrats filed first, of course, they'd be accused of fomenting skullduggery. But Baker spoke of "integrity" and "consistency" and "finality," warning of "mischief" and "bias." He mentioned nothing about the analogous statute from Bush's home state. The Texas Election Code presumably had envisioned "mischief," but nonetheless allowed for hand counts with the vaguest of standards—the overarching principle was "any clearly ascertainable intent of the voter," which included but was not limited to a dimpled chad.

At his sixteen-hundred-acre Prairie Chapel ranch near Waco, Texas, with his dog Spot and running mate, Dick Cheney, at his side, Bush told reporters that he was trying to be "responsible." "I keep using the word 'responsible,'" he said, "because I think the people of America understand that there's a very good chance that Dick and I will be the president and vice president." The unfortunate transposition of "president" and "vice president" was just the kind of verbal goof that got Bush so relentlessly teased.

Bush's lawsuit was assigned to U.S. District Judge Donald Middlebrooks, who'd been appointed by President Clinton in 1997. Though the fifty-three-year-old Middlebrooks was a registered Democrat, he was respected throughout the Florida bar, and Bush lawyers, though they had hoped for a Federalist Society type, believed Middlebrooks would be fair. The judge put the case on a fast track, as the canvassing boards continued their counting or deliberating whether to count. The way the federal system worked, any ruling by Middlebrooks could be brought to the 11th U.S. Circuit Court of Appeals—the most conservative federal appellate court in the nation, and the same court that overturned an Alabama election a few years earlier, a fact that had occurred to Olson at the outset. Any decision by the 11th Circuit could then be appealed to the U.S. Supreme Court, which had the option to hear the case or not. There was one justice of the Court with special responsibility in this region: Anthony Kennedy. The different federal circuits of the country are each assigned to a justice, who's in charge of emergency petitions reaching the Supreme Court from that particular jurisdiction's courts, both federal and state. Kennedy's 11th Circuit turf covered the southeastern United States, including Florida. He could not help but notice the events unfolding in his bailiwick. Should he fear the runaway train headed in his direction? Or relish the chance to be the hero, to rescue his country from constitutional calamity?

The next day, the *New York Times* ran an Op-Ed piece championing the role of courts. "In a nation as litigious as ours, lawsuits over close elections are no novelty and will continue to occur," it read. "But this creates no crisis, even in a close presidential election. . . . Getting this right is more important than getting it over with." The author was Larry Tribe. His ardent article almost made him sound like he was representing Al Gore. Actually, he was, though the *Times* didn't mention it.

Tribe was in the bathroom of his Cambridge, Massachusetts, home Saturday around noon when Ron Klain called from Tallahassee. It was two hours after Bush's emergency federal lawsuit had been filed. Klain was one of Tribe's many protégés out of the Harvard Law School. In the mid-1980s, Tribe's wife, Carolyn, had met Klain while both were working on Congressman Ed Markey's unsuccessful run for the U.S. Senate. She was sufficiently impressed that she introduced him to her husband, and Tribe, as he put it, "made sure that the admissions office didn't lose track of him." Klain and Tribe remained close over the next decade and, when Klain needed a lawyer to match Olson in federal court, Tribe was the only name he really considered. Much had changed in the eighty hours since Gore unconceded and the Florida wars began. "At the beginning, I didn't think about Larry at all," Klain says. "Constitutional law never crossed my mind."

Like so many arcane specialties—Hegelian philosophy, string theory, Basque Separatist haute cuisine—American constitutional law lends itself to true mastery by only a few. With fewer than a hundred constitutional cases a year being argued in the U.S. Supreme Court, there isn't much demand or room for perceived expertise. The fifty-nine-year-old Tribe was nonpareil as both scholar and litigator, even though his activist philosophy and professorial style could be grating at times. Tribe's résumé was daunting: math prodigy as a Harvard undergraduate; law clerk to Justice Potter Stewart; at twenty-seven, a Harvard law professor; at thirty-seven, the author of the still-definitive treatise on constitutional law; and advocate before the U.S. Supreme Court a remarkable twenty-nine times, winning eighteen of those cases outright and making a bundle of money along the way. He might've made it himself to the High Court. That is, until he thrust himself into the Washington political vortex in 1987, helping Senate Democrats defeat the Court nomination of conservative icon Robert Bork.

Klain told Tribe of the existence of Bush's federal case—he hadn't seen the formal complaint—and asked for a gut sense. Tribe asked for ten minutes to think about it, Klain called back, and Tribe spun out an outline based on federal judicial deference to state law and processes— "federalism" or the old "states' rights," as they called it on the other side. Any relief Bush wanted from a federal court he could seek in state court, which was in a better position to know the state's own laws regardless. Tribe had argued along these lines before—most notably in 1987 on behalf of Pennzoil in its titanic showdown with Texaco—but he was more typically in federal court urging intervention rather than restraint. He had made a nice living from defending an American's right to "make a federal case" out of all sorts of grievances. There was some irony in his now thinking of getting a federal judge to declare himself humble—just as the role reversal for Ted Olson had been strange. Klain explained that the court timetable was extraordinary—a hearing was scheduled for that afternoon. Could Larry get on a plane to south Florida right away?

Tribe's personal feeling was that he was very busy and this wasn't a case, despite the electoral context, that was going anywhere—he thought it was going to be legally DOA. But his wife, who usually served as the brake on his enthusiasms and overbookings, this time advised him to go full steam, and said she'd join him in Florida later in the day. "It was the first time in thirty-five years of marriage that she packed my suitcase," Tribe recalls.

He got on a Delta flight out of Boston and worried much of the trip that he was on a wasted mission. "I thought enough had gone wrong in that campaign that it wouldn't have shocked me if I arrived there only to be told the argument was half over." Instead, when Tribe got to Florida, he found out the court hearing had been put off until Monday morning.

Tribe's hiring was an illustration of both Klain's influence and the impossible chain-of-command problems that the crushing time pressure created. Warren Christopher and Bill Daley didn't know Tribe was even under consideration until Klain informed them he had put Tribe on a plane. Neither did Gore, interestingly; since he was an acknowledged micromanager, would not the selection of a key lawyer count as a major strategic call? Christopher and Daley were concerned that Tribe, who was remembered by many conservatives as the professor who had put the intellectual dagger into Robert Bork, was too hot. Klain told Christopher and Daley he wanted the best lawyers he could get, noting he'd also brought on Bill Bradley's campaign counsel and operatives from the old Michael Dukakis presidential run. Since Bradley had challenged Gore in the primaries and Dukakis was a forbidden name among Democrats, Klain thought hiring their people gave him cover within his party. His selection of Tribe prevailed, though in the endgame of the thirty-seven days, the high command's trust in him would vanish.

With a Dickensian cast of lawyers before him—seven for Bush, including Olson, twenty-three for Gore and other parties—Judge Middlebrooks heard oral argument. The law loves a coincidence: The courtroom happened to be the same one where the federal case of Elián Gonzalez was heard and where Manuel Noriega, the former Panamanian dictator, stood trial. Because it was a federal courtroom, there would be no TV cameras.

The hearing went a little over two hours. While Tribe and Olson were on their game—smart, responsive, articulate—the case wasn't at all hard to present. It was the high-minded jurisprudential equivalent of the snippy exchange that the candidates themselves had engaged in late on Election Night. Olson told the court that selective hand recounts were "unreliable," "subjective," and "inevitably biased," and therefore clearly unconstitutional. Tribe told the court that Olson's objections were "utterly quotidian" and that Olson's client was seeking to "enshrine in darkness what the will of the people was," and that Florida's law was clearly constitutional. (Take that, you quotidian enshriner of darkness!) The best moment of the argument came after it. Tribe and Alan Dershowitz, his Harvard colleague, who was representing several Palm Beach voters, raced for the TV lights waiting outside the courthouse. Tribe won, proving that quick wits always beat a motormouth.

Within an hour, Middlebrooks ruled against Bush in a twenty-four-page decision, a length that suggested he'd worked through the issues well prior to the hearing. The judge professed to take "great comfort" that his own ruling would be reviewed by higher authorities, but his opinion manifested little equivocation on the relative legal merits of what at one point he referred to as a "garden-variety election dispute." (There's an old motto ascribed to trial judges—"sometimes in error, but never in doubt"—that Middlebrooks seemed to be honoring.)

The arguments before him were "serious," Middlebrooks wrote. "The question is *who* should consider them." Not him, he said in effect. "Under the Constitution of the United States, responsibility for selection of [presidential] electors ... rests primarily with the people of Florida, its elections officials and, if necessary, its courts. The procedures employed by Florida appear to be neutral" and of the kind ordinarily immune from "federal legal challenge"—unlike, say, practices aimed at depriving racial minorities of the right to vote.

But what of Bush's claim about *selective* hand recounts? The judge wasn't buying. "The state election scheme," according to Middlebrooks, was "reasonable and non-discriminatory . . . designed to protect the integrity and reliability of the electoral process . . . by providing a structural means of detecting and correcting clerical or electronic tabulating errors" in counting ballots. Moreover, Florida's manual-recount provision had no animus—it did not "limit candidates' access to the ballot or interfere with voters' rights." Instead, the law "strives to strengthen rather than dilute the right to vote by securing, as near as humanly possible, an accurate and true reflection of the will of the electorate" and "resides within the broad ambit of *state* control over presidential election procedures." Article II of the Constitution itself made explicit the authoritative role of each *state*, as opposed to the federal judiciary, in decreeing how presidential electors were chosen. There was even a benefit, Middlebrooks found, to an electoral system run by localities. "Rather than a sign of weakness or constitutional injury, some solace can be taken in the fact that no one centralized body or person can control the tabulation of an entire statewide or national election. For the more county boards and individuals involved in the electoral regulation process, the less likely it becomes that corruption, bias or error can influence the ultimate result."

In less than two days, Middlebrooks had crafted one of the most thoughtful legal opinions of those thirty-seven days that determined a presidency. Little noticed by the commentariat, it was a compelling defense of judicial restraint, of staying in the wings when so many in the crowd were calling for a command appearance. Middlebrooks understood the value of *not* deciding cases. "Federal judges are not the bosses in state election disputes," he wrote in conclusion, slyly quoting another federal judge, J. L. Edmondson. Why sly? Edmondson, the "Scalia of the South," was a member of the 11th Circuit, the appeals court that might be reviewing his decision. Middlebrooks well knew that. Gore phoned Tribe to congratulate him on his victory, but the vice president's high regard for the professor would not survive the thirty-seven days.

Middlebrooks's firm dismissal of Bush's claims was just the first in a memorable sequence of episodes that day and the next that shaped the ensuing month. The political and legal issues had been joined—or, rather, where politics failed, lawsuits rushed in. Bush had invoked federal court and chalked up a loss; Gore was on his way to state court to buy more time for recounts; and, between them, four counties continued to get themselves bollixed up in recount minutiae—it was a wonder they had managed to put on an election at all back on November 7.

Ron Klain likened the entire ordeal to the opening of a James Bond movie, "where you're driving along and the guy in front first pours oil on the road, then nails, then glass, and then spits out black smoke." Every day, Klain complained, "there was a different obstacle thrown in our way." Baker was no Goldfinger, but he'd intended it just that way.

four

All About Katherine

Section 102.112(1) of Florida's statutory code directs every county's canvassing board to certify its election returns and forward them to the secretary of state by 5 P.M. on the seventh day after an election. The law even established a two-hundred-dollar-a-day fine for late returns, payable by each board member out of his or her pocket. For the presidential race of 2000, that meant a deadline of Tuesday, November 14. In turn, the secretary of state would tally up the numbers, add in the last of the overseas absentee ballots due in by Friday, November 17, and then a ceremonial state commission would certify the outcome and declare a winner.

How on earth a large county could possibly have its numbers ready by November 14 in the case of a manual recount was anybody's guess, but that's what Section 102.112(1), in its infinite wisdom, required. Such was Florida election law, 124 pages of it, where so many provisions entered the law books just before midnight on the last day of the legislative session. Whether this was by design or negligence depended on whom you asked and who was getting screwed at that moment. Otto von Bismarck once observed that there were two things people should not see being made—sausage and laws. In that spirit, a former majority leader of Florida's House of Representatives liked to call his state's leg-islation a "clusterfuck."

The November 14 date represented just one of the many advantages George W. Bush had going into the second week. Assuming he remained in the lead when the fax machines were turned off in the secretary of state's offices that afternoon, and assuming the overseas absentee ballots went his way—which everybody expected, given how many of them were from the U.S. military—then Bush would be certified the winner of the Sunshine State's electoral votes. The only way for Al Gore to pre-vail would be a post-certification court challenge.

Such a "contest," as state law called it, was a different animal from the recount proceedings before local canvassing boards. Those earlier proceedings, termed "protests," were inherently political, even though a judge sat on each board. They necessarily connoted local discretion and possibly varying standards. By contrast, a "contest" was a centralized case, before a single judge, that would take place in a Tallahassee court-room, with any ruling being appealable to a higher court. A contest was supposed to be governed by the neutral rules of a magistrate, who pre-sumably could ensure that standards were followed and that the process was fair. The judge would have broad equitable powers to make things right, so if, for example, further recounting was needed, he could order it. Because the judge had statewide jurisdiction and would be supervis-ing any recounts, in theory any disputed ballots would be decided by him—that was the definition of equal treatment and a far cry from the possible disparities of different canvassing boards.

If you're Al Gore, that shouldn't have sounded so bad—who cared, then, if the Tuesday, November 14, deadline lapsed? There would be recourse thereafter, and under judicial supervision. The PR quandary, though, was the formal certification for Bush. That reflected an official declaration of victory and would be trumpeted by headline writers and Bush himself. Would the public then tolerate litigation that might look like chicanery? No, Gore and his commanders believed, the certifica-tion had to be blocked and the November 14 deadline erased from the calendar.

Deadlines in the law are a funny business. Arbitrary as they are, you have to have them nonetheless, or else the world of commerce and gov-ernment and social relationships would be chaotic. But the questions of which deadlines you really have to follow and which ones you don't are tricky and, one might say, arbitrary. If you don't pay by the contractual cutoff, you may be in breach. If you don't file your lawsuit within the statute of limitations, you may not get to sue. If you don't pay your taxes on time, they may put you in the pokey. Unless maybe you were just a day late, or were wrongly advised by your attorney, or the mail truck fell into a ditch. It all just depends on what the law says, which usually means what a judge says it says. In labor negotiations, for example, there's even a term for ignoring a deadline: It's called "stopping the clock."

So what about the deadline for Florida's county canvassing boards to send in their returns to the secretary of state for final tabulation? The law did say November 14, but it also provided for hand recounts that couldn't be done in heavily populated counties within that time frame, especially if the request for a recount came late in the seven-day period between Election Day and November 14. Does one exalt rules over purpose, form over substance? Moreover, the text of the statute, amended and re-amended over the years, had built-in confusion. One section of the election code stated that the returns of any county canvassing board missing the Tuesday deadline "*shall* be ignored" by the secretary of state. But another section, without elaborating, says such returns "*may* be ignored"—but don't have to be. Laws have sloppiness in them all the time. It's primarily a function of negligence rather than premeditation. That's why the good Lord invented judges.

In the case of Florida's muddled law, what's the right answer, who decides, and who decides who decides? Florida's secretary of state, Katherine Harris, ruled that November 14 was the absolute cutoff and that it was her decision to make. Her office sent a letter to Palm Beach that read like a threat. "No county canvassing board has ever disenfranchised all the voters of its county by failing to do their legal duty to certify returns by the date specified in the law." You're worried about *some* votes not being counted? she was telling the board. Worry about them *all* not being counted.

The only exception she'd countenance was a natural disaster, like Hurricane Andrew barreling into the Florida coastline. "A close election" wasn't sufficient grounds. "The law provides for automatic recounts, protests, and manual recounts, and it plainly states when this process must end." Yet where did her exception for Really Big Rain come from? The election code envisaged no such thing. It was a matter of interpretation and, once Harris allowed the exercise of judgment to become fair game for evaluation, she had opened the door.

Al Gore decided to go to town on Katherine Harris. It was fine to argue "will of the people" and "count every vote," but perhaps the folks out there watching on TV needed a better story line. Every moral crusade needs a villain and, for the Gore side, the forty-three-year-old Harris seemed to fit the part. She was the dupe of the party, a political hack. "Commissar Harris," jeered Gore's press secretary, Chris Lehane. Publicly, the line got him in trouble with his bosses; privately, they roared. The vice president himself took Lehane aside the next day and shared a chortle.

Harris, never a household name, wasn't expecting to be in the maelstrom. True, she had been a co-chair of George W. Bush's campaign in Florida, but so were eight others, including Jeb Bush, the governor. Jeb might be engulfed, but not her. Sure, records did show that there had been a two-minute call on Election Night from her cell phone to the executive mansion in Austin, but that, she said, had an innocent explanation: She'd been with the state Republican chairman, Al Cardenas, at a GOP party and his cell batteries had died and she let him borrow her phone.

No, she was only the secretary of state, and while she ran for the office in 1998 in part to "restore integrity to Florida's elections" (put this under the heading of Be Careful What You Wish For), she didn't have in mind becoming the electoral czarina of the South. Harris thought being secretary of state would be a place-holder until a better job came along—maybe a seat in the U.S. House or Senate?—and it would be a fine place to get wired in the capitol, much better than her previous spot in the state senate. While biding her time, she'd take advantage of the secretary of state's role in overseeing matters of cultural affairs, historic preservation, and the arts. That would give her control of tens of millions of dollars over orchestras, ballets, libraries, and museums, which would be a lot more interesting than immersing herself in elections. Who could make a name for herself signing ministerial can-

vassing documents every November? With her M.P.A. from Harvard's
Kennedy School of Government, she also hoped to make a special effort
to promote Florida business and trade abroad; she repeatedly promised
to make Florida "the Hong Kong of Latin America."

In her two years in office, following an odious and costly Republican
primary, she got to do just that, accumulating more than $100,000 in
travel expenses, according to the *St. Petersburg Times*. There were trips
to Mexico, Rio de Janeiro, Canada, and Barbados; a visit to Australia in
honor of the $350,000 "Florida Pavilion" at the Olympics; and stays at
pricey Washington and New York hotels. Closer to home, the paper
reported, she twice billed the state for reimbursements of $2.32, to cover
mileage from the capitol to the Tallahassee airport. What she may have
lacked in PR savvy she made up for in accounting prowess—though
even her critics acknowledged that her peregrinations boosted Florida's
profile. Who knew how much more she'd do, come the presidential
election?

A fourth-generation Floridian and multimillionairess (every $2.32
helps), Harris was a granddaughter of the late Ben Hill Griffin Jr., who'd
been the closest person the state had to a Rockefeller besides the snow-
birding Rockefellers themselves. Over the course of the twentieth century, Griffin built a citrus-and-cattle empire totaling 275,000 acres and a
fortune of more than $300 million. He served twelve years in the legisla-
ture as a Democrat, ran for governor (losing in a primary to Reubin
Askew); and donated enough money to the University of Florida that
the Gators put his name on the football stadium. Harris never let anybody forget she was part of the Florida aristocracy, and it helped her rise
quickly from real estate agent to state senator to secretary of state. (People forgave her that wacky, ill-advised stint in the early 1990s leading the
audience in the chicken dance at a Sarasota nightclub.)

But whatever her missteps and ambitions, Harris got herself carica-
tured by Gore's supporters, as well as by much of the media, because of
her physical appearance on TV. Sometimes it was her stiff demeanor,
sometimes it was her size 2, but mostly it was the makeup. Cruella De
Vil, Vampira, Morticia, Tammy Faye Bakker, Dustin Hoffman as Toot-
sie, fodder for a latter-day Brothers Grimm—these were some of the
nicer things that Gore staffers and other lampoonists came up with.

Compared to Harris, Theresa LePore, the "butterfly lady," received a free pass.

One *Washington Post* article particularly savaged Harris, based on an infamous TV appearance. "Her lips were overdrawn with berry-red lipstick—the creamy sort that smears all over a coffee cup and leaves smudges on shirt collars," snickered the fashion critic of the paper. "Her skin had been plastered and powdered to the texture of pre-war walls in need of a skim coat. And her eyes, rimmed in liner and frosted with blue shadow, bore the telltale homogeneous spikes of false eyelashes. Caterpillars seemed to rise and fall with every bat of her eyelids."

"Okay, I made a mistake that day," Harris says now. "So, shoot me."

Mr. Blackwell put her on his Worst-Dressed List (right behind Mariah Carey). It was all well and good and accurate for editorialists to note that none of this would've happened if she had been a he (though any man wearing that much makeup would make for a fun story), but she set herself up for the ridicule. Hey, Warren Christopher's wizened face, which one senior Bush aide likened to a mortician's, wasn't his fault. At least Lehane's dig about "Commissar Harris" was gender-neutral. Republicans called the attacks "character assassination."

Harris made no attempt during the fall race to conceal her fealty to George W. Bush. She had campaigned for him during the New Hampshire primary, she wrote checks, she was a Bush delegate at the convention, and on Election Night she was celebrating with the state GOP brass at the Tallahassee Doubletree. It was only after she'd gone home to bed that she found out about Gore's un-concession and the automatic recount provision of Florida law; she returned to her office, bleary-eyed, in a sweatshirt and jeans to meet with her staff.

When she reiterated in a press release on Monday, November 13, that she would enforce the 5 P.M. deadline the next day for the canvassing boards, Harris planted herself in the center of the storm. "The President Maker," announced one headline.

It was a role she seemed to loathe and relish at the same time. On the one eyelash, she knew she was chief elections official of the state, and that Republicans viewed her as Bush's potential savior. For all the jokes from late-night TV, she could turn for solace to the dozens of bouquets delivered every day to her office, or the 750,000 e-mails offering sympathy and support over the course of a month. She loved to recount stories, like what happened when she brought her bounty of flowers to a nursing home one Friday night. She met a white-haired woman, who commented how she'd seen Harris on TV and thought, "You're so small and here you were carrying the weight of the world on your shoulders." The old woman apparently was thrilled by the meeting and said she was going to tell her family about it. As Harris was leaving the facility later, though, a nurse came running up.

"I've got to tell you this, ma'am," the nurse said. "That woman's son just called us and his family is distraught over their mother. They think she's overmedicated because she just called them and said, 'Katherine Harris just brought me flowers.'"

Harris, too, didn't mind being able to summon the likes of Christopher and Bill Daley for a meeting or greet them by name at a restaurant. For someone who a decade earlier was imitating poultry at a nightclub, this was heady stuff. By the end of the thirty-seven days, polls showed her name recognition in the state was second only to Jeb Bush's. Quick, name another state cabinet officer who ever was asked to go on *Saturday Night Live*. (Harris thought about it, then declined.) "Difficult as it was," she said afterward, "I wouldn't let anybody take this away from me—being part of history."

There apparently was no escaping it. Two months after the recount, Katherine Harris was still enjoying her fame. Her alma mater, the Kennedy School at Harvard, had even invited her to be a guest at their functions at the exclusive World Economic Forum in Davos, Switzerland. Here was a chance to slip away and enjoy the Alps and a world-class gathering of thinkers and global leaders. What fun! When she sat down at the JFK School's dinner, however, who was right there next to her? Another guest: Mary Boies, wife of David and an accomplished lawyer in her own right. To this day, Mary Boies says she doesn't know if Harris noticed her name tag. They didn't talk at all. Harris recalls nothing. As Mary Boies tells it, "I think her view was, 'This just can't be happening—and so it isn't.'"

That was the other part of Harris's emotions. During the crisis, she often felt under siege, grumbling privately to friends that the GOP wasn't adequately defending her. To all those who would listen, she wallowed in self-comparisons to Queen Esther from the Old Testament. In the story of Esther, good triumphs over evil because of the courage of a beautiful orphaned maiden of Persia who risks everything to save the Jewish people. Harris identified with the tale. "If I perish, then I perish!" she occasionally lamented to her aides. Adept at a PC keyboard, she'd do automated searches of her e-mails to find references to Esther, then reply to well-wishers that the queen provided her "comfort and guidance."

Reflecting on her fascination with the biblical figure, Harris said it helped her persevere. She understood it might seem odd to outsiders that she dealt with stress this way or by going home and watching TV, which time and again was talking about . . . her. Harris has a sense of humor and knows that, no matter what else she does in politics, her obituary someday will lead with a reference to chads. She still keeps in her anteroom the voting-machine gag someone made for her. It's the deluxe Fisher-Price Sesame Street Farmhouse Shape Sorter, complete with Elmo and friends — modified for Florida elections. In the left farm door goes a "Democrat"-shaped ballot, in the right goes the "Republican"; the silo's for "Independents"; and in the window goes a ballot for "None" — can you match your ballot to the correctly shaped opening?

But then she's back to talking about Esther again. "Esther was always someone I admired, just like Vashti, the queen before her, who was banished because she wouldn't dance for the king," Harris says. "My thought was, you know, that quote, 'Who knows but that you're created for a moment such as this.'" In her lavishly decorated office at the capitol, with tiny Flags o' the World lined up on her desk, Harris keeps a cloth copy of the Book of Esther by her side. It's in Hebrew. She's Presbyterian. "Maybe *you* can read this," she suggests to me, knowing I'm Jewish.

Esther loomed large enough on her mind that she also volunteered, "When I'm in Israel, everybody always thinks I'm Jewish," and that she agreed to marry her current husband, Anders Ebbeson (who's Swedish-born), on the condition "we could live in Israel someday." She adds, "My parents don't know where I get this from. *I* don't know where it comes from."

The weird thing about referring to Esther so much was that the story also involves the wits of a great man, her uncle Mordecai. *Esther had help.* Without getting into all the historical details, most rabbis will tell you it was Mordecai who pulled the strings for her and plotted her strategy in the palace. That's probably not the analogy Katherine Harris had in mind when she thought of Queen Esther.

Nor did J. M. "Mac" Stipanovich, the Mordecai of her story. The fifty-one-year-old John McKager Stipanovich was Tallahassee's, and maybe the state's, best Republican lobbyist-lawyer and all-purpose political fix-it man. He was certainly the most prominent, as colorful as anyone in the state capital. In incestuous Tallahassee, most of which he could see from his glass-walled offices ten stories above North Monroe Street, Mac knew everybody and everybody knew about Mac—his pearl-gray goatee, his Latin class, his obsession with golf or skiing or whatever sport he'd just taken up, his days as a Marine intelligence officer in Vietnam, all in addition to his political prowess. The Bush-Gore clash of 2000 was just another interesting episode in a rich life; "the recent unpleasantness" was how he'd always refer to it months later (an artful allusion to what Southerners used to call the Civil War).

Most just called him Mac; some referred to "Mac the Knife" for both his cutting wit and his ability to cut to the chase and get stuff done; and a few in the media were partial to "Mac the Quote," because the man could talk and charm. His candor could get him in trouble, as in 1999, when the state's legislative session ended and he was overheard telling the governor, Jeb Bush, "I got everything. I don't know what the poor people got, but the rich people are happy and I'm ready to go home." The Democrats, and some Republicans, assailed him for the crack (just whom did they think lobbyists represented?), but everybody soon forgot and Stipanovich was welcome in most precincts around town.

Stipanovich had been a strategist for both Jeb Bush and Bob Martinez, the Republican governor in the late 1980s. He'd also helped a woman named Katherine Harris unseat the incumbent secretary of state in 1998. So, now, if she needed advice on what to do after Election Day 2000, who better to call? Once the recounts began, Harris instructed her two senior aides—Clay Roberts, the director of the elections division, and Ben McKay, her chief of staff—that no one in the office should be talking to Bush or Gore representatives about anything other than administrative details. She said later she applied that directive to herself.

But would the rule apply, say, to an outside political operative brought in to help the secretary of state? Harris's artful response suggests her opponents underestimated her.

On the Thursday after Election Day, Stipanovich's cell phone went off while he was in Latin class at Florida State University—he still had time for pursuing a master's degree in medieval French history (course reading: *The Hundred Years War*), even with plans in the works for building a Cat's Paw dinghy and entering a mullet-tossing contest with his homemade trebuchet. His law partner, Ken Sukhia, was on the line. Sukhia was a former U.S. attorney with close ties to the Florida Republican machine. That day, he was in Gadsden County preparing a recount challenge for the Bush campaign. Sukhia wanted Stipanovich's counsel on Gadsden and he wanted input from Bush's inner circle, with whom Stipanovich was familiar. Stipanovich agreed to call the state GOP head-quarters in Tallahassee, where the Bush command had set up shop—Jim Baker, Ben Ginsberg, George Terwilliger, Bob Zoellick, Margaret Tutwiler, Joe Allbaugh, and, when they were in town, Don Evans and Ted Olson.

What happened next was the source of much reportorial speculation during and after the thirty-seven-day whirlwind. Who did Stipanovich talk to there on that day and beyond? Connected though he was in Tallahassee, it wasn't as if he had close relationships with national players like Baker. The answer points to Randy Enwright, a top political consultant and the former executive director of the state Republican party. On Election Night, Enwright had been a key provider of information to Bush's people in Austin. When fifteen or twenty elections officials gathered at Harris's office at the capitol after Gore withdrew his concession, Enwright was there comparing their respective vote totals, and he arrived at the tentative 1,784-vote margin for Bush before they did. (No one from the Gore campaign was there.)

Enwright, forty-eight, knew the local players and more of the ground game in the Florida counties than anyone on the Bush side. He was the GOP's version of Michael Whouley. Years earlier, running Poppy Bush's 1988 primary campaign in Missouri, Enwright was a minor hero for having won a foot race up ten flights of stairs at the state capitol to file papers for his candidate first, which meant getting top line on the ballot. He was the type of details guy needed in a recount struggle. When Baker had a question about a precinct in Broward or Volusia, it was Enwright to whom he turned. On the third floor at the red-brick Republican headquarters—right next door to the Teddy Roosevelt Society—Enwright had a desk twenty feet from Baker's office. If anyone doubted his zeal for the candidate, they had only to look at the twenty-minute home movie a staffer put together during the thirty-seven days. Enwright pops into the screen four or five times with a broad smile and the same line: "We're *still* not counting!"

Stipanovich acknowledges he talked on November 9 with a member of the Bush campaign at the Tallahassee headquarters. "I was asked whether I was going to get into this fight, or just stand around parsing Latin verbs," Stipanovich says. It wasn't a hard choice. He figured out that Harris's office was woefully undermanned—no public-relations help and little political experience—and called McKay, her chief of staff. He was happy to have Stipanovich.

"I'll be back in time for the next class," Stipanovich told his Latin instructor.

Stipanovich freely confirms his role as Mordecai—or Rasputin, depending on which historical metaphor you prefer. He did help Harris plan her moves, "bringing the election to an end, forcing it down the funnel, bringing it in for a landing"—which, of course, cornered Gore until the sands of the hourglass ran out. He admits to being a partisan, but says any notion of a cabal is laughable. "Neither campaign had a strategy beyond winning," he says. "Everything was tactics—and they changed from hour to hour. What you did on Thursday wasn't what you had decided to do on Monday. The notion that we could predict what would happen two weeks down the road is bull."

If he admits he was in fact a voice behind the throne, then why not also dispense with the question of his contacts with the Bush campaign and whether he coordinated their agenda with Harris's actions? Stipanovich says he works in a company town and it's not right to say more. He steadfastly declines to say whether the person he talked to at Bush Central was Randy Enwright, on Thursday, November 9, or on any day in the recount period. Is that silence not probative? Stipanovich just says, "It's fair to assume that if somebody didn't commit murder, and you ask them, 'Did you kill your grandma?' they'd say, 'No, I did not.'"

Enwright won't comment either. But the two of them did know each other, and Republicans familiar with both say Enwright provided a conduit through which the campaign could communicate with Stipanovich and, through him, with Harris.

What, then, about Harris's directive that her office establish a firewall from both candidates? Did she give Stipanovich the same instructions?

Harris dodged the question. "You know Mac—everybody wants to be the hero of their own story."

What does that mean? Did she tell him to avoid contact with Bush's people or did she diligently avoid addressing the issue?

"She couldn't give me instructions," Stipanovich says. "I didn't work for her."

Did he know of the instructions to her staff?

"Yes, and I thought it was proper." Indeed, Stipanovich says he told the Bush camp, as well as Jeb Bush's office, that they shouldn't contact the secretary of state for "anything other than what they were entitled to as a matter of law." Jeb Bush had recused himself from any formal role in the post-election process, but several key staffers—including his general counsel and press secretary—took unpaid leaves to work for his brother during the recounts.

Even if those folks didn't call Harris's office directly, couldn't they still contact *Stipanovich*?

"I suppose they could."

Did Harris know that?

"I suppose she did."

It wouldn't take a cynic to conclude that whatever else one thought about Katherine Harris's face and eyes, she had perfected the wink-and-nod. Through Mac Stipanovich, she had arranged deniability.

If Gore was looking for evidence of favoritism, Harris's decision to enforce the Tuesday, November 14, deadline was it. The election code was a hash, so went the argument, and she had wiggle room to let the canvassing boards submit late numbers, all the more so since the last of the overseas absentee ballots weren't due in until Friday. Thus, the earliest any winner could be certified in the presidential race was at least Saturday. Why the big rush? It "looks like a move in the direction of partisan politics and away from the nonpartisan administration of election laws," Christopher charged at a press conference.

Harris responded that the law gave her "no leeway," and that she was honoring process. Elections, she said, were "a balance between the desire of each individual voter to have his or her intended vote recorded, and the right of the public to a clear, final result within a reasonable time. It is the duty of the Florida legislature to strike that balance, and it has done so." Trouble was, it really hadn't, because its election code said two different things.

Now it was time for the Democrats to go to court. At almost the exact same time on Monday that the Bush team was telling a federal judge in Miami that hand recounts should cease, Gore's lawyers were in state court in Tallahassee seeking extra time. The case was assigned to Judge Terry Lewis of the Leon County Circuit Court, who became one of the few participants in the circus who seemed to derive strength and stature from the glare. It wasn't that he'd done nothing controversial on the bench: In 1999 he had struck down as unconstitutional a Florida law requiring underage girls to notify their parents at least forty-eight hours before getting an abortion. Or that he had no political background: He was appointed by a Democratic governor and his friends say they have little doubt he voted for Gore. But the Tallahassee bar regarded him as fair-minded, and neither campaign believed it would have an edge in his courtroom. In a local course he taught to other judges, Lewis had a philosophy of judging: "Everything in judging is a continuum," Lewis explained. "For some, the ends justify the means. And for some, the means justify the ends. It's always a balance. I fit into the middle."

A favorite judge of his is the one from *Miracle on 34th Street*, who's asked to decide if there's really a Santa Claus. A political adviser tells him that if he rules there isn't, the judge won't even make it to the primaries. "You'll get just two votes—yours and that district attorney's." The judge shakes his head and, as he heads back into the courtroom, says, "No. The D.A.'s a Republican." The judge then tells the litigants he's decided to have an open mind on the subject.

Says Lewis: "It's a great scene."

Lewis didn't exactly fit the Grishamesque profile of a Southern jurist. He was known for taking the bench in a suit, rather than robes, and his easygoing way sometimes indulged lawyers to talk and talk and talk. Mustached and trim, he looked a decade younger than his forty-eight years. Off the bench, he could be found sporting about town in his black PT Cruiser, or on the tennis and basketball courts of the local church. Like others in the Florida limelight, thanks to cable TV, Lewis developed a momentary global following. Florida's "sunshine laws" opened the doors of virtually every state proceeding to cameras, including courtroom action. Lewis got hours of face time. His fans sent him all manner of correspondence, including one e-mail from Kentucky that his wife, Fran, saved for the family scrapbook: "You have a luxurious mustache, judge—you are *a fine-looking man*!" This more than made up for the wackos who called up to leave such pleasant messages as "I hope you burn in hell, but have a long, miserable life until then."

Lewis was also a novelist, having published *Conflict of Interest* in 1997. The legal thriller, set in Tallahassee, was about an alcoholic attorney appointed to defend the person accused of slaying the reporter that the attorney used to date. "Gripping . . . taut . . . rings with authenticity all the way to its heart-stopping conclusion!" raved *Publishers Weekly*. Lewis's rulings in the case of *Gore v. Harris* were not as spellbinding, but they were object lessons in modest, dispassionate judging. They would've fit well into the book Lewis happened to have in chambers right next to his own *Conflict of Interest*. Its title: *Famous Elections*.

Joined by Volusia and Palm Beach Counties, Gore asked Lewis to extend the deadline of the following day and stop Harris from certifying the election results. As much as this might truncate the limited time they'd have for legal actions after a certification, Gore's generals thought any pronunciamento of a Bush win was too big a PR hit to risk. Lewis heard three hours of argument from the lawyers. Representing Gore was seventy-year-old Dexter Douglass, the Atticus Finch of Tallahassee. He also was a diehard Democrat who liked to quote his father thusly: "If the Lord Jesus Christ ran as a Republican, you'd better have voted Democratic." Douglass had been the cattle-raising, white-haired consigliere to Lawton Chiles, the late Democratic governor, advising him on judicial appointments and all matters legal; he'd presided as well over the state constitution's revision committee, which made him well versed in the statute books. Harris rated Douglass a dear friend; her executive

assistant came from his small law practice. Even Jim Baker knew him—
they'd hunted wild turkey together.

That kind of professional portfolio, along with his Tallahassee drawl
and courtly mien, gave him an instant presence. There wasn't a judge in
the jurisdiction who hadn't heard, or heard of, his homespun anecdotes
and homilies, usually involving an alligator or preacherman or, on occasion, commentary more risqué. (Douglass hated the New State Capitol,
calling it "the only erection Reubin Askew ever had.") As to the
presidential-election controversy, Douglass made sure to come to
Lewis's courtroom well stocked.

Harris's legal position was that the statute authorized an exception to
the deadline only for natural disasters such as Hurricane Andrew. "Let
me tell you," Douglass serenaded Lewis. "This is not only a hurricane.
This is a bark-splitting north Florida cyclone with a hurricane tacked
on." Douglass said the issue before the judge was whether "Florida
stands for an honest vote that people in other countries can look at to
say the United States has honest elections—or are there elections where
some bureaucrat writes a letter and says, 'You lose, your vote doesn't
count.'" He then asked for a seven-day extension, while county lawyers
proposed other time periods, which had the unintended consequence of
pointing up that any judicially created new deadline essentially had to
be pulled out of the ether. Judges have equitable powers and legitimately
do those sorts of things, but good ones get antsy when they're reminded
how arbitrary their rulings may be.

Bush's lawyers were Barry Richard and Michael Carvin. Richard
was a Tallahasseean and middle-of-the-road Democrat, the son of a former Miami Beach mayor and an ex–state legislator himself. TV viewers
came to know him as the well-coifed lawyer whose silver mane got
mentioned in the media as often as Harris's war paint. Despite his
Democratic affiliation, Richard had represented Jeb Bush's administration, and the Bush campaign in Austin signed him up hours after Gore's
un-concession. He later said he did it just the same way he'd have represented the vice president if he'd called first—a lawyer was a lawyer.
Teased about siding with Bush by a Democratic friend working for
Gore, Richard bantered back: "Whatever you guys do, make sure I can
make some money out of it."

Richard was an appellate specialist, highly respected within the state—and recognized around Tallahassee as the proud fifty-eight-year-old father of baby twins—but mostly unknown in national legal or political circles. That low profile, along with a mild manner, contrasted him with Carvin, a gladiatorial Washington litigator and GOP partisan who was an alumnus of the Reagan administration and had worked with Ted Olson. But between their wildly opposing styles, they made little headway against the judge's skepticism. What was the good of demanding results on Tuesday when no winner could be declared until later in the week anyway? Lewis asked. "You do a certification and you don't say who the winner is?"

The next day at lunchtime, Lewis issued his eight-page decision. Despite his obvious frustration with the badly drafted statute and his own view that waiting a few days for votes carried with it little downside, the judge declined Gore's request for an injunction ordering all late returns to be counted. That, he held, would require him to "rewrite the statute which, by its plain meaning, mandates the filing of returns by the canvassing boards" by 5 P.M. on Tuesday. The boards would be required to submit whatever numbers they had. However, Lewis also ruled that Harris had to weigh the acceptance of late returns on a case-by-case basis. She could ignore them, he wrote, but could "not do so arbitrarily—rather only by the proper exercise of discretion after consideration of all appropriate facts and circumstances."

In short, Lewis was acknowledging that the Florida legislature had set up an electoral regime that pitted "the desire for accuracy" against "the desire for finality." Someone had to strike the balance. "I give great deference to the interpretation by the secretary of state," who he reminded the parties was the "chief election officer." But interpret she must, instead of limiting a deadline exception to natural disasters, since "an Act of God has long been considered to excuse even the most mandatory of requirements." Determining "ahead of time" that all returns would be ignored, unless caused by natural disaster, "is not the exercise of discretion. It is the abdication of that discretion." Lewis offered some of the kinds of commonsense questions Harris might make allowance for: What if returns were late by five minutes, or fifteen? Or if there were a power outage? Did it matter when the initial request for a recount was made?

As he explained later, Lewis was signaling the Gore side that they might yet beat Harris's attempt to bring down the hammer, but only with compelling *evidence* that she was abusing her discretion. Otherwise, he'd give her "great deference." He really couldn't have been any clearer. Not all judges are nice enough to tip their hands. The last paragraph of Lewis's opinion contained some other friendly advice. It was barely noticed, but in view of what happened, it was prescient. "I also note that although the canvassing boards cannot properly contest an election," Lewis wrote, "an unsuccessful candidate" *can*, including on the ground that "a number of legal votes sufficient to change or place in doubt the result of the election" were rejected.

Lewis was practically inviting Gore not to pursue his complaint at this stage in the process, for whatever time he bought now he'd be forfeiting in the "contest" period later on. The losing candidate could only initiate that phase after the election results were formally certified. It would be crunch time then, when a court would be assessing the entire election—the results and methodology of any recounts, the Palm Beach butterfly ballots, allegations of racial discrimination in some precincts, the validity of absentee ballots. Because a presidential election did seem to impose unique time constraints—the Electoral College does cast its votes on a date certain, Congress tallies up the results on a date certain, and a winner presumably is inaugurated on January 20—Lewis was telling Gore he could come back into Leon County Circuit Court in a week or two, perhaps even before the same judge in the same courtroom, and save himself valuable time. Lewis wasn't being a partisan. He didn't say how he'd rule, merely suggesting to a litigant that time was being wasted. "If I was their lawyer," Lewis says, "I would have let it go and not appealed. I understand why they did it, but in hindsight I think it was wrong."

Gore was facing yet another conundrum. Florida election law, with its conflicting "shall" and "may" language, was unquestionably a mess. Now, conspiring with federal requirements on presidential races, it had constructed an irreconcilable calendar for Gore. In the hope of pulling ahead, how far should he go to get votes included before Harris certified? How much time would he really be allowing at the back end? It wasn't as easy as Lewis saw it. For, even with a longer contest period, there was no guarantee that another judge wouldn't just dillydally until the last minute anyway.

Lewis's ruling allowed both camps to claim they won. Gore's people said the judge was demanding reasoned judgment; Bush's counterparts argued the judge all but said he'd ultimately defer to Harris. Did not! Did too! It was another round of the spin games that played out in dueling news conferences, on TV and radio talk shows, and, most important, in the off-the-record try-to-sell-them-anything conversations that Bush and Gore cronies would have all around the state capital. The media maw beckoned—the beast needed to be fed. By one estimate, there were 334 press outlets covering Florida. Ben McKay, the chief of staff for Harris, remembers that media bookers knew only two questions to ask him: "Will you appear, and are you appearing on anybody *else's* show?"

At the GOP headquarters, staffers kept a giant toteboard tracking who was due on which network and when. Ben Ginsberg, the campaign counsel, got razzed for being a media hound, but it was Barry Richard whose firm kept track of his media "hits." At the end of the Florida show, Richard's tally showed 2,753 TV appearances for his mane and 1,141 more print references. (For the record, Ginsberg didn't request a recount.) Ginsberg says his favorite press clipping was in the *Berkshire (Mass.) Eagle*, where he'd once worked. The paper ran a photo of Richard talking to the media, with Ginsberg standing beside him. "Bush attorney Barry Richard before the cameras," read the caption. "Bald man at right is former *Eagle* reporter Ben Ginsberg."

The spinning spun out to places far and wide, including Washington, where congressional leaders took the leads the campaigns provided. Clearly, Gore was trying to "steal" the election, unless you believed that Bush was the one doing so. House Republicans met Tuesday in a private caucus and complained that Bush—not seen since Saturday, when he emerged from his Texas ranch with his dog Spot, daughter of Millie— was losing the PR war. Trent Lott, the Senate majority leader, strangely seemed to boost Gore by noting that back in 1800 it took thirty-six ballots in the House of Representatives to select Thomas Jefferson over

Aaron Burr after a tie in the Electoral College; Lott was implicitly acknowledging that Congress was capable of settling a presidential election dispute if it had to.

At Harris's offices, the staff pondered how to deal with the court ruling, but shared the same chuckle that thousands of other Americans with Web access enjoyed that afternoon or thereabouts. The Net had long since replaced the watercooler, or even late-night TV, as the best place to hear the latest joke. The national debate over Florida election deadlines was ample fodder. "World Series Not Over Yet!" read the headline on a mock AP story that even Harris circulated. "The New York Mets announced today that they are going to court to get an additional inning added to the end of Game 5 of the World Series. 'We meant to hit those pitches from the Yankee pitchers,' said the Mets batting coach. 'We were confused by the irregularities of the pitches we received, and we believed we have been denied our right to hit.'" The Mets, of course, had lost to the New York Yankees two weeks earlier.

Meanwhile, given Lewis's order that counties send in their latest tallies, Harris could run the numbers and officially announce the current margin between Bush and Gore. As MSNBC's on-air countdown clock ticked down to the deadline, Volusia County actually completed its manual recount, with five minutes to spare, and new write-in ballots were found for Jesus, Mickey Mouse, and "the Cable Guy." Gore had a net gain of ninety-eight votes. Miami-Dade finally got into the action by conducting a sample count of several precincts and then deciding against a full hand recount.

The new numbers? One week after Election Day, one week after the gap had been 1,784 votes, it was now down to 300. (Different newspaper accounts at the time claimed it was 288 or 286, the secretary of state's abacus notwithstanding.) The conventional wisdom about recounts producing comparable pickups for all candidates just hadn't worked out in Florida. Theories varied, but the likely reason was that so many more voters who had trouble with ballots—first-time voters or residents of counties with poor equipment or supervision—were Democrats. In the constant pairing of good and bad news throughout the post-election, for Gore this was the day's counterpoint to Lewis's ruling that gave Harris another shot.

■ ■ ■

Harris and her staff, with Stipanovich never far away, took advantage of it. Shrewdly, they placed the burden on the canvassing boards to come up with justifications why she should give them more time—and to do so posthaste, without a chance to sabotage her by stalling. The boards would have less than a day to submit written pleas (another deadline!). Maybe they'd couch their reasons in terms of "the will of the people" or the exigencies of big counties, or maybe they'd be straight up and say something like "because the voters in our county can't read or are just nincompoops." In any event, the canvassing boards would have to divine what might be an acceptable reason. She certainly wasn't going to tip them off about what she had in mind or what her legal research was indicating.

She had retained her own big Florida law firm, Steel Hector & Davis, to advise her, and over the next month it did so extensively enough that it later billed the secretary of state's office more than $682,000. Steel Hector had a mixed political lineage. Bill Clinton had named three of its partners to the federal bench and a youthful Janet Reno once worked there, but so, too, did Jeb Bush's general counsel. The firm was run from Miami by Joe Klock, who was a Democrat but voted for George W. Bush. (On Election Night, after Gore's un-concession, he had playfully e-mailed congratulations to Bush, then retracted them a few minutes later.) Klock was a competent meat-and-potatoes litigator, but could never live down an incident at his firm in 1983. His mentor was Talbot "Sandy" D'Alemberte, now the president of Florida State University. D'Alemberte was a pro-bono-minded partner back then. Klock wrote a stern memo about billable time. Whereupon D'Alemberte, a onetime member of an American Bar Association committee on the "resolution of minor disputes," punched him in the nose—"Klocked" him, as it were. The two made up, and D'Alemberte paid Klock's medical tab, but when the name of either came up, that story was never far behind.

Klock told Harris what she'd hoped to hear: The only precedents for accepting late returns beyond what she'd said earlier—mechanical error or natural disaster—were proof of voter fraud or gross dereliction by election officials. So she'd been correct all along, she concluded. While the precedents didn't cover the full universe of possible reasons to extend a deadline, they did reflect what judges and other agency heads had already contemplated. That was sufficient for her. Mere voter mistake or confusion wouldn't be enough to extend the deadline.

When the canvassing boards of Broward, Miami-Dade, and Palm Beach on Wednesday didn't offer any of the excuses she'd deemed acceptable, Harris summarily rejected their requests and repeated she'd certify the presidential election—just as she'd planned—come Saturday, after the last of the overseas absentee ballots were tabulated. For those who believed Harris was single-mindedly trying to wangle a Bush victory, it was a curious call. Why not simply keep mum and certify on Saturday, a fait accompli that could be the coup de grace? Gore would then have to put Pandora back. Judge Lewis had even provided her that opportunity, when he said there was no need to certify the election twice (once before the overseas absentee ballots were counted, once after). By announcing her intentions, Harris was either trying to be fair or just miscalculating the benefit to Bush of freezing the tally.

Harris went on national TV to announce her decision, which came shortly after the state's highest court, the Florida Supreme Court, without comment, denied her request to halt all manual recounts. (This helped prompt on-again off-again Miami-Dade, Palm Beach, and Broward to switch gears yet again and eventually begin recounting, which in turn led to a new kind of skirmish—it wasn't just dimpled or pregnant chads, but "eaten" chads, whereby Gore observers allegedly chowed down the little perforations that had fallen off ballots. No chad? Presto! No evidence of shenanigans.) The timing of Harris's choice to go on TV suggested an intention to drown out the judicial setback, which it unmistakably did. This was the prime-time appearance that would forever emblazon her face on the national consciousness.

It was quite a night on the tube that Wednesday. Harris's live statement just after nine was sandwiched between Gore's on the evening newscasts at 6:35 and Bush's at 10:15. From a hearth at his NAVOBS residence, in tempered tones that contrasted with his press secretary's "Commissar Harris" taunt, Gore went on with an offer to drop all litigation if Bush accepted hand counts in the remaining three counties. Gore also said he'd agree to a full statewide recount. Bush, speaking in front of a portrait of Sam Houston, rejected both proposals. But caught off guard by his adversary's stunt, Bush had to motorcade from his ranch to the mansion in Austin for a suitable, official backdrop and proximity to the satellite trucks—thus the interlude of more than three and a half hours. (Governors don't get helicopters.) Gore purposely interrupted only the nightly news, but Bush "walked straight into the middle of a CBS miniseries about the O. J. Simpson trial," as a *New York Times* television critic mused, "a bizarrely perfect mingling of media sagas"; over on NBC, Bush was cutting into a *Law and Order* episode that mentioned Larry Tribe. Within twenty minutes of his statement, Bush was in a van heading back to his ranch.

On Thursday, Gore's lawyers returned to the Leon County Courthouse, a few blocks from the capitol. They were confident that Judge Lewis would agree that Harris had shown such contempt for the spirit of his order that he'd rule against her. They figured it couldn't hurt that her lawyers looked silly telling the judge that Harris thought the counties were moving too slowly in their counting—since Palm Beach, for example, had stopped because Harris herself told them a recount was illegal. To their considerable surprise, however, Gore's lawyers got nowhere. In a brief opinion on Friday morning, Lewis refused to find that Harris had acted arbitrarily. *"On the limited evidence presented,"* he wrote, "it appears the secretary has exercised her reasoned judgment . . . and made her decision. My order requires nothing more." Again, he had telegraphed his decision, his last words at the hearing twenty-four hours earlier being, "Do you have any more evidence, counselors?"

Lewis wasn't saying he agreed with Harris. In fact, he disagreed. But it wasn't his judgment being exercised, and he understood that. All he had before him were Gore's legal papers. "There were no affidavits on how long it might take to count or whether, statistically, it would make a difference," Lewis recalls. "It was a no-brainer. They didn't give me enough to do much. Why would *my* date be any better than her date? And remember, apart from Gore, there may have been *other* parties who wanted to file a contest to the election, and that couldn't happen until after certification."

Did imprecise lawyering on Gore's behalf matter? Not really, if one goes by practical consequences. After all, Gore wound up getting the extra time. If he made a mistake in this first lawsuit, it was, as Lewis noted, bringing it to begin with.* The larger question, however, is to what extent the incredible time pressures, and weight of being behind, led Gore's legal think tank to misstep. Lawsuits usually take months or years to conceive and execute. Few things are left to chance. Courtroom surprises and evidentiary oversights are rare, especially when the caliber of lawyer gunnery is high. In their first significant legal encounter with Bush, unless one included the abbreviated federal case in Miami, Gore had come up short.

It wasn't for lack of lawyers. Despite the travails with Holland & Knight and that many Jeb-rigged Tallahassee law firms wanted no part of Al Gore, Ron Klain had assembled an impressive militia. Its divisions ranged from the trench warriors who'd initially come to monitor the county canvassing boards, to the K Street brigade from central Washington, to Florida lieutenants like Dexter Douglass, Kendall Coffey, election-law guru Mark Herron, and Mitchell Berger, an influential fund-raiser and name partner in a Fort Lauderdale law firm. (Berger's Tallahassee offices, and then Douglass's storefront, eventually housed the legal team, with armed guards out front.) Running the campaign, of course, was Klain, along with Bill Daley and Warren Christopher. And, on the potentially critical federal front, there was Larry Tribe.

But even Tribe couldn't be in two places at once. If he were going to continue with the federal case, which Bush was planning to appeal to the 11th Circuit in Atlanta, then he couldn't take on the state case that had begun in Judge Lewis's courtroom and that Gore had decided to appeal up the judicial ladder to the Florida Supreme Court.

A few days earlier, when the decision was made to sue Katherine Harris, Klain had anticipated the problem posed by two tracks of litigation. Dexter Douglass was fine to handle an emergency hearing in Leon

---

*It's by no means certain that a longer contest period would've been of use. Various courts—including the U.S. Supreme Court—might simply have used the extra time in deliberations and opinion writing, and decided cases at the last minute anyway.

County and he was great to have behind the scenes gaming the various judges that would be hearing appeals. But with all respect to him, Douglass lacked the perceived ability to intellectually manage an ever-changing welter of facts and fit them into enigmatic law—the gifts of only a few courtroom combatants. Nor did he always have perfect pitch with the media. Who might?

After the federal ruling in Miami, Klain called Walter Dellinger, his O'Melveny law partner, a Duke law professor, and a former solicitor general under President Clinton. Next to Tribe, Dellinger was considered as good a constitutionalist as the left had. Along with Tribe, he'd been on various pundits' short lists for a U.S. Supreme Court vacancy in a Democratic administration. (Though eminently qualified, Tribe was far too radioactive as a result of the Bork hearings to ever get nominated; on the other hand, as recently as the Democratic convention in August, Dellinger's name had been bandied about as a potential Gore nominee to the High Court.) Gore knew him primarily through his brother-in-law, Frank Hunger, who had also been a senior Justice Department official under Clinton.

"Who is the best appellate lawyer in America not already working on this right now?" Klain asked Dellinger. They were like Rotisserie Baseball managers, assembling the best lineups in history. "Just who can we call out of the blue and expect they'll be on a plane in an hour?" The answer might've been Dellinger himself, but the chairman of Klain's law firm had suggested to Klain that two partners (Klain and Christopher) working on Gore's fight pro bono was quite enough. (Memo to the firm boss: What millions you lost in fees you reaped in incalculable publicity.)

The name that Dellinger and Klain quickly arrived at was Joel Klein, who had just left the Justice Department, where he'd run the antitrust division and taken down Microsoft. What if Klein wasn't available? The first runner-up: David Boies, who had done the actual trial in the Microsoft trust-busting case on behalf of the government, and was regarded within both his profession and the media as the best corporate litigator of his time, well worth the $750-an-hour tariff to the companies that could pay it. Boies's vivisection of Bill Gates, in twenty hours of depositions, made the Microsoft chairman look like a fool and was the centerpiece of the government's case. Its artistry lay not only in technically picking apart the great man, but doing it in a way that was neither rude nor mean-spirited. Some winning cross-examinations end with one mortal blow. Most succeed by a thousand cuts. Boies knew how to do it without the victim even realizing it, until it was too late. "The Michael Jordan of the Courtroom," declared the *National Law Journal*.

The press adored Boies—"the cult of Boies," the envious Republican lawyers called it—and he swiftly displaced Daley and Christopher as the public voice of the Gore recount campaign. His hits far exceeded those of Barry Richard or Ben Ginsberg, the media darlings on the other side. He was friendly, accessible, and nimble. He even seemed comfortable at the mike, standing tall and looking to all the world like he was just having a conversation with you, rather than pontificating on the future of the nation. He had dinner with reporters on a moment's notice and he'd use them to test out ideas, making them seem like part of the team. He was genuinely brilliant and a five-minute conversation with him could reap more insight than fifty minutes with some of the spinners around town. The only trouble with the saturation coverage of Boies was that there were limited stories to include in the barrage of profiles each media outlet had to produce and pawn off as new.

There was Boies the undiagnosed childhood dyslexic who used a prodigious photographic memory to compensate; Boies the bridge hustler and Las Vegas gambler; Boies the randy law student exiled from Northwestern for having an affair with a professor's wife; Boies the youngest partner ever at Manhattan's starchified Cravath, Swaine & Moore, who bolted to start his own litigation boutique when the firm wouldn't let him represent George Steinbrenner; Boies the thrice-married father of six (he had the first as a teenager), hearty beef eater, and rumpled dresser with suits from either Macy's, Sears, or Lands' End, depending on who's writing the piece (size 39, for those bearing gifts); Boies the man who loves to dine at *très élégant* La Caravelle but scoops off all the yucky sauces they put on the entrées; and the Boies who sails the seas on a seventy-eight-foot sloop, bicycles with his family in the south of France, journeys cross-country with his kids in the Jeep Wrangler, and still has time for his ranch north of San Francisco.

There was also the Boies who defended IBM for years from antitrust attack, but who still doesn't use a computer; Boies, the man who fourteen years earlier, based on such work as his defense of CBS against

General William Westmoreland's libel suit, had been featured on the cover of the *New York Times Magazine* with the cover line "The Wall Street Lawyer Everyone Wants"—a piece now framed in the guest bathroom of his 10,000-square-foot hillside Georgian mansion in the leafy suburbs of New York; Boies the take-no-prisoners litigator who unsuccessfully offered to settle for $12,000 from a local wine merchant who allegedly cheated him (Boies buys a lot of wine), then squeezed the juice out of him in court for six and a half times that; and Boies the champion of Napster, Calvin Klein, Garry Shandling, Don Imus, and a Palm Beach woman whose ex-husband kidnapped her children and fled to Guatemala.

Journalists could play mix-and-match with these biographical tidbits and produce an instant, readable sketch of his stardom and eccentricities. The only problem was getting even a little detail wrong and, in the process, undermining whatever else they'd written. Margaret Carlson of *Time* magazine thought she had a choice morsel when she revealed to readers in late November that Boies would arrive at the Microsoft trial "with a bag of bagels and eat only the insides of each, leaving the crusts piled on his plate." Unfortunately, as Boies himself liked to point out, he's famous at the deli counter for just the opposite—eating the crust of bagels, and leaving the innards in a remainder pile. Oh, well.

With his record, how could Boies not have been Klain's and Dellinger's first choice? It was simply a matter of Klein being a familiar Washingtonian. Though Boies and Dellinger were together at Yale Law School for a year after Boies transferred there, they weren't close and Klain didn't know him at all; regardless of Boies's legend, Klein seemed the safer choice. As in the hiring of Larry Tribe the prior Saturday, Gore didn't make the retainer decision.

Klain went to call Klein, and Dellinger, Boies. Klein, however, was en route to his honeymoon (with Nicole Seligman, one of Bill Clinton's impeachment lawyers, who had defended the president in the well of the Senate). Dellinger reached Boies, who leaped at the chance to represent Gore and, like many other Gore lawyers (as well as Jim Baker on the Bush side), would do it for free. As he left for Tallahassee, Boies promised his doting wife, "I'll keep a low profile for as long as I can." She was always concerned he drove himself too hard and, at fifty-nine, should take more care. That night, a few hours later when she turned on the TV, the first thing she saw was her husband in front of the microphones.

Boies and Klain soon talked and realized they shared some political and Democratic pedigree. Boies had been chief counsel to the Senate Judiciary Committee in the late 1970s, when the Democrats were in control. Klain had the same job a decade later. (In between them, among others, was a fellow named Stephen Breyer, who in 1994 would go on to the U.S. Supreme Court. Small world.) The task of this newest lawyer come to town was to pilot Gore's case straight to the Florida Supreme Court.

The strategies of both sides were now transparent. Gore needed to harvest more votes; Bush wanted an end to the counts. Those opposite goals could yet be resolved by the political process: the candidates themselves and their parties, buffeted by public opinion, as well as down the road by the U.S. Congress, which the Constitution ultimately entrusted to resolve disputed presidential elections. Instead, the Bush-Gore battle veered into two judicial collisions—one in federal court, now before the 11th Circuit in Atlanta, and one on its way to Florida's highest court.

Both campaigns were playing a mutual game of offense and defense. It just depended on the forum. In federal court, Gore wanted judges to stay on the sidelines, while Bush pushed for review, whereas in state court, Bush wanted the judges to defer to the political actors and Gore urged intervention. Each side had placed its chips on a different bet, but either way the presidential race was going to be won on a judicial table.

"Judicial activism"? "Judicial restraint"? These were meaningless designations in Bush versus Gore. They typically were. Those who fought the great social-policy conflicts in court—over abortion, civil rights, economic and environmental regulation—just appropriated the label that best suited their political agenda. Activism today, restraint tomorrow—there was nothing in and of itself wrong with this. Political judgments need not be ideologically or philosophically consistent. It's often in their nature to be ad hoc, based on compromise and shifting coalitions rooted in who's got the votes and when.

The problem arises when the battles move to the courts, which are not supposed to be just another political forum, based on the momentary whims and passions of the political class. Neutral, abiding principles and fidelity to the long view are the touchstones of law. All the attempts by Al Gore and George W. Bush to wrap themselves in the mantle of the Constitution were merely laughable. The only connective tissue in their respective legal claims was the determination to win.

First came the "Official Florida Presidential Ballot." Then the "Palm Beach Hokey Pokey," playing on the Internet and on talk radio. These were creations of a Democratic heart and demanded a riposte. Out of Muskegon, Michigan, from a thirty-eight-year-old insurance agent named Rich Taylor, came the soon-to-be-ubiquitous "Sore-Loserman" logo, morphed from the "Gore-Lieberman 2000" campaign sign. "Sore-Loserman" was a lot easier to put on a coffee mug than an entire ballot. At the GOP headquarters in Tallahassee, there were rows of boxes of "Sore-Loserman" T-shirts for volunteers. The Great Florida Recount Struggle as constitutional crisis? Sure. But while we were at it, why not make a few bucks at the same time?

five

"The Gang of Seven"

Now what? At best, Al Gore's legal brain trust hoped the Florida Supreme Court would decide that Katherine Harris had been wrong to exclude late returns and order her to amend her formal certification. But getting the justices to prevent her from certifying in the first place? And requesting them to do it right away, since it was now Friday and Harris had promised to bring down the gavel the next morning, would be impossible, so why bother asking? Dexter Douglass, the Tallahassee lawyer who, behind the scenes, had helped put many of the Florida justices on the court, repeatedly advised Gore not to appeal Judge Terry Lewis's ruling. Douglass was quoted in the *New York Times* suggesting that the Democrats go straight to the "contest" phase of the post-election, where any recount would be judicially supervised and governed by the same methodology and standards. It almost got him fired by Gore. That kind of bickering within Goreworld*—perhaps

---

*As Michael Whouley and others had long called it. In President Clinton's universe, there were the "FOBs"—Friends of Bill. From time to time, that nomenclature led to the "FOAs"—Friends of Al. Why that never stuck, and why the wackier-sounding "Goreworld" did, is an unanswered question in the political lexicon.

inherent in being the candidate behind—made it a different kind of operation from George W. Bush's.

After Lewis ruled against them in the lower court, Gore set up a conference call between Tallahassee and his residence in Washington. It was the bleakest moment since the motorcade on Election Night. On the line along with the vice president were Joe Lieberman, Warren Christopher, Bill Daley, David Boies, Ron Klain, and others. The politicos were telling the lawyers they had to move for an immediate injunction from the Florida Supremes. "No way," Boies and Klain counseled. Injunctions required a litigant to show "irreparable harm." That was an extraordinary burden; for example, in Florida it meant "we'll give you a stay of execution while you press your appeal, because otherwise you'll be dead when we render an opinion." Gore wasn't facing the electric chair. He retained all his rights and remedies. If the top court disagreed with Judge Lewis, or if a lawsuit prevailed during the contest phase, then Harris would be forced to add on recounted votes later. Yes, Gore would suffer a "devastating" political setback, as Klain put it, in the sense that "a hundred editorials the next day would say Bush is the certified winner and Gore should drop out. But that's not irreparable harm."

So Gore accepted the advice. But three hours later, as Tallahassee began to close down on a Friday afternoon, the seven justices of the Florida Supreme Court gave Gore what he hadn't even bothered to ask for. "On its own motion" and "to maintain the status quo," the court, by a 7-to-0 vote, ordered Harris not to certify. Then came the striking last sentence of the one-page order: "It is NOT the intent of this order to stop the counting and conveying to the secretary of state" of any ballots. There was no judicial order in place saying otherwise, and the court itself had stated in an appeal the day before that manual recounts could continue pending the appeal. Why, then, the sentence with the "NOT"? It was the juridical equivalent of shouting.

Gore loved it. Talk about wild oscillations: He'd gone from the valley to the peak emotionally. As Klain explained, "at noon that Friday people were beginning to write our political obituary." Gore mocked his lawyers on the phone: "Our first great legal victory came on something you said we could never get!" Throughout the ordeal, Gore's staff liked to say, "The worm keeps turning." Mark Fabiani, the communications director, now added, "That worm is getting awfully dizzy." Gore learned of his reprieve minutes before he was supposed to speak to reporters about the Lewis ruling. Up and down the roller coaster went.

The all-caps "NOT" in the court's stunning order only fueled Bush's fears, for it looked as if the Democrat-dominated court was reaching out. Jim Baker pooh-poohed the significance of the decision. An "interim order of the Florida Supreme Court," he sneered, "has been portrayed to you by my good friend Secretary Daley as the biggest thing since night baseball." But Baker was alarmed. It's difficult enough getting courts to refrain from doing what your opponent asks, without having to worry they'll do twice as much. When the court ruling came down, Bush himself was on his way from the ranch to Austin for what was to be a Four Seasons post-certification celebration that weekend. In the seal of the Florida Supreme Court, embedded in the floor of the marble-columned rotunda, is Themis, a consort of Zeus and the goddess of justice. She's blindfolded to symbolize the impartiality of the law, carrying the scales of justice in one hand and a drawn sword in the other. To the GOP, she seemed a lot handier with the latter. The gratuitous "NOT" turned out to make the court look bad. But when they signed the order, some justices commented later, it never occurred to them.

The court announced it would hear oral argument come Monday, just three days later, which was remarkably swift in the world of appellate litigation. Technically, there were several election cases before the court—Palm Beach and Volusia Counties' request for clarification on when hand counts were appropriate, Harris's demand for the end of all counts, and Gore's appeal of the November 14 deadline for submitting numbers—but the crux was simple: What could the secretary of state do next and when?

Despite Dexter Douglass's warning that Gore might be robbing Peter to pay Paul—that the delay in certification would shorten the chance for a later lawsuit contesting the results of the election (though also Bush's time for defending it)—the inner circle was certain it was the right course. Bush would be denied the psychological advantage of a certified win. He could not claim to be the president-elect. And the more new facts Gore could "put on the ground" before certification, which meant more votes for the vice president, the better his chances were. If he pulled ahead, the tumblers would click in and the public-relations dynamic would shift his way. Bush, loser of the popular vote, would face inexorable pressure to withdraw—far more than Gore confronted when he trailed. Such, at least, was the argument. And even if Gore didn't go into the lead, he stood a chance of reducing the margin. A few hundred here or there really might make the difference.

With litigation in play and Florida election law in dispute, few could have illusions that the state's highest court would not be pulled into the action. The chief justice himself, sixty-one-year-old Charles Wells, had an inkling after Election Day that "the gathering storm" would wind up in his court. In a Marco Island speech to a group of state attorneys general, he opened with a line about there being a "great confusion" in Tallahassee. He was being coy—the pretext for his remark was that the coach for the Florida Gators had yet to announce the starting quarterback for the big game the following week against the Florida State Seminoles. But everybody in the audience understood what he was really referring to.

"I knew we'd get the case one way or the other," Wells later reflected in private.

In the same procedural context in another state, the court might have been regarded as a neutral, nonpolitical arbiter. Maybe, maybe not. Over the past four decades, courts at all levels—federal and state, trial and appellate—have become more politicized than at any time in U.S. history. While there had been moments earlier—FDR and court-packing, even as far back as the Civil War and the early nineteenth century, when de Tocqueville rendered his classic observation about American political questions inevitably turning into judicial ones—it wasn't until the 1960s that the cynicism firmly took root, and with justification. Impartiality was only a rumor.

Not all judges were "politicians in robes," but some of the doctrinal frolics of Earl Warren's and William Brennan's U.S. Supreme Court, with lower courts in tow, gave judges a bad rep. "Activists," they were called, which usually meant they were simply issuing decisions their critics disagreed with. That became abundantly clear when conservatives, appointed by Richard Nixon and Ronald Reagan, wrested control of the judiciary, issued their own aggressive interpretations of the law, and were called activists by those in the earlier generation who couldn't wait to see judges fill the breach. "Activism" wasn't so much the problem as personal hauteur and institutional hubris. Ask a judge to step in, and he or she rarely paused to consider, "Why me?"

State courts weren't immune from the public perception that they were merely a third *political* branch of government. The Florida Supreme Court that would hear the Bush-Gore election cases was in a particularly bad spot. In a state run by a Republican governor and legislature, it was seen as the refuge of Democrats. Six of its members had been named by Democratic governors and the seventh was jointly appointed by a Democrat and a Republican. Two justices were women, one of them black; the most senior justice on the court was also black; only four of the seven were white men. Such analysis, based on party, gender, and race, was simplistic, but that's what Republicans chose to see. "At best," says Ben Ginsberg, the Bush campaign counsel and a leader of the legal recount team, "we thought it was going to be a populist court."

The bottom line was that the court liked to rule for abortion, against school vouchers, for affirmative action, against the death penalty. The decisions, of course, were never cut-and-dried. It wasn't a thumbs-up or thumbs-down Colosseum, any more than any judicial tribunal is, but by and large that was the public's view and it was shared by the GOP. The politicization of the judiciary helped make it so. When too many courts for too long do the bidding of the political branches, the effect is corrosive—even the reputations of good courts are eaten away. Few are always good or always bad, but the courts that are most often bad—the ones that seem bent on reaching particular results and not explaining why—tend to drag down the good.

The Florida Supreme Court had come a long way, having gone through some horrific times as recently as the mid-1970s. One justice was forced to resign the day before the Florida legislature was going to impeach him for trying to throw cases; he was later disbarred, and at the time he died was a fugitive from drug-smuggling charges. Another justice allowed the lawyer for a utility company to write the draft of an opinion in a utility case; the chief justice then tried to cover up the unethical ex parte contact between the justice and the lawyer. These embarrassments led to the end of elections for Florida's justices, replaced by a merit-based system. A nonpartisan screening panel, made up of lawyers and judges, nominated finalists from whom the governor made the appointment; after six years, justices had to go on the ballot for "retention." No one has yet been voted off the bench. Whatever citizens thought of the new process, it didn't produce any more crooks.

Nonetheless, warfare between the Florida Supreme Court and the other two branches of Florida's state government, located just up from and across South Duval Street, was open and bilious by late 2000. Legislators had earlier considered bills to let Governor Jeb Bush appoint two new justices—court-packing by another name—and reduce the court's jurisdiction in certain criminal appeals. The latter had enveloped the justices for twenty years, as capital cases—including lawsuits over the state's mortifyingly error-prone electric chair—dominated Florida headlines and the court's docket. By an estimate one justice gave in April 2001, the court still spent 30 percent of its time reviewing pending executions. Republicans contemplating the court's entry into the presidential mess saw only disaster. From their promontory at the capitol, and at the GOP party headquarters, they expected not justice, but only Themis's avenging sword.

"The Gang of Seven," the court's harshest critics dubbed it. "Judicial provocateurs," said Karl Rove, the chief strategist for Bush.

"I've been disappointed in some of their activist opinions," Florida's incoming House speaker, Tom Feeney, said at the time. "They've been too willing to substitute their judgment and political bias for the legislature and the people's will." Concerned that the Florida Supreme Court might act similarly in resolving the presidential dispute, Feeney and other GOP lawmakers began considering ways to substitute their judgment for the court's.

On Saturday, November 18, Katherine Harris announced the final tabulation of overseas absentee ballots, which didn't have to be in until ten days after Election Day. The Florida Supreme Court had ordered that she not certify the presidential election, but nothing precluded her from giving updates on counting, especially when the new numbers pushed her candidate further ahead. While she did so without the fanfare that would've accompanied a certification making Bush the president-elect, pending a contest proceeding, she still acted. A secretary of state seeking to seem neutral might have declined to announce anything until the highest court in the state resolved both the timing question and the issue of whether additional hand counts were to be included. By contrast, the running tickers across the bottom of the CNN and MSNBC screens were unofficial data mined from journalistic sources; Harris had nothing to do with those.

The Saturday vote totals showed a net gain of 630 for Bush, considerably more than either side had been predicting. That more than tripled Bush's Florida margin over Gore to 930. It also underscored Gore's strategic point that if minute-to-minute public relations mattered—and he religiously believed it did—chipping away at the lead as soon as possible was vital. This was an argument for immediate hand recounts now rather than a contest down the road.

Bush's pickup of 630 came from a pool of 2,223 overseas absentee ballots counted since Election Day, of which many, but not all, were from military personnel. (Others were from embassy officials, businesspeople, retirees in Israel, and tourists on extended trips.) More significant was the number of ballots that had been rejected by canvassing boards across the state for failure to meet technical requirements such as a properly dated postmark on the mailing envelope. That total was 1,977, which represented 47 percent of all the overseas ballots submitted after Election Day. And in counties that Gore had carried, the percentage was much higher; Broward, for instance, threw out 77 percent.

This was no statistical anomaly. Gore's ground operation had successfully challenged the overseas ballots where they believed it was tactically in their candidate's interest to do so. It was a shrewd maneuver, well executed by Gore's observers only recently trained by *The Recount Primer*. But tactical gains can have political costs, and that soon would become brutally apparent. If you're claiming that "every vote counts," but then contend that, well, some shouldn't count—and those happen to belong to Americans serving their country, the very people for whom you aim to be commander in chief—you risk looking like a Pecksniffian fraud. Maybe you can convincingly distinguish technically deficient overseas absentee ballots from domestic butterfly ones, but good luck.

Saturday, November 18, in Tallahassee was notable for a reason beyond reshuffling the presidential vote total. This was the day of the big football game—the Florida Gators from Gainesville against the hometown Florida State Seminoles, a battle between two teams in the national Top Ten. Once a year, the rivals fought for state football supremacy. This was war, and every back page of every sports section trotted out the clichés about families divided, families torn. "I think people in the Swahili tribes in Africa are tuned in," the Gators' quarterback Jesse Palmer told one newspaper. And this year the event had metaphorical implications: Forget about Bush and Gore. Here was the contest that *really* mattered. There would be a winner declared at the end and, best of all, there weren't any lawyers, except in the VIP skyboxes, where David Boies and Jeb Bush and Joe Klock and Katherine Harris cavorted, along with two justices of the state supreme court—just six of the record eighty-three thousand that filled the brick stadium that night. Terry Lewis came, too, though he fortunately didn't run into any of the justices who were in the middle of reviewing his ruling. Best T-shirt spotting: "Electoral College? They don't even have a football team!"

True, there was a big court case in forty-eight hours, but this was *football.* How big was football? The chief justice of the United States, William Rehnquist, has Gilbert and Sullivan stripes added to his black robes. The chief justice of the Florida Supreme Court? Charlie Wells had orange-and-blue robes, in honor of his beloved Gators, which weren't the team in town, but people sort of forgave him that. And, though he kept the colors in his chambers alongside dozens of other Gator memorabilia, Wells had the decorum to never actually wear the colors in the courtroom. (Rehnquist used his adornments even as he presided over the Senate impeachment trial of Bill Clinton.) This year's game was so big in the state that the Florida Supreme Court received scores of e-mailed complaints from people who thought the Bush-Gore arguments had been delayed two days because of football. It would be the first in a litany of electronic salvos aimed at the court. Sometimes the messages had the same wording, suggesting they emanated from a common source, like the Internet call to arms against the justices sent out by Florida's own Charles Colson, the former Nixon aide who set up the "plumbers" unit and went on to found the Prison Fellowship Ministries.

Ben Ginsberg recalls the FSU-Florida game being the only time in ten days he'd been out of GOP headquarters "for a meal or anything approaching normalcy. I remember going into the stadium through a student entrance, and guess what? They were talking about normal things like football, dates, and booze, and not obsessing over the recount." However, when the game ended after 11 P.M., Ginsberg stayed in the VIP area to wait for traffic to subside. At eleven-thirty, the TVs in the boxes went to *Saturday Night Live*, which was skewering Bush and Gore to rave reviews. "Very funny," said Ginsberg.

The only folks unhappy with the game were the reporters and lawyers who got tossed from their hotel rooms in favor of the fans who'd made reservations a year earlier. Jim Baker got the heave-ho from the Doubletree and settled in at a garden-apartment efficiency just across from GOP headquarters; for some reason, Warren Christopher was able to keep his suite at the Governors Inn. The local hostelries were concerned enough about squatter guests that they consulted the police in advance about eviction procedures. What kind of gratitude is that in exchange for all those room-service tabs?

Florida State won handily, 30–7. In other football action that Saturday, George W. Bush's Yale defeated Al Gore's Harvard, 34–24.

Aside from the football revelry, the main event in Tallahassee that weekend was writing legal briefs. All the parties—Gore, Bush, the secretary of state, the attorney general, the Palm Beach and Broward canvassing boards—had under forty-eight hours to submit their papers. All told, 458 pages would be filed on Saturday and Sunday. Gore's position came down to asking the court to do precisely what he'd asked the federal judge not to: take command. Bush's wanted the justices to keep out of the political thicket, which is exactly the opposite of what he'd wanted from the federal court.

The fifty-page brief on behalf of the vice president demonized Harris. "The eyes of the nation—indeed of the entire world—are on Florida," it opened. "The right to vote is at the core of our democracy and the president is our nation's head of state. There is an overwhelming interest in ensuring that every vote is counted."

And who was thwarting that? "Instead of seeking to facilitate the resolution" of Florida's confusing election statute, the brief went on, "the secretary of state had chosen repeatedly—in at least five different ways—to try to stop or delay the lawful manual recount of ballots." Her meddling included her letter to shut down the Palm Beach count on the ground that hand recounts were illegal except when machines broke; her statement that she'd reject any vote tallies after November 14; her refusal to accept the explanations of three heavily populated counties for late returns; and her request to the Florida Supreme Court itself that it issue an immediate halt to all recounts pending appeals. If the recounts had been taking place in George W. Bush's Texas, Gore's attorneys noted by way of comparison, an extremely liberal statute would govern. Not only were manual counts "preferred" to electronic counts under a provision Bush signed into law, but the standard for counting a ballot was any evidence of "any clearly ascertainable intent of the voter." Although Texas law didn't control Florida elections, it obviously discredited Bush's attack in Florida on hand counts and chads.

"Taken as a whole," Gore's brief argued, Harris's "approach has been Kafkaesque. She has tried time and again to direct the counties to stop counting—and then, once these directives have been set aside by the courts, she has sought to reject votes because of the counties' failure in obedience to her directives to complete the counts on a timely basis. . . . Any delay by any of the counties is in large part attributable *to the secretary herself.*" The brief contained arcana on the statute, including an exegesis on the definition of "tabulation"—does it mean counting generally or just counting by machines?—but at its heart was a ringing plea to the Florida justices to make right what a partisan state executive official had done wrong "in the heat of a political controversy and contrary to the practice in this state for more than 150 years."

In a forty-six-page reply, in between their own discursive expositions of statutory construction, Bush's lawyers tried to show their case was simple enough. "Finality and uniformity are essential to the orderly administration of a democratic process," they wrote. "The very right to vote itself is subject to mandatory deadlines." They offered an obvious example: people trying to vote after 7 P.M. in Florida. Were they denied their right to vote because the polling place had closed down? "No matter how compelling the reason for the voters' tardiness, or how diligently he or she sought to meet the deadlines, lateness will not be excused, because all voters must abide by the same rules."

In the "heated circumstances" of Florida, the Bush brief stated, "when so much is at stake for the state and nation, it is essential for this court and all public officials to be faithful to the rule of law." That meant deferring to the judgment of Florida's chief election official. The way Gore wanted it, Harris not only lacked discretion to accept returns after the deadline, she lacked discretion to *reject* them. Could that really be what the legislature intended when it commanded that late filings "shall be ignored" by the secretary of state?

This view, of course, was based on the fiction that legislators actually were aware of what they were doing when they added language to the election code that appeared to conflict with prior text, just as they supposedly had to be aware it was impossible to conduct manual recounts in counties with hundreds of thousands of voters. But it didn't matter that legislators might be fools. Courts were obliged to let legislatures do as they pleased, short of violating the state or federal constitutions. That was rooted in democracy. It was better to let elected politicians make mistakes that could be readily undone by new statutes than entrust judges to manufacture, in effect, their own legislation. Such at least was the subtext of Bush's legal position. For her part, Harris's brief hyperventilated that the current "state of affairs," which had been "initiated" by Palm Beach and "pursued" by Gore, "has rendered the entire voting process just short of anarchy." In her view, if anyone was being "Kafkaesque," it was them.

As much as Bush was defending Florida's deadline and arguing the merits of state law, though, he was looking above and beyond the state supreme court. Given what his lawyers regarded as the court's overall liberal bent, they assumed Bush would probably lose come Monday. The court's self-initiated stay on Friday against certification had basically tipped its hand. The brief had to go through the motions on matters of state law on which the justices would base a decision; it was possible they'd step back from the brink and avoid the case. However, if that didn't happen, there was another appellate option. The Florida Supreme Court was the only game in Tallahassee, but it wasn't the only one in the nation. At the top of the judicial ladder, there was the U.S. Supreme Court, if the nine justices in Washington deigned to take the case.

It was true enough that the Florida Supremes, like most top state courts, typically got the last word in a case. Yet on unusual occasions, when federal law and the federal constitution were involved, the U.S. Supreme Court would jump in. Wouldn't a presidential election be such a time? As a procedural matter, to preserve the ultimate appeal, Bush had to raise the federal questions in his brief to the Florida Supreme Court, no matter how uninterested and unconcerned the local justices were likely to be. So, while Gore's papers didn't mention a single federal case or statute, Bush's legal team borrowed extensively from the federal claims they had already raised in federal court in Miami at the beginning of the week—selective hand counts violated "due process" and varying chad standards were a denial of "equal protection" under the Fourteenth Amendment. And then Bush's lawyers broached two brand-new issues involving both federal statutes and the United States Constitution.

First, they cited the Electoral Count Act of 1887, which effectively forbade states from changing the rules of a particular presidential election *after* Election Day. Congress passed that act to avoid a repeat of the Hayes-Tilden presidential deadlock eleven years earlier. Back then, four states—including Florida (of course)—submitted two slates of presidential electors to the Electoral College. The race eventually was decided by a special commission created by Congress, consisting of Supreme Court justices, senators, and House members; the commission's job was to choose among the competing electors. To prevent another such stalemate—Hayes-Tilden lasted almost seventeen weeks—the Electoral Count Act, in inexplicably tortuous clauses, promised states that Congress would conclusively honor any slate of electors it submitted under two conditions: The slate had to be agreed upon six days before members of the Electoral College met in their respective state capitals (in 2000, this was December 12) *and* the state had to have in place before Election Day a procedure for resolving electoral disputes.

In Florida, the procedure was spelled out in the election code that had spawned such a mess. There were provisions for hand counts and deadlines. There was a role for the secretary of state and a role for the courts. Now the question was whether having a new deadline for certifying a presidential winner, or clarifying what markings on which kind of ballot constituted a vote, was tantamount to a change in election procedures or merely a way to facilitate the law already in place on Election Day. Bush argued that this was a change and, therefore, violated the Electoral Count Act, which superseded any Florida law.

Second, Bush's lawyers brought up Article II, Section 1 of the Constitution, which gave to state legislatures the exclusive power to pick the "manner" by which presidential electors were chosen. Every legislature in the country happened to set up a system whereby citizens voted for president and the winner received the electoral votes. But in the end, it was up to the legislature, which by implication meant it was *not* up to the courts. Then again, to the extent that Article II says "each state" was in charge of its own presidential electors, wasn't it curious for Bush to assert that, no, it was a federal matter? Even if a state supreme court might get it wrong—by possibly overstepping its role in reconciling conflicting meanings within a statute—wasn't that preferable to federal intervention over this most sacrosanct of state prerogatives, as Article II itself recognized? In short, invoking Article II cut both ways. But the larger strategic call by Bush was to try to lay the groundwork for a successful appeal to the U.S. Supreme Court, however improbable that seemed to be. Mentioning the old Hayes-Tilden law, as well as Article II, was bait to lure the nine justices' doctrinal interest. Or, if one were a cynic and believed the justices just needed an excuse to step in, then injecting these federal questions into a state court appeal would be a big enough hook to let them reel the case in.

In the western shadow of Reubin's Erection, the capital's architectural monstrosity, the Florida Supreme Court was a model of Jeffersonian Greek Revival, right along the sidewalk of central Tallahassee. With its six tall columns at the entrance and big dome atop the rotunda, the pastel beige-and-white building conveyed the atmospherics befitting a state tribunal of last resort—majestic and grand, but subdued as well. Its original walls, cast in monolithic concrete, were almost two feet thick. But around the courthouse on Monday, November 20, the scene was like Ringling Brothers, with all the satellite equipment, demonstrators, and gawkers commingling on this little stage; there were even tents for the performers from Televisionland. Nearly two weeks of battling—from Austin to Nashville to Washington, from various counties among Florida's sixty-seven to venues around the capital city—were now focused on one courtroom.

The whole country would have the chance to watch, with all the networks preempting the soaps—and *Judge Judy*—to cover the Bush-Gore swamp fight live. Gore tuned in from the vice presidential residence, Bush from the governor's offices at the state capitol in Austin. The Florida Supreme Court is among the most open anywhere, its proceedings always sent out over satellite and the Internet. The courtroom itself has the usual elegant properties—high ceilings, oil portraits of past justices, a dark-paneled bench (bulletproof, because a chief justice during the 1980s got nervous)—but also the traits of a studio, with four tiny permanent remote-controlled cameras, two on pillars near the rear of the courtroom and two recessed in the wall behind the bench. If you didn't look for the cameras, you wouldn't notice them or the acoustical renovations that had been made for better broadcasts. (The court emphatically believed that televising arguments before it was a good idea, though Chief Justice Charlie Wells was amused to learn from his daughter, Ashley, a law student at Northwestern, that not everyone recognized his accent. After the argument, one of Ashley's classmates told her, "I didn't know your father was from *Kentucky*.")

The courtroom sat only about two hundred, so there was bound to be squabbling over those seats. Tallahassee had been overrun by journalists and lawyers, and the court argument was going to be the big show they'd want to tell their grandchildren about. How many times would a supreme court ever be hearing a case that could determine the American presidency? (Answer: four, over the next twenty-one days in Tallahassee and Washington.) Most of the seats went to lawyers, court personnel, campaign officials (including Jim Baker and Warren Christopher), and ordinary plebes who had lined up outside all morning in the cold wind.

But the Florida court set aside twenty-eight seats for media, to be allocated by lottery. No news organizations could have more than one seat, no matter how important or loud they thought they were. Only one "entry" in the drawing was permitted each organization, no matter how many affiliates; that meant, for instance, that NBC and MSNBC couldn't each submit a request. The lottery, which the court itself ordered, consumed hours of time for the court's public-information officer, Craig Waters. "Judging from the contents of the lottery box," Waters recalls, "ABC News was well on its way to staking out its own zip code." With no appreciation of irony, ABC had tried to stuff the ballot box, as it were—with every available correspondent and producer the network had in Tallahassee. Waters had to sift through the entries and weed out all but one, so that their chances wouldn't be any greater than anyone else's. He additionally had to research corporate ownership to see which media had the same parentage. The quarrels and worries over those rules—was it fair that a big-city newspaper with a platoon of reporters got no preference over the *Vero Beach Press-Journal*?—were almost as entertaining as the ones over the Florida election code. Waters's favorite was the Reuters reporter who showed up for credentialing with his baby on his hip.

Just after 2 P.M., the seven justices entered the courtroom through the curtains behind the bench. They sat, as always, by seniority, except for the chief in the middle. To his right was the longest-serving justice, Leander Shaw; then to the chief's left, bow-tied Major Harding; and so on. "Hear ye! Hear ye! Hear ye!" intoned the marshal, Wilson Barnes, bringing the courtroom to order. "The supreme court of the great state of Florida is now in session. All who have cause to plea, draw near, give attention, and you shall be heard. God save these United States, the great state of Florida, and this honorable court!" For two hours and twenty-five minutes, the justices and ten lawyers, in sequence, debated the case. The main combatants were David Boies for Gore (introduced to the court by Dexter Douglass, as if the justices needed a reminder that, though he wasn't arguing today, he still was part of Team Gore), and Michael Carvin and Barry Richard for Bush. (Ted Olson watched from the gallery.) Joe Klock would speak for Harris.

For those nonlawyers among the millions watching, the oral argument must have been a revelation. Unlike the theatrics of trials like O.J.'s, or slightly more plausible courtroom scenarios that unfolded during prime-time shows like *The Practice*, Case No. SC00-2346 was a measured, nuanced exploration of the legal issues. Yes, Lara Flynn Boyle would've made them more entertaining, but that wasn't the point. Americans got to see, at least in form and tone, that the clash over the presidency could be discussed rationally—that neither Rush Limbaugh nor Geraldo Rivera defined the standard. Even if one still concluded the presidency might be better settled in a purely political forum, it was impossible not to be impressed by the dialogue in court this day.

The choreography of appellate advocacy is unlike any other in the law. There is no jury to impress, no witnesses to grill, little chance for grandiloquent speechcraft. The lawyers are there to answer the judges' questions from the bench. Many jurists will tell you the lawyers themselves aren't significant at all—they're merely vehicles through which the judges talk to each other. By asking this question or challenging that answer, judges can test out their own theories or lobby for someone else's. The dance between attorney and judge rarely foretells how a court will decide, only giving hints about the contours of a ruling.

But the justices already had a sense of where they'd come down, well before their regular formal conference that followed oral argument. They had extensive briefs and they could read the record of what had transpired in the lower courts; as one of the justices put it privately, "it was like reviewing the death warrant in a capital case." In fact, at its chief justice's behest, the Florida Supreme Court had been monitoring the parade of election lawsuits that had begun in Palm Beach and spread across the state. For these judges to be unfamiliar with the issues of recounts and deadlines, they'd have to have been trapped on the space shuttle. There was nothing improper with the justices having a decision in mind before hearing from the lawyers. It has to be that way in rushed cases, when an opinion has to be issued almost immediately. In the federal case in Miami the prior week, Judge Donald Middlebrooks couldn't have ruled right after hearing from the lawyers unless he'd begun writing earlier. Being open-minded doesn't mean being an empty vessel. Some Republicans later complained that the Florida Supreme Court had prejudged the case. No wonder three justices had been spotted at the Gators-Seminoles game on Saturday night! "They probably had their opinion already written," Ben Ginsberg quipped.

Some joke. On the way to the oral argument on Monday, Ginsberg got a copy of an e-mail the campaign received from someone plugged into the court. "They've made up their minds," the e-mail stated. "You lose."

Whether it was a leak or just someone blowing off steam, the mere idea that the justices had reached a preliminary consensus before argument proves not that they'd been unfair or prejudicial, but only that they were pretty convinced early on they were correct. What they'd concluded was that Al Gore was right—and that Katherine Harris needed to be judicially spanked.

■ ■ ■

The clues were there during oral argument. In their colloquies with the lawyers, 162 exchanges in all, the justices kept returning to the timing issue: What was the absolute deadline for recounts in order to have Florida's presidential election returns accepted by the Electoral College? "What I'm concerned about," Wells explained in his delivery that lingered on every third or fourth word, "is the rights of those voters who may not have their votes counted if we don't honor the recounted votes, and the rights of all voters who might have their rights denied if the certification doesn't get in within the time limit." In short, what would be the electoral point of no return for the state of Florida?

The question assumed hand counts were legitimate under the circumstances, even if the state's chief election officer found otherwise. And it assumed Katherine Harris was also wrong about the November 14 deadline; Justice Barbara Pariente all but called Harris's exercise of discretion a ruse. Gone was the "whether" issue about recounts. All that remained was "when"—if an acceptable remedy could be fashioned, Gore was going to prevail in the appeal. The Florida justices had narrowed their focus to schedules, not their own institutional role relative to the state legislature. The Bush-Harris legal position was DOA at the court before Carvin or Richard had a chance to advance it.

Boies was happy to discuss dates—anything was better than the Tuesday past. The deadline he repeatedly cited was December 12, six days before the Electoral College met and twenty-two days hence—a veritable eternity in the day-to-day, minute-to-minute struggle. This was the date mandated by the Electoral Count Act by which states had to get their acts together, in order to prevent Congress from possibly rejecting a slate of presidential electors. December 12 was a so-called safe harbor, but it was *not* a requirement ordained by either the U.S. Constitution, the Florida constitution, or even Congress itself. It was only in the nature of a benefit offered, with no penalty other than the absence of the benefit—sort of a no-risk offer. Any electoral slate determined thereafter simply would not be immune from congressional examination in a close election. That might seem like a big deal in theory, but did anyone really believe that in practice the electoral votes of one of the most populous states in the Union might go uncounted altogether? The distinction between a safe harbor as freebie or absolute requirement was vital, but Boies didn't make it. Boies figured: Why should he? If his client got the time to count, Gore would overtake Bush and hand *him* the witch's hourglass.

Wells pressed Boies on whether he agreed that December 12 represented the outer bounds.

"I do, Your Honor." He said this despite there being no state law or executive pronouncement to that effect.

Boies's concession of the date as a constitutional line over which no recount could cross would come back to haunt him in two weeks at the U.S. Supreme Court. It walled him in from ever offering such dates as December 18 (when the Electoral College convened), January 6 (when Congress met in joint session to count the electoral votes), or even January 20 (Inauguration Day). Indeed, January 20 was the only date mandated by the federal Constitution (in the Twentieth Amendment)—the other dates were mere statutory creations, which could be changed.

But to the extent the justices were going to come up with a new timetable, thinking about December 12 was critical. Any certification of the election—whether it included all, some, or none of the results from manual recounts—had to happen in time for the contest phase of Florida law to play out. A contest lawsuit needed time for trial and appeals. That had to be completed by December 12, according to Boies's answer. Justice Fred Lewis wanted the lawyers to work back from that day to arrive at possible cutoffs for the recounts in three counties and then a certification. Boies grudgingly suggested a week after a court ruling.

Even if the December 12 date was obeyed, what of all these new cutoffs, which obviously weren't mentioned in state law, affecting Florida being entitled to the benefit of the "safe harbor"? Were not these new cutoffs arguably the kind of post–Election Day change in the rules that the Electoral Count Act prohibited? Perhaps the court wanted to consider the argument that it was free to ignore any conceivable application of the Electoral Count Act in these circumstances in the election code, since it was debatable whether the court's rendering of conflicting provisions amounted to a "change" in law at all, as opposed to a routine, unremarkable exercise of statutory construction of the sort that courts performed for a living. Or, regardless of the Electoral Count Act, maybe fashioning new cutoffs by judicial decree was a usurpation of the U.S. Constitution itself. After all, Article II did delegate to state *legislatures* the manner by which presidential electors were chosen. Unfortunately, neither Boies nor the Florida justices took up any of these questions. Nor, critically, did the court wrestle with counting standards: What criteria could various canvassing boards use to determine a voter's intent? Did Florida want its chads swinging, hanging, or what? If that had been resolved—if the justices had established a uniform standard—they might have defused Bush's equal-protection attack that the U.S. Supreme Court later accepted.*

The court did raise the issue of a statewide recount, but Boies passed on the invitation to push such a judicially imposed remedy. "We are not urging that upon the court," he told the justices, even though Gore had proposed precisely that in his televised offer to Bush five days earlier. Boies's miscalculation was twofold. It reinforced the appearance that Gore was less interested in "counting every vote" than in manipulating the system. And it gave fodder to other judges down the road, who were skeptical about Gore's strategy. Justices of the U.S. Supreme Court, for example, eventually voiced concerns about the equal-protection implications—that voters' rights were a function of which county they lived in. And the Florida Supreme Court itself did order a statewide recount of undervotes eighteen days later—a remedy that wound up being too little, too late. Hindsight is easy. But, between them, Boies and the seven justices left a lot on the table that aided and abetted the U.S. Supreme Court leaping in.

As to be expected, the Florida argument had its pointed digressions. In one momentary sidelight, the court asked why Bush's lawyers had gone outside the state courts to launch a federal lawsuit against Florida's election procedure. "You don't think that the state court has within its jurisdiction to decide whether a statute is being constitutionally applied?" Pariente asked Carvin, in a clear dig at Bush's federal litigation demanding a halt to all recounts. Litigants, of course, can go to different courts in different jurisdictions to pursue their rights. Pariente was just taunting Carvin, who acknowledged, as he had to, in eight words that

---

*Does that mean Bush would then have lost at the U.S. Supreme Court? Of course not. If the justices were predisposed to Bush, they'd find another rationale to rule in his favor. But eliminating the equal-protection problem would've made the job tougher.

state courts obviously did have the power to pass constitutional judgment. Then Carvin changed the subject.

Poor Michael Carvin suffered the brunt of the court's hostility toward the Bush-Harris legal position that manual recounts were hopelessly subjective, but he hardly did much to help himself. He hemmed and hawed; he lectured; he interrupted the bench; he professed to be unfamiliar with the Texas chad statute, which was right there in the briefs. Unlike the smooth Boies, whose absence of notes at the lectern made him seem like the consummate listener, Carvin fit the stereotype of the arrogant out-of-towner. Don Imus, the talk-show host, made him the whipping boy for the Bush argument, likening Carvin to a "thinner, less good-looking Chris Farley," who went "up there and sweated as much as he could" and was "as ill-prepared as possible." It was a cheap shot—Carvin had had a bad day—but he would not be seen again in these parts, giving way to Barry Richard in the second round before the Florida Supreme Court in early December. Imus needled Richard as well, calling him "Little Richard," the rock-and-roller with the pompadour; Richard got his hair trimmed forthwith.

On this Monday, November 20—almost two weeks after the election—you really did need a scorecard to track the legal action. In Palm Beach, Judge Jorge Labarga issued his ruling on the butterfly ballot. Gore hadn't himself brought the lawsuit, in keeping with his strategy to concentrate on recounts. But he and his lawyers had closely watched the case, aware that it could be decisive.

It would not be. There would be no do-over in Palm Beach County, even if it was clear that the ballot design had confused enough voters to cost Gore the election statewide. Labarga reached out to be sympathetic. "This court is well aware that the right to vote is as precious as life itself to those who have been victimized by the horror of war," he wrote. Nonetheless, "the plaintiffs in this action cite no case law authority in the history of our nation, nor can the court find any, where a revote or new election was permitted in a presidential race." Though the judge recognized that states, rather than the federal government, ran elections, he found that a presidential election was special, governed by Article II of the U.S. Constitution as well as the Electoral Count Act.

There was one day, and one day only, to cast a vote for president. In essence, Labarga was declaring the primacy of federal law in the dispute. This was not what the Gore legal team wanted to hear, especially on the same day it was arguing before the Florida Supreme Court.

The justices would get the appeal of Labarga's ruling by the end of the following week. Meanwhile, they had to decide the main election case they had just heard. It took them just over twenty-nine hours.

At 9:45 on Tuesday evening, the Florida Supreme Court issued its forty-page decision. Unanimous and unsigned—an indication that the justices wanted to speak with a single institutional voice—it was nearly a complete victory for Al Gore. "The will of the people," rather than "hyper-technical reliance upon statutory provisions," has long been "our guiding principle in election cases," wrote the court. Voters, not the candidates, "are possessed of the ultimate interest and it is they whom we must give primary consideration." A citizen's right to vote is "the right to be heard." By "refusing" to recognize that right "for the sake of sacred, unyielding adherence to statutory scripture," the justices held, "we would in effect nullify that right."

From this soaring but vague prose, the court, invoking its "equitable powers," ordered that the results of any manual recounts be included in the state's certified presidential tally. Broward, Miami-Dade, and Palm Beach thus could keep counting. There was one condition: The new numbers had to be in within five days, by Sunday, November 26, at 5 P.M.—explicitly allowing time for a contest proceeding. The justices seemed to have created that new deadline out of the ether—and recognized it as much, expressing "reluctance to *rewrite* the Florida election code" in the same sentence in which it invoked "equitable powers." Courts did that on occasion, wielding the "equitable" authority that judges needed to honor legislative intent, cover unforeseen circumstances, or fulfill the spirit of abstract constitutional language. Such was often a legitimate exercise of judicial power—most agreed, for example, that Miranda warnings to criminal suspects helped effectuate the Fifth Amendment's ban on self-incrimination—but it, too, was what gave judges a bad name for "making" law rather than "interpreting" it. The Florida Supreme Court often cited itself as "the temple of justice." One never heard that kind of vainglory from the legislature across the street.

Where did the Florida Supremes come up with a five-day extension? Once they concluded in their internal discussions that Harris was wrong to enforce the November 14 date, they decided they had three choices. They could give Harris another chance, which would take time and inevitably produce another round of litigation. They could invent a new date, even though they had no testimony or evidence—trial, not appellate, courts presided over those kinds of things. Or they could attempt to calculate the time the counties would've had if Harris hadn't issued her incorrect advisory opinion that said hand recounts were unauthorized except when machines malfunctioned.

The justices chose the last option, and it continually perplexed them later on that they were accused—most prominently by Jim Baker—of having made up something. Indeed, Larry Tribe admitted to the U.S. Supreme Court that the new date looked to him "like an exercise of the chancellor's foot." The Florida justices wouldn't say anything for the record, but they privately told others they thought the attack by a former secretary of state—and a longtime member of the bar—was grossly irresponsible. All that their remedy had done, as the justices explained in a subsequent opinion (written after the U.S. Supreme Court threw out their ruling), was to "put the parties in the same position they would have been" when Harris on November 13 advised the counties to stop counting. That was five days before she was going to certify. Now, the court was just adding back the lost time (though it also effectively included the seven additional days it took for the justices to come up with a ruling). November 26 "was not a new 'deadline,' and has no effect in future elections," the court said. "It was simply a date in accordance with the requirements that had been established prior to the election and in order to construe all the provisions" of the election code "as a consistent whole."

While this was a reasonable defense of the new date, it also came twenty days *after the fact,* in the opinion the justices wrote after the U.S. Supreme Court sent it back for a rewrite in much the way an elementary-school teacher tells Johnny to try again. Had they explained the date when they first came up with it—and addressed why it didn't amount to a change in the rules that ran afoul of Article II of the U.S. Constitution and the Electoral Count Act—it might've taken the wind out of Baker's bluster. But the Florida justices never saw the howling gale coming. Their failure to anticipate the criticism and to figure out how to render an opinion that rang with legitimacy—which courts, more than the other branches of government, crave—was not a comment on their intelligence. Instead, it was a reflection that appellate opinions in momentous cases are best not written during all-nighters pulled by judges thirty and forty years past their college days.

Ascribing partisan motives to the justices had no basis and, in fact, some of the justices were not fans of Al Gore. But even without partisan criticism, the Florida Supreme Court ruling had other deficiencies. In the name of getting the electoral process moving forward to a resolution, the justices ducked the other constitutional question that would come back to bite them: By what standards should canvassing boards evaluate punch-card ballots? Their opinion never discussed standards and didn't even mention "equal protection"—the federal constitutional problem lying in wait. The court would have a hard time blaming this omission on time pressure. The opinion itself, midway through, acknowledged the need to "examine the interplay between our statutory and constitutional law at both the state and *federal* levels." Yet that is the last reference in the opinion to the U.S. Constitution. Where's the promised "examination"? Infallible as supreme court justices may be because their decisions are final (as the old dictum from U.S. Supreme Court Justice Robert Jackson observed), did they not have a proofreader?

It just didn't seem that big a deal to the Florida court. "Neither side has raised as an issue on appeal the constitutionality of Florida's elections laws," the opinion stated in an introductory footnote. Well, that wasn't so. Admittedly, Bush's lawyers hadn't dwelled on the equal-protection issue posed by recounting in some but not all counties; and so far they hadn't even raised the issue of standards and all manner of chads. But the lawyers had nevertheless broached the subject and the justices ignored it at their peril. They were motivated to avoid federal questions because they thought that would insulate them from review by the U.S. Supreme Court. Maybe that was plausible in an ordinary case, but Bush could be expected to raise the federal issues again on appeal. Would it not have been better to dispel them ahead of time?

Boies agreed with the Florida court. "There is no basis to appeal this to the U.S. Supreme Court," he said, following the ruling. "Any appeal to the U.S. Supreme Court would be denied."

Judge Terry Lewis accepted his rejection by the Florida high court with equanimity. But he still says he was "shocked." Lewis understood that lower court judges were in the business of being reversed and this was just another example. But he didn't buy the reasoning. "You know you're in trouble when you rely on 'broad equitable powers' to justify your decision," he says.

Lewis belonged to the same Rotary Club in Tallahassee as Major Harding. "Nothing personal," Justice Harding gently told him the next time they saw each other. "We have as much right to be wrong as the next court." It was a rare display of humility from a jurist during the thirty-seven-day standoff.

The Bush campaign, though always pessimistic about the Florida Supreme Court, fumed. The candidate himself talked of the court "usurping" authority. Minutes before midnight on Tuesday, Jim Baker issued a statement that sounded as if it came from a former general rather than a former secretary of state, speaking with more venom and emotion than he'd previously shown in the Bush-Gore confrontation. Lacing his comments with references to "judicial fiat," Baker then upped the ante. "Two weeks *after* the election," he said, "the court has changed the rules and has invented a new system for counting the election results. No one should now be surprised if the Florida legislature seeks to affirm the original rules." While the idea had been kicking around GOP circles since the stalemate began, this was the first time a Bush representative gave it currency—failing to note, of course, that any move by the legislature risked violating the Electoral Count Act.

Baker was practically begging Florida legislators to step in and name their own slate of presidential electors, something that state law gave them the right to do in certain instances. It would be a perfectly legal step that the U.S. Congress, if the election came to that, could then evaluate in deciding who ultimately received Florida's twenty-five electoral votes.

But Baker's invocation of the legislature's prerogative raised the question of what the Bush campaign was doing in the courts to begin with. If Bush, through Baker, believed that a presidential election in the end rested with the judgment of the legislative branch—at both the state and federal levels—he might have appeared more principled if he'd taken that line in the litigation Gore instigated, and he might've wondered how he could bring suit himself in federal court. That's pie in the sky, obviously, because principle wasn't the point. Winning was. And with an adverse Florida Supreme Court ruling in hand, unpredictable recounts looming, and the strong possibility that the U.S. Supreme Court wouldn't interfere, the Florida legislature represented Bush's best hope for the moment. Jeb Bush—that Florida governor who had recused himself from the state's electoral matters—echoed Baker's views. "It's pretty clear the legislature has a role in this, should it get to that."

Talk of the legislature commandeering the election enraged Gore's team, who thought Baker's attack on the justices and his mention of the state House and Senate were uncharacteristically overbearing. Gore himself feigned magnanimity. Had he lost his appeal at the Florida Supreme Court, he would've been forced to give up the fight. Now, with Joe Lieberman at his side at the vice presidential mansion, he promised to avoid an end run around the judiciary, renouncing "any effort" to persuade Bush electors to switch their votes in the Electoral College. Gore praised the Florida justices for honoring "the will of the people." And in words he would soon come to regret, he complimented them for "wisely" setting a deadline for recounts "in order to preserve a reasonable period to resolve any remaining questions."

Ron Klain learned of the ruling from a fax machine at Mitch Berger's law firm in Tallahassee. One by one, the pages trickled out with the decision. Klain was ecstatic—and got his only nosebleed of the thirty-seven days. "Ruined a perfectly nice white shirt," he says. Klain had to read the opinion flat on his back, in a corner, where he hoped he wouldn't get stepped on during the celebration.

The world got word of the Florida Supreme Court ruling from Craig Waters, the court spokesman. Standing at a podium on the courthouse steps, fenced in by cameras and microphone booms, Waters announced the outcome in bare bones—166 words of it. He offered no comment and took no questions. Yet the forty-four-year-old Waters, a lawyer by training and onetime journalist, instantly became another of the mini-celebrities created by the media cyclone.

All the planet's eyes were fixed on the front of the courthouse. There were three sets of huge metal double doors at the entrance, just like the ones guarding the Emerald City (one still bore a bullet hole fired at the building in 1974, a reminder of earlier troubled times). Because the justices didn't hold press conferences, there wasn't anything to feed the impatient media beast. So, each time Waters emerged from the courthouse, the pack descended upon him in expectation of major news. Earlier that afternoon, when he showed up on the steps without an announcement, CNN cut in with a live shot and the silly headline "No decision whether to release a decision tonight."

It got sufficiently ridiculous that the networks were breaking into regular programming whenever Waters went out on the steps. He only found out about this from a friend relaying his mother-in-law's complaint on one occasion that "Dan Rather had interrupted her soap opera" to report that "Craig Waters was telling reporters that he had nothing new to tell them." In fact, Waters was out there at the request of one reporter with questions about court procedure, but Waters was immediately mobbed. Waters did have an office in the courthouse, but it was near the justices' chambers, and reporters weren't allowed inside.

As a result, Waters never again went out the front of the building except for formal statements. And, at the suggestion of an ABC producer, he got the justices' permission to give the press a thirty-minute alert for the statements. Right before he'd come out the doors of Oz— with gatekeepers on both sides—the podium was hauled out. It quickly became the cue for TV producers. The podium kept moving farther up the stairs as the media crowd got bigger. Eventually, it was placed just in front of the north doors, allowing Waters to finish a statement and rush back inside. For his one-on-one meetings, Waters used the basement entrance in the back, which the media swarm never staked out. "Only people who really know me understand how difficult an experience the whole thing was," Waters says. "One of the ironies is that this public role was given to someone who, at one point in his life, could not even give a public speech."

Waters made *Larry King Live, Good Morning America*, the Greta Van Susteren show, the BBC, and the front page of *USA Today*. He participated by phone in a class at the Harvard graduate school of education. Over at the GOP headquarters in Tallahassee, they referred to him as "Secret Squirrel," the Hanna-Barbera cartoon character from the 1960s who played the zany crime-fighting agent of the rodent kingdom. Secret Squirrel wore a trench coat and a big hat with the eye holes cut out. Waters's ensemble had neither, but he apparently squinted just enough to occasion guffaws among the Republicans who associated him with the bad news coming out of the court.

Given the bizarre e-mail sent to him, some of which mistook him for a justice, the court's marshal assigned Waters a security officer any time he left the premises and Waters tried to avoid appearing in public. Friends ran his errands and brought him meals. The notoriety faded after the election was finally decided, but during the Christmas holidays in his hometown of Pensacola—prime Republican territory—he says he was remembered with nasty comments and gestures. But the nice folks got an autograph. "It was all very, very surreal," he says.

The fact the court deliberately chose to have a public face at all was unusual. Some appellate courts convened to announce their rulings from the bench, but most just issued their opinions and none used a spokesperson. For its presidential election cases, the Florida justices opted for what they believed was a fairer and more accessible approach, since there were practical limitations on their press office's ability to distribute hundreds of copies of an opinion simultaneously, and electronic release through the Internet put on-scene reporters without wireless Web access at a disadvantage; as it was, the court's Internet server kept crashing under the burden of requests for data. On the Tuesday night the court ordered the new certification deadline, its Web site received 3.5 million hits—more than seventeen hundred times the usual. (Waters had to maintain two identical servers. Demand for the election-cases page was so high he couldn't take it offline to be updated. So he'd edit a backup page—an exact duplicate—then substitute it for the main one and update the other. That also minimized the danger posed by hackers, for whom the Florida Supreme Court home page would be an inviting target during this period, though the biggest obstacle to a scoundrel was the sheer volume of traffic on the Web site—it would take much patience to open the elections page to make mischief.)

The Florida Supreme Court had historically been a leader in openness—it championed cameras in the courtroom, electronic availability of all filings, live Webcasts—but the prominence of its spokesperson had its critics. The most significant was in Washington, where the U.S. Supreme Court had long preferred decorum to sunshine. The Court typically did announce its rulings in open court, but that was all—it had no cameras inside and its press liaisons were forbidden to say much of anything on the record. The White House press secretary gave daily press briefings; the public information officer of the U.S. Supreme Court could tell you Justice David Souter's middle name (it's Hackett), but that was about it. The notion that a spokesperson would have announced a ruling from the great marble steps was heretical.

So when the chief justice of the United States, William Rehnquist, saw an obscure man named Craig Waters step up to a podium in Tallahassee and speak for the Florida Supreme Court, it infuriated him. This was no way for any court to behave and certainly not a state court of last resort. This sort of debasement would never be allowed to happen at the institution over which he presided. Yet it would soon put pressure on the Court to lift part of the veil that had always shrouded it.

Craig Waters wasn't the only one at the Florida Supreme Court to experience the vicissitudes of fame. By the end of the year, after the American presidency had been resolved, Justice Barbara Pariente was reduced, as she laughingly put it, "to being No. 22 on *The New Yorker*'s end-of-the-year quiz."

"Who is Barbara J. Pariente?" the question read, right after the one about Strom Thurmond.

The incorrect responses were: "a) the woman for whom Newt Gingrich left his second wife (for whom he'd left his first wife)," "c) a friend of Linda Tripp's who said of Tripp's plastic surgery, 'It looks like she's had a head transplant,'" and "d) the little girl who was first in line to buy the new Harry Potter book."

For a transplanted New Yorker like herself, it was an honor to make the quiz. But it highlighted how quickly the Warholian public forgets.

■ ■ ■

Legal defeats were piling up for George W. Bush all over the place. He had now lost before the Florida Supreme Court and in the preliminary federal skirmish in Miami. And Bush had been rebuffed in his appeal of the latter case: A few days prior to the Florida Supreme Court ruling, the 11th U.S. Circuit Court of Appeals in Atlanta unanimously and summarily denied his request to block all hand recounts on grounds they were unconstitutional. "States have primary authority to determine the manner of appointing presidential electors and to resolve most controversies," wrote the full twelve-judge court, which had among its members seven Republicans appointed by Presidents Reagan and Bush. This was more than enough reason, the judges said, for a federal court to stay out this early in the state process. In short, the 11th Circuit was expressing doubt that the feds had any role. This was notable skepticism from a conservative court.

But Bush still had another route to possible federal intervention. The U.S. Supreme Court was the next and final rung in the federal ladder above the 11th Circuit, and it also had the power to review the Florida Supreme Court if it believed that court had intruded on federal constitutional or statutory domains. Those were matters of judgment, of course, but it was solely up to the nine justices in Washington to make the call. That was just another striking attribute of the U.S. Supreme Court's power. It alone was the master of its docket—it decided which cases it wanted to hear and how far its own jurisdiction should go. Despite its professed respect for the prerogatives of state institutions—which Boies referred to when he said there was "no basis" for the U.S. Supreme Court to get involved—the Court could do as it pleased in matters of constitutional law, subject only to the obloquy of law professors. The decision of every other court in the land could be reversed—so, too, the actions of the president and the Congress—but not the U.S. Supreme Court. Short of an amendment to the Constitution to undo a ruling, an event that almost never happened, the justices were supreme indeed.

There was another remarkable aspect to their authority. The Court's exercise of power was derived not from a specific constitutional grant, such as Congress's ability to pass legislation or the president's to command the armed forces, but from the assumption that to make the

American structure of government work, one of the three co-equal branches of government had to be the final arbiter of what the law meant. It was the Court that articulated that assumption early in the Republic's history and claimed the role for itself.

In time, the other branches acquiesced in the arrogation of power. But such assent was based on respect and the convention that judges ruled on principles rather than political whim. It had to be that way because the courts had "no influence over either the sword or the purse," as Alexander Hamilton famously put it in *The Federalist Papers*. Securing their authority by intellect put judges in a unique constitutional position: They had neither might nor the imprimatur gained from a ballot box, but the presumed principled basis for their actions gave them special legitimacy. This combination, noted the great scholar Alexander Bickel forty years earlier, made the Supreme Court "the least dangerous branch" of the government, even as he acknowledged it was also "the most extraordinarily powerful court of law the world has ever known." In one of the twists of the American system, the justices—unelected, unaccountable, serving for life—were supposed to personify the Constitution.

As *Bush v. Gore* headed their way, would the justices enter the fray and pick a president? Or resist the temptation and decide *not* to decide?

s i x

Numbers

Al Gore's November 21 victory in the Florida Supreme Court was merely a means to an end. Whatever the self-righteous chatter about Counting All the Votes—ostensibly a paean to process, a rampart of fairness—recounting in the three south Florida counties would amount to nothing if Gore didn't pull ahead. Winning was the Promised Land; anything else was just wasted time in the desert.

And, at this point, Gore remained down by 930 votes.

Because the justices ruled that recounting could continue while the appeal before them was pending, Broward, Miami-Dade, and Palm Beach had done just that. The proceedings were public—the obscure local officials observed and harassed by national party apparatchiks—with all three rings of the electoral circus covered live on TV. The scorecard showed that Gore had so far picked up a net of 106 votes in Broward, 157 in Miami-Dade, and only 3 in Palm Beach. The counties were all at different points in their recounts. In Miami-Dade, only a fifth of the 614 precincts had been gone through, and the stack of ballots for the board totaled 10,000. In Palm Beach, more than 8,000 ballots were left to consider. And in Broward, the canvassing board had completed an initial review of ballots in all precincts (despite taking part of Monday, November 20, off, in order to watch the Florida Supreme Court argument on the tube). The board had yet to inspect the disputed ballots—the nearly 2,000 in varying degrees of pregnancy or detachment. But under somewhat mischievous circumstances, Broward had already liberalized its standards, so Gore had cause to be newly optimistic. No longer would two corners—"hanging chads"—be required. Now, a dimple would do, as long as it reflected the "intent of the voter."

The change was suggested by Andrew Meyers, Broward's chief appellate lawyer, who, in one of the side briefs to the Florida Supreme Court, had asked the justices to announce a chad standard. They declined to set any guidelines, but Meyers did convince the Broward canvassing board to unanimously discard the two-corner rule and go with dimples. Reasonable people could, and did, differ on standards on both what constituted evidence of intent and whether the rules should be established halfway into the game, so Broward's decision was debatable. Not so Meyers's role in it. He shouldn't have been involved in the first place. It wasn't just that his county duties didn't include advising the canvassing board—or that his desk sported a Gore-Lieberman campaign button. His wife, Dawn Meyers, practiced at Mitch Berger's law firm—the one that, along with Dexter Douglass's, was Gore's legal headquarters in Florida. She even assisted the Gore team. Whether or not Meyers discussed Broward business with his wife—and according to him he did not—he no longer could claim to be disinterested. Had the Broward canvassing board known Meyers had a conflict of interest, it probably never would have let him say a thing in his official capacity.

The tallies thus far left Gore nearly seven hundred votes shy of overtaking George W. Bush. In the five days of pell-mell after the Florida Supreme Court ruling, as the litigation possibly headed toward Washington, the byplay in the three Florida counties set the arithmetic stage. No judge was going to decree which candidate won. The presidential election would always come down to numbers. But lurking around with the undervotes and overvotes of Broward, Miami-Dade, and Palm Beach was another category of contentious ballots affecting every county in the state—several thousand overseas absentee ballots that arrived after November 7. These, too, would be fought over in hand-to-hand, envelope-to-envelope combat.

In most states, all absentee ballots had to be in by Election Day. This would allow an expeditious count. After all, absentee ballots typically had to be tallied manually. But Florida, home of so many things weird, wasn't in the category of "most states." In Florida, any absentee ballot from overseas, civilian or military, didn't have to be in until ten days past Election Day. That was November 17 in 2000. The only statutory requirement was that the ballot envelope be postmarked on or before Election Day, stopping unscrupulous types from voting with the knowledge of where a race stood—say, just for example, in a case where the margin between candidates for the American presidency was several hundred votes and a few cartons of new ballots could make the difference.

The Florida rule, dating to 1982, was forced on the state by the federal government, which worried that Floridians serving in the military wouldn't have enough time to get in their votes. In most states, that wasn't a problem because the ballots could be mailed out well ahead of time. Florida, however, had a late primary season, so the names of the candidates in the general election sometimes weren't resolved until October, which, in turn, dictated that ballots could not be mailed abroad until Halloween. Absentee ballots were crucial in Florida due to its military bases and the fact that members of the armed forces liked to claim official residence there because of the tax laws.

Overseas absentee ballots—OABs, in the counting jargon—were the last trove of virgin ballots that both sides might be able to mine. Gore hoped for a run of support from American nationals living in Israel, but it was Bush who was in the best position. Military folks tended to vote Republican. How the fight over OABs played out potentially meant a decisive number of votes: If Bush won more of them, he might develop a large enough lead that continuing challenges by Gore would become politically untenable. If Gore eliminated enough OABs, he might overtake Bush during the recount, thereby altering the media and public-opinion dynamic, and forcing any court that were to declare the recount unconstitutional into the position of undoing a Gore lead and anointing Bush president. But, just as important, OABs laid bare how both sides played the post-election game. If anyone had any doubts that Bush's respect for electoral rules and Gore's reverence for votes were facades, OABs would dispel the illusions.

Mark Herron was a big-firm Tallahassee lawyer with Democratic connections, specializing in ethics and election law. He had defended the party in grand jury proceedings, as well as before Congress when it was looking into funding misadventures by Bill Clinton's presidential campaign in 1996. Herron joined Gore's recount team the afternoon after Election Day, part of the inner circle in Tallahassee that included Ron Klain and Nick Baldick, the campaign's chief ground operative in Tallahassee.

While the others concentrated on petitioning selected canvassing boards for hand recounts, Herron was asked to look at OABs. Rumors had begun to circulate in both camps about get-out-the-vote efforts *after* Election Day—both on aircraft carriers and in Israel. The Democrats knew about the ten-day extension, but little else about the law governing OABs. Herron's job was to become the instant expert. Like a good lawyer, he set out to draft a memo.

Herron quickly discovered yet another morass of Florida law. The ten-day extension grew out of a lawsuit by the federal government against the state. As part of the settlement, the U.S. State Department issued rules on OABs in Florida. For the ballots to count, the envelopes containing them had to be postmarked—or signed and dated—by Election Day. But a Florida statute passed several years later mentioned only postmarks and the federal government never challenged it. So, was signing and dating an overseas absentee ballot no longer sufficient in Florida, because that's what the Florida legislature seemed to say? Or would that be a "hyper-technical" interpretation that disenfranchised voters and thwarted the popular will, since some overseas mail wasn't postmarked? How could Gore argue it one way with these OAB rules and just the opposite with the ones Katherine Harris was trying to enforce? How could you avail yourself of legislative stupidity one moment and seek to override it the next? Gore would have to deal with these conundrums shortly. Herron had only to explain the vice president's options, including the most aggressive tack of challenging any OAB not properly marked.

Before doing even that, Herron had to clear out of his law office,

Akerman, Senterfitt, & Eidson. For taking on Gore as a client, he had basically been tossed out of the firm, in which he'd been a partner for a decade. When Herron went to his office on Thursday afternoon, November 9, he found a memo from the managing partner, Charles Schuette, obviously hastily written: "Please see me before anyone commitments [sic] to represent any interest, adverse or otherwise, dealing with either the Bush or Gore campaign [sic] or the election." Like other law firms in Jeb Bush's Florida, Akerman Senterfitt didn't want political entanglements, particularly the kind that went against Jeb.

Herron called Schuette. He believed the memo, though addressed to "all firm attorneys," was targeted at him; nonetheless, he played it straight. "I'm afraid I've been working for Gore for a day and a half," he told Schuette. "If the firm wants, I will resign effective Election Day and you can tell the world I haven't been here since."

That's what he did and they said. The charade played out absurdly the next day, Herron's birthday, when at his office party he announced his resignation—effective three days earlier. "Law firms are peculiar creatures," Herron says. "I don't miss partners' meetings with two hundred of my closest friends."

Mark Herron's memo was innocuous enough, but he soon wished he'd never written it. Gray-haired at fifty, who needed this kind of grief? Dated November 15 and addressed to Democratic lawyers observing OAB counting in the sixty-seven counties, the four-page, single-spaced document dispassionately analyzed the rules for ballots and the procedures for "protesting" them. Any challenge, for instance, had to be made before the ballot was removed from the envelope in which it was mailed. The memo gave, without embellishment or spin, ten bases for a challenge, all derived from Florida law: the voter never formally requested the ballot; the voter didn't fully fill out the form requesting a ballot; the voter didn't sign the ballot envelope, or the signature didn't match up with the one on the registration books or the ballot-request form; the ballot envelope wasn't notarized; the voter had already voted; or there was a problem with the postmark, including a late postmark, a domestic postmark (which included Puerto Rico and Guam), or the absence of any postmark. On this last vital matter, the memo acknowledged that a signature and date might be acceptable instead of a post-mark, but the memo gave election-board observers no guidance on whether to abstain from challenging in these cases.

Herron could have taken a tactical page out of *The Recount Primer,* which the campaign had studied from the outset. His memo could've been positioned as a strategic paper to suppress ballots; it could have said to attack any ballot not in strict compliance. In that sense, it would have read no differently than the advisory opinion Katherine Harris's office had issued early on about the propriety of manual recounts. Most would interpret it as a partisan screed, but it would've been within the bounds of advocacy, since Herron was a Democrat working on behalf of the Democratic candidate. But the fact was, he didn't write it as a brief. "Milquetoast" is how Herron would later describe it. He mapped out the options for the political chieftains to evaluate. It would be up to them to make policy; for example, Michael Whouley, the campaign's chief strategist, wanted to go after any suspect ballots.

So it was with unmitigated astonishment that Herron watched his memo become a lightning rod, for which he got zapped. The memo had been faxed to more than one hundred Democratic lawyers and political operatives spread out among the counties. And Murphy's Corollary on confidentiality applied: In the age of Xerox, any document not sup-posed to get into enemy hands, will. "We never anticipated that some-one was going to take the damn thing and give it to the Republicans," Herron recalls. But it wasn't as if this was viewed as dynamite. Even Clay Roberts, the director of the Florida division of elections and a deputy to Katherine Harris, told Herron the memo was "a correct state-ment of the law."

Nobody leaked the Herron memo. It was taken from plain sight. Ed Fleming, a GOP field lawyer in Pensacola—home of the great naval air station—had heard rumors of "an orchestrated, concerted effort by the Democrats against military voters." (Republicans liked to call OABs "the military ballots," which wasn't entirely accurate because it lopped off American civilians abroad, but such is spin.) On Thursday, the day after Herron distributed his memo, Fleming called Tom Dannheisser, an attorney for Santa Rosa County, to find out if he knew anything.

"Oh, yes, we've got a memo just like that," the lawyer replied. Dannheisser represented the local canvassing board as part of his duties, so the Gore campaign had sent it along in preparation for the OAB count at the end of the week.

Fleming filed a public-records request under Florida's sunshine laws and promptly had the Herron memo. If Gore hadn't forwarded it to a public official, it might never have wound up with the Bush team. Fleming then faxed it along to Craig Unger, the Tallahassee lawyer driving the OAB train for the Republicans. The thirty-three-year-old Unger was a former special counsel to the Florida House and realized the memo had immense political utility. He passed it along to the GOP inner circle. By lunchtime on Friday, November 17—hours before the deadline for overseas absentee ballots—the memo was in the hands of Ben Ginsberg, Don Evans, and, finally, Jim Baker. By the end of lunchtime, the story was cresting over the national media.

"GOP Cries Foul As More Than 1,100 Ballots Discarded!" read an AP story. The Bush campaign arranged for a statement from Norman Schwarzkopf, the Desert Storm general and now a resident of Florida: "It is a very sad day in our country when the men and women of the armed forces are serving abroad and facing danger on a daily basis," he said, "yet because of some technicality out of their control they are denied the right to vote for the president of the United States who will be their commander in chief." Was it not "unfair," the general asked, that postmarks and other formalities applied when "at the same time" other ballots in Florida had "already been counted twice . . . and a third time"? In Austin, the increasingly voluble Republican governor of Montana, Marc Racicot, accused Gore of "going to war" against American soldiers. "We learned," he said, "how far the vice president's campaign will go to win this election." Bush himself eventually weighed in, asking Gore to ensure that "our men and women in uniform overseas should not lose their right to vote."

Herron felt the onslaught the next night at home. His sixteen-year-old son called him from the big football game between the Gators and Seminoles. "Have you heard the Republican Marty tape?" the son asked?

"Who the hell is 'Republican Marty'?"

The son explained that Marty operated a popular phone hotline that provided taped messages about Florida football, GOP politics, and other world affairs. Herron's son called in to find out Marty's take on the game. Instead, he got an earful about his father's memo and, according to the son, Marty said, "We got to hunt this Herron guy down." There was no specific threat made, but Herron filed a police report— "just in case somebody did hunt me down, they could figure out who did it." (Nothing came of it, but the forty-four-year-old Marty Glickman involved was arrested in mid-April 2001 on charges he gave LSD and money to underage girls in return for sex. Several weeks after his arrest, Glickman committed suicide, apparently by ingesting pesticide.)

Herron later laughed about what Republican Marty had done to him. But at the time, he said, "My world changed."

It got worse the next day.

Joe Lieberman, Gore's running mate, was doing *Meet the Press* with NBC's Tim Russert on Sunday, to be followed by other network appearances. OABs were certain to come up in the discussion. Russert followed the headlines and was a charter subscriber to the rumor mill. That's part of what made him an effective interviewer and *Meet the Press* the hottest public-affairs program on TV. But Russert also liked being the star of the show, which meant theatrics; it was more *I'm Tim* than *Meet the Press*. Lieberman had been briefed on the brewing OAB tempest the night before and again for a few minutes before going in the studio. While he said afterward that he had no recollection of seeing the Herron memo, he was surely familiar with the hard-line stance associated with it. Among the central players in the campaign, wouldn't Lieberman be most receptive to this position? When litigating the butterfly ballot was debated two weeks earlier at the vice president's residence, it was Lieberman taking the aggressive approach.

After exchanging pleasantries with his quarry, Russert wasted no time. Waving the Herron memo before Lieberman as Exhibit A, he asked, "How can a campaign that insists on the intent of the voter—the will of the people, not disenfranchising anybody—accept knocking out the votes of people in the armed services?"

"Tim, I haven't read that memo. That's the first I've actually seen it."

But what of its substance?

"Let me just say that the vice president and I would never author-ize—and would not tolerate—a campaign that was aimed specifically at invalidating absentee ballots from members of our armed services."

Russert invoked clips from Norman Schwarzkopf and a military postal official who noted the difficulty of sailors obtaining a postmark while aboard a battleship. In light of those testimonials, Russert demanded, would not Lieberman, "today, as a representative of the Gore campaign, ask every county to re-look at those ballots that came from armed-services people and waive any so-called irregularities or technicalities?" Would Lieberman direct Democratic lawyers to "drop any objections to overseas ballots from armed services personnel"?

Lieberman could have finessed the question or simply answered it, "No, they're not technicalities, to the extent someone may have cast his vote after Election Day." That was more than a theoretical possibility. The Democrats had persuasive circumstantial evidence that the GOP had launched a get-out-the-vote effort after November 7. Of the 4,200 OABs that arrived past Election Day, almost half came in during the first three days, indicating that, even where they lacked postmarks, they had likely been mailed well before Election Day. For the next four days, the number of OABs dwindled in the sixty-seven counties around the state. But, then, close to 2,000 more ballots showed up. Was this just a strange statistical distribution, or did it not suggest that these OABs had been mailed well *after* Election Day? If it walked like a duck and voted like a duck, it probably was a duck.

Some of these ballots had late postmarks and presumably could easily have been disqualified. But Katherine Harris had issued a statement that late postmarks should be ignored if the envelopes had signatures and a date filled in by November 7. And, of course, many OABs didn't have postmarks at all, either because of dumb luck or because the senders arranged to use a military post office, which doesn't postmark letters unless a sender specifically requests it. (The Pentagon's own monthly newsletter, "Voting Information News," repeatedly advised the military, "Have the postal clerk hand-stamp the ballot envelope verifying the mailing date.")

Such an explanation by Lieberman wouldn't prove that any suspect ballots were Republican rather than Democratic—though there was ample anecdotal evidence that it was the GOP talking more about ways to get-out-the-overseas-votes after Election Day. Nor could it have totally dispelled the sense that the Democrats wouldn't be challenging overseas ballots at all unless they thought they skewed to Bush. But it nonetheless would have made a strong case for why close inspection of OABs was legitimate and in no way an attack on American servicemen.

There was other information to wave back in Russert's face. The Democrats had a spreadsheet that showed overseas absentee voters with mailing addresses in California, Hawaii, Kansas, North Carolina, and Virginia, as well as Florida; when their envelopes had postmarks, they were from those states. Two ballots, from a husband and wife, were sent into Clay County from a Maryland fax machine. As show-and-tell documents went, this would've been plenty to rebut Russert. Ballots from a *Maryland fax machine*?

Instead, Lieberman caved in. "If I was there," he said, "I would give the benefit of the doubt to ballots coming in from military personnel generally." By now all the OABs in theory had been tallied—the counting had been completed the day before—but Lieberman volunteered to go back in time, a gift-wrapped concession to the GOP for which he got nothing in return. "Take another look," he directed the Florida canvassing boards. "Because, again, Al Gore and I don't want to ever be part of anything that would put an extra burden on the military personnel abroad who want to vote."

The senator went on to recant slightly—no, late ballots shouldn't count—but it still was the "benefit of the doubt," a phrase he used four times, that should govern. The import of Lieberman's TV appearance— "the adventures of Joe Lieberman," Herron mockingly called it—was clear. He had tanked any chance for his campaign to keep litigating against overseas absentee ballots that likely were going Bush's way, and he had effectively encouraged the GOP to try to reinstate ballots that had already been rejected. Other Democrats, most significantly Bob Butterworth, the Florida attorney general, hopped on the Lieberman bandwagon. He sent a letter to elections supervisors across the state, urging a lenient standard. Regardless of Gore's chances for the presidency, it seemed the politically safe move.

Republicans had their own memo. When he first saw what Herron wrote, Fleming fired off an eight-page letter to Tom Dannheisser with an alternative view. "Should ballots without a postmark, but which arrive by midnight, November 17th, 2000, be counted?" Fleming asked. "Yes. Disallowing these ballots would violate federal law, both in letter and spirit, and would subject the person so excluding to criminal sanctions," something he claimed four more times. Though Fleming would later argue that mentioning "criminal sanctions" only illustrated how strong the federal interest was, the fact remained that his letter read like a threat. Tim Russert never took the GOP to task over it.

Herron watched Meet the Press with Nick Baldick and his Tallahassee troops at the campaign's little rented ranch house on East College Avenue. They knew Lieberman was going to be on, but had no inkling what he'd be talking about. When Herron heard Russert mention his name, followed by Lieberman's answer, he got a pit in his stomach. "I was not feeling good," Herron says. It wasn't so much that Lieberman had sold him out, because he hadn't. Lieberman didn't criticize Herron or his memo, but he didn't defend it either. "The memo didn't say what the Republicans were claiming it did," Herron reflected later. "In no way did it attack military voters."

Herron stormed out of the house, half dazed, half enraged. "Republican Marty" was one thing, getting whacked by the would-be vice president–elect was another.

For his part, while he did apologize to Herron privately during the Jefferson-Jackson Dinner in Miami the following June, Lieberman says he has no regrets. Though his staff said afterward he was a victim of bad briefing, Lieberman insisted what he did was not only morally correct but tactically shrewd. "My position highlighted the inconsistency of what the Republicans were doing."

Perhaps in theory, but that didn't seem to be the message that got out. In the days that followed, the Gore campaign was on the public-relations ropes and many canvassing boards—particularly in north Florida, land of the big military bases—were sheepish over having tossed OABs. "It was a huge boon for us," says the GOP's Ginsberg. "Lieberman's appearance was a break in their ranks."

"We were put on the defensive," Whouley says. "We were taking so much 'incoming.'" This was the person, after all, who never tired of reminding his compatriots that "the point of a recount is to win."

Jay Leno joined in. "It's one of the big toys this year—the Al Gore doll," he said in his monologue. "You wind it up and it refuses to count the vote of the GI doll."

Since certification of the election results would not be taking place until November 26—because of the Florida Supreme Court ruling that came two days after Lieberman's *Meet the Press* debacle—the Republicans smartly went back to fourteen counties, as well as to lower courts. If Gore was going to use the extra time to harvest votes in Democratic strongholds, it was just fine with the GOP to use the bonus round to retrieve disqualified overseas ballots. Given the Florida Supremes' views about "hyper-technical reliance upon statutory provisions," as well as Lieberman's freshly advertised patriotism, how might Gore respond? He might argue that the clock for counting OABs had already struck midnight, but as a PR matter, it wouldn't have survived the laugh test. Not after the Florida Supreme Court had just obliterated another deadline. Turnabout was fair play. No, the only option would've been to try to hold the line on the merits of the rules.

"The campaign got a deer-in-the-headlights look," says Herron, illuminating the unspoken conflict within Goreworld over both tactics and expectations of prevailing big-time in the manual recounts under way. "The world had shifted from underneath us. Litigation was popping up all over the state and we couldn't get a real decision whether to stay away from it or go in and forcefully argue our position that military people weren't entitled to special rights to the exclusion of everybody else. The federal law didn't do that anyway." What was the outcome? "We punted the issue to the Republicans." Says Baldick: "We were rolled."

As several Republicans in Congress introduced bills that would retroactively include all overseas military ballots in the Florida totals, the GOP ran with the ball and put more votes on the board. Several Florida counties reversed course—a few citing Lieberman's retreat—and now included OABs that had been rejected because they lacked a postmark or other required documentation. By the time Katherine Harris certified the vote, Bush's net gain among OABs was 109; in one heavily Republican county, Bush picked up 45 votes to Gore's 9. Escambia County took ballots dated as late as November 13, six days after the election; Santa Rosa County accepted four that arrived after November 17, the final deadline; the Maryland faxed ballot was accepted by the Clay

County canvassing board. "It was like, 'You should take ballots that are postmarked from Kansas, because maybe Dorothy landed there on her way back from Oz, or Europe or an aircraft carrier,'" says Charlie Baker, one of the key Gore field directors working with Baldick and Whouley.

Media accounts referred to the electoral windfall for Bush as "Thanksgiving stuffing." More accurately, it was the turkey produced and directed by Joe Lieberman. "We didn't hang tough," says Whouley. "I have all the respect in the world for Joe Lieberman, who was very much a warrior during this whole thing. He had very much wanted to keep a lot of the options on the table, including the butterfly ballot. But this was disheartening and very frustrating."

Eliminating the 109 net votes for Bush, or some portion thereof, would still have left Gore behind. But late in the thirty-seven days, Bush's margin dropped down near that total—before the U.S. Supreme Court intervened for the second and final time.* Without the votes that Lieberman's turkey enabled, Gore might've pulled ahead. Would such an event—the pivotal instant the Gore forces were working toward all along in the recounts, when the victor and vanquished flipped positions, when the hunted suddenly became the hunter—have altered history? Would it have discouraged the U.S. Supreme Court from reversing the outcome? It was one thing to stop a recount that had kept Bush in the lead throughout, but quite another to turn back the tumblers. In the post-post-election parlor game, that was the most-asked question and the thing that drove folks like Mark Herron mad.

On November 22, the morning after the Florida Supreme Court ruled for Gore and extended the time for recounting in Broward, Miami-Dade,

---

*Virtually all media accounts used a 176 total for the new net Bush OABs—but that was the total of the 109 OABs plus 67 votes from four other counties. Nassau County decided to ignore its automatic recount right after Election Night and go with its initial tabulation, resulting in a Bush pickup of 51 votes. Citrus, Collier, and Pinellas Counties netted Bush 1, 14, and 1 votes, respectively. None of this particularly matters—why else do you think it's in a footnote?—but it serves to illustrate the muddle that Recountland had become. If neither the

and Palm Beach, the Gore campaign could not have been more pleased. They had triumphed in the litigation and the U.S. Supreme Court seemed only a last-ditch hope for Bush. Overseas absentee ballots were being reconsidered by various canvassing boards, but the numbers didn't seem consequential to Gore, compared to what was now going to be harvested in south Florida. All that remained was tallying up the victory.

The Wednesday euphoria barely lasted until lunch. Ron Klain was in his cubicle at Mitch Berger's Tallahassee law offices and got up to forage in the kitchen. "I noticed on one of the TV sets that CNN was covering a meeting of the Miami-Dade canvassing board," he says. Surely the network was just showing file footage, since whenever there had been a meeting, Kendall Coffey, a Gore lawyer, told him so. Not today. After chaos ensued when they began recounting, the board called for a meeting.

"The first thing that I heard was something about 'stopping the counting,'" Klain recalls. "I went nuts. I paged Kendall and asked, 'Why aren't you at the meeting?'"

"What meeting?" replied Coffey.

"Like the one on CNN right now."

"They aren't having a meeting."

"I'm watching the meeting."

"They couldn't be having a meeting, because if they were having a meeting, they always gave me notice, and I didn't get any notice, so there can't be a meeting."

"Turn on CNN—*please.*"

When Coffey did, after this absurd exchange, he hurled a series of expletives at the TV, and then raced over to the county government center. By the time he arrived, the meeting had ended and the canvassing

courts nor the secretary of state nor the canvassing boards nor the press could agree on numbers that were susceptible to rational calculation, who could possibly expect consensus on the trickier legal and political issues? Had the statewide recount at the end of the thirty-seven days gone forward, there would've been further adjustments to the OAB totals. On December 8, the same day that the Florida Supreme Court ordered the statewide recount, a federal judge in Florida directed canvassing boards to reconsider certain OABs. Since this reconsideration never took place, it's not clear whether either candidate would've netted a few dozen or even a few hundred additional votes.

board had decided to stop the recount they'd begun two days earlier, hours after the Florida Supreme Court had given its approval to continuing to count. Since Election Day, in the span of two weeks, the county had begun to count, then stopped, started again, and now stopped again.

Why the stop this time? The board itself said it just could not meet the state supreme court's Sunday deadline, even if it tried to manually go through only the 10,750 undervotes. It was a plausible explanation from bureaucrats. After all, Miami-Dade had gotten started later than Broward or Palm Beach because it kept changing its mind. But Gore loyalists believed there was a more sinister reason. They believed that somehow the Democratic mayor of Miami-Dade, Alex Penelas, was behind the canvassing board's reversal, that he was administering payback for the Cuban-Americans among his constituents who were still stewing over the Clinton administration's handling of Elián Gonzalez. It was an accusation the thirty-eight-year-old Penelas denied and one that the conspiracy theorists couldn't substantiate. "The board was willing to go forward one minute, then not go forward the next," Chris Lehane, Gore's press secretary, said later. "Clearly something occurred down there. You know the famous saying, 'You go to bed and there's no snow on the ground, and you wake up and there is snow on the ground—you can only conclude it snowed.'"

There was another, more credible explanation—or partial explanation—for the board's unanimous action: Republican scheming to block manual recounts. Litigation hadn't worked for the GOP, the view went, so it resorted to bullying. When the canvassing board first gathered Wednesday to begin the counting process, it was confronted by several dozen Republican demonstrators. They weren't spontaneously assembling members of the body politic, but well-tailored GOP professionals who had been flown in earlier from around the country—hotels and meals courtesy of the party—to observe recounts across Florida. Now they were bused to the Miami-Dade government center. In the sense that they'd been rounded up, they were no different from the junior congressional staffers and law-firm associates the Democrats had recruited in the days after the un-concession. The twist here was that the demonstrators were being put to good use. Their job was to disrupt and they succeeded beyond anything they'd imagined.

With little planning for security and crowd control, county officials were overwhelmed by the shoving and heckling. "Let us in!" the protesters cried, as they pounded on doors and windows to the recounting room. Was the canvassing board duly intimidated into giving up the recount? Its members said they were not. But assuming they were, was it the result of a Republican plot? That's harder to buy. If GOP strategists were this clever, why hadn't they sent other packs of wolves to Broward and Palm Beach? The most reasonable way to understand Miami-Dade is that the board never had its heart in a recount, whether because it believed there weren't enough votes to make a difference or because it didn't think the law called for a recount. And the Florida Supreme Court's new deadline only made a recount seem that much more unreasonable.

Gore's lawyers went back to the Florida Supreme Court Thanksgiving morning, imploring the justices to order Miami-Dade to resume counting. Lieberman was especially adamant within the Gore camp that rule by mob had to be countered. Citing "scores of noisy demonstrators engulfing the counting floors," "vituperative attacks" on elections staff, and "physical assaults" on Democrats, the Gore brief painted an ugly scene and said the Miami-Dade canvassing board was being forced to thwart the "will" of the county's voters—precisely the opposite of what the court had ordered.

Bush didn't even have to file a response. The justices—most of them on their way to turkey dinners and unreachable for parts of the day—talked by conference call and summarily rejected Gore's motion in a unanimous, one-paragraph order. Most of the justices, according to what they told others, were troubled by the events down south. But to force Miami-Dade to act under the circumstances—where the court would be ruling on the spur of the moment without benefit of a lower court first examining the facts, where Gore was now asking that decisions by local canvassing boards be ignored (which was the opposite position he took in fighting against Katherine Harris), and where there remained a contest proceeding for Gore to pursue—seemed rash to the court.

Later on, a few of the justices were miffed that their decision to stay out of the Miami-Dade fray earned them no credit for neutrality in the relentless public-relations game, just as when they ruled the following week against any challenge to Palm Beach County's butterfly ballot and against Gore's effort to expedite the contest litigation presided over by Judge N. Sanders Sauls. If the justices were only Democratic partisans stacking the deck against Bush, they would've ruled for Gore in all three cases. Instead, they dealt him a critical defeat in Miami-Dade from which there was no appeal, given that the Democrats could hardly go to federal court with a straight face. But as far as the justices were concerned, the GOP didn't much notice. The fact that they didn't, and the fact that any justices cared, showed just how bitterly politicized the court battles had become.

"*The decision by* the canvassing board to stop counting," Klain says, "was the single most dispositive event" in the thirty-seven days. "It was a huge shift in morale and momentum," Baldick says.

Maybe Gore would've picked up enough votes in a Miami-Dade recount to move past Bush, though the media-sponsored counts long after the fact suggested Gore not only wouldn't have netted the requisite number, but might have lost ground. However, even if the votes weren't there for Gore, at the time he emphatically thought they were, and he spent resources over the next three days trying to get the Miami-Dade canvassing board to reconsider. As it turned out, given what was happening up Interstate 95, those were resources that might have been put to better use in Palm Beach, where the recounting turned into an even bigger mess than it had been ten days earlier — way back when the secretary of state and attorney general dueled it out with advisory opinions. Moreover, had Miami-Dade finished, it would have obviated the need for Gore to include the county in the eventual contest litigation, which, in turn, would've vastly simplified that proceeding in front of what turned out to be an unsympathetic judge.

In fact, the contest might not have had to demand any more counting at all. And that would've changed the entire complexion of the appeals to the Florida and United States Supreme Courts that ultimately decided the presidency in mid-December. To understand the progression of interlocking events, and why halting the count in Miami-Dade was an electoral tipping point, you have to wade through the machinations and mechanics of the other two counties.

By Sunday, November 26, the deadline for certification, Broward was done. They'd managed to go through half a million ballots, mostly without the logistical gyrations affecting Palm Beach to the north and Miami-Dade to the south. There were arguments and histrionics—and the iconic photograph of the eye of canvassing board member Judge Robert Rosenberg using a magnifying glass to inspect punch-card ballots—but the recount steamed along. Under the liberalized standard adopted midway through, at the behest of a county lawyer with a spousal tie to the Democrats, Broward mined 1,146 more ballots. Gore's net gain was 567.

Now, having factored in Bush's late pickup of 109 OABs, as well as Nassau County's decision to disregard its own automatic recount (netting Bush 51 votes) and some minor adjustments from small counties, Bush's overall lead was down to 537 votes.

Palm Beach was also finished with its recount, over in the amphitheater at the county's warehouse-sized Emergency Operation Center. Trouble was, the canvassing board had spent so much time debating standards—and made the remarkably unwise decision to take Thanksgiving Day off, a move the Gore people later would point to as a benchmark of their bad luck throughout the siege—that they missed the Florida Supreme Court's 5 P.M. deadline. In order to prevent the secretary of state's staff from having to work that Sunday, if Katherine Harris preferred them not to, the court's ruling had given her the option of receiving final vote totals on Monday morning. But Harris, who'd been effectively told by the justices that she screwed up, wasn't about to give the renegade counties an extra night to count. Actually, she wasn't going to give them an extra second. This time she had a deadline that the opposition had cooked up, and they were going to live, or die, by it.

Roughly five hours before the deadline, the Palm Beach canvassing board figured out it couldn't get through the remaining pile of disputed ballots, even after staying up all night. The chairman, Judge Charles Burton, wired Harris for an extension. If he was like the college student who had left a term paper to the last moment, only to discover that an analysis of the New Deal couldn't be written in eight hours, Harris was like the professor who reveled in teaching the lad a lesson. Around her office, there were a few cackles when Burton's fax came in and Harris said no. "In accordance with the explicit terms of the Florida Supreme Court," she smugly wrote, "your request . . . is denied."

Her "reliance on the Florida Supreme Court is really bogus," Burton angrily told reporters. "I don't know what the difference is between sending it at 5 P.M. or at 7:30 P.M." The difference was getting your results included in history. For the second time in the 2000 presidential election—who would've thought the infamy of the butterfly ballot could be topped?—Palm Beach elections officials were laughingstocks. This time, they had cranberry sauce on their faces, for their mistake wasn't born of an oversight, but of a conscious decision to skip counting on Thanksgiving.

Minutes before the deadline, the Palm Beach board sent in what results they had—virtually the whole recount, with the remaining precincts set aside on a spreadsheet so Harris could see how close the county was to finishing. There were less than a thousand ballots left to resolve. Two hours and a few minutes later, the board was done. As a result of a far stricter chad standard than Broward had—no pregnancies or dimples in these precincts, so that only about 8 percent of Palm Beach undervotes were turned into votes, compared to 26 percent in Broward—Gore had a net gain of around two hundred votes.

Around two hundred? It was bad enough that the percentage rates in the two counties could be so different, but Recountland was such that the parties couldn't even agree on the exact number of actual votes, and it would become the source of further litigation. At least four different numbers made legal papers, press reports, and public statements. The most common were 174 and 215, while 176 and 214 had proponents as well. Part of the confusion may have come from the scribbled partial results Palm Beach initially sent in, but it was mostly emblematic of the chaos of Florida election procedures and never-ending spin from the combatants. Months after, Gore's representatives still said their candidate picked up a net of 215 votes, while county officials (based on an audit), as well as Bush's lawyers, cited 176 as the correct figure.

Such nitpicking didn't even address the issue of standards. Thousands of dimpled ballots never became "votes," so they were the source of endless verbal scrums. But both sides agreed that a more lenient standard in Palm Beach would've netted Gore somewhere between 500 and 1,000 more votes—enough to put him into the lead when added to the 174, 176, 214, or 215.

The one thing, though, that the Palm Beach canvassing board could claim over neighboring rival Broward was continuing celebrity. Almost nobody recognized Broward's chairman, Judge Robert Lee, whereas perpetually bronzed if also sleepy-faced Burton was making it into Jon Stewart jokes on Comedy Central and months later would be seen hobnobbing at the White House Correspondents Dinner in Washington. Plus, there was Donato Dalrymple, the famous fisherman from Elián days of yore. Dalrymple showed up at the Palm Beach count just to "check it out."

Against the backdrop of Broward and Palm Beach, Gore's commanders say the Miami-Dade board's vote to fold its tent was disastrous. For starters, Gore might've pulled ahead with a net gain of only a couple hundred votes, in which case it would've been Bush contemplating a formal contest. But leaving that aside, if Miami-Dade had completed its count on time, the only issues during the contest phase for Gore would not have involved further counting and the attendant wrangling over standards. Palm Beach, in fact, had finished counting. It was just late, so the legal issue once again would've been about deadlines. "With a lawsuit by us about things other than counting," says Ron Klain, "the second U.S. Supreme Court case would not have existed or would have been entirely different." The Court ruling was about one question only: Were differences in county counting standards in a judicially supervised contest unconstitutional, as a matter of "equal protection" under the Fourteenth Amendment? That question would've disappeared had Miami-Dade completed its count on time.

Gore's legal claims over chad standards might also have been aided by Miami-Dade going forward on that Wednesday. If the county had used the same liberal standard that Broward had, then Palm Beach's stricter standard would have constituted the exception. Gore's lawyers would've then argued that in the name of consistency, Palm Beach needed to conform to the other two counties (which might have netted Gore many hundreds of votes). Of course, a judge could find that Broward and Miami-Dade should've used Palm Beach's test, but at least Gore could persuasively make the opposite case. Then, the Florida Supreme Court, in the second case it heard, would have been faced with a simple either-or choice, rather than being asked to pick standards out of the air. Either way, Bush's claim to the U.S. Supreme Court on December 11—that a statewide recount might wind up using sixty-seven different standards—would not have existed.

The Wednesday before Thanksgiving also proved eventful to the Bush campaign, though in a more frightening way. If anyone had any doubts that Florida's stalemate was stressing out the participants, they had only to look to the Republican vice presidential candidate. At three-thirty in the morning, at his suburban home outside Washington, the fifty-nine-year-old Dick Cheney felt an odd sensation in his chest. An hour later, he was admitted to the George Washington University Medical Center and was told he'd had a mild heart attack—his fourth coronary, though his first since quadruple bypass surgery in 1988. Bush's boil might have been funny in the days after Election Night. This was not. "Oh God!" reacted Bush, when he got the news from Don Evans, the campaign chairman. "What's going to happen next?"

As Cheney underwent a two-hour procedure to open a blocked artery, the surgeons listened to music on the radio, only to be interrupted by news bulletins about Dick Cheney's heart problems, for which the reports were hopelessly behind. The doctors had the surreal experience of hearing a play-by-play of their treatment of their patient, even if the coverage wasn't right. Only in the late afternoon did the hospital and campaign acknowledge that Cheney had indeed suffered a heart attack rather than the innocent-sounding "elevated enzyme levels." Earlier, Bush himself specifically said his running mate had not had a heart attack, which aides later explained was based on faulty information. Trying to reassure the public, Cheney did the Larry King show by phone that night and said he'd be out of the hospital before the weekend. "I can report," he joked to King, "that when they got in there, they didn't find any pregnant chads."

If they had, the Democrats would likely still be counting them.

On Sunday evening, November 26, Katherine Harris finally got to do what she'd been trying to do for nearly two weeks. At 7:25, before a lightstorm of flashbulbs and a national TV audience (except on NBC, which opted for the more melodramatic *Titanic*), she carried out the formal act of certifying George W. Bush the winner of Florida's twenty-five electoral votes.

From the darkly paneled Cabinet Room of the capitol, Harris could hear the cheers outside the building. Along with the two other members of the state elections commission—the ministerial body from which Jeb Bush had recused himself—Harris applied her embossed seal to the document attesting to these words: Bush, 2,912,790; Gore, 2,912,253. The margin of victory was 537 votes. Jeb's recusal only went so far—he still would sign, an hour later, the "certificate of ascertainment" that the Electoral College required. That document might be decisive later on if Congress ever had to choose between competing slates of electors, just as happened in the Hayes-Tilden race of 1876. (If the two houses of Congress disagreed about which slate to recognize, federal law gave preference to the slate "ascertained" by the governor.)

The elections commission normally handled the certification without fanfare—a staffer went around to obtain the needed signatures. This time, Harris said, "because of the great interest in our actions, we are meeting publicly." It didn't hurt that she got some more TV exposure, this time without anyone calling her Cruella, despite her bright red thousand-dollar suit. In brief and unusually barbed remarks, Harris got in a few more swipes at the Florida Supreme Court, which, she said, "created a new schedule for filing certifications and conducting election contests, rather than implementing the schedule enacted by the legislature." Then she went after the Palm Beach canvassing board for missing the 5 P.M. deadline. Her acrimony notwithstanding, she trumpeted the "triumph" of "democracy" and "the rule of law." And in what's become the political oratorical equivalent of "Have a nice day," she signed off with "God bless America."

Mac Stipanovich's wife and daughter watched the ceremony from the front row of the Cabinet Room. He saw it from the War Room in Harris's suite of offices, one floor above. Not a bad way to celebrate his fifty-second birthday.

It might've gone differently if Miami-Dade had continued its count and Palm Beach had finished on time and included more dimpled ballots. As the grandfather in "Peter and the Wolf" gravely asked, "What would have happened *then*?" Harris probably would've certified Gore the victor (she says she would have), with all the accompanying qualifiers. Or perhaps she would have refused, claiming the Florida justices had debased the process, and dared Gore or the state attorney general to take her back to court. Or just maybe she would've resigned in protest and become a GOP martyr for the ages. Is the last possibility only speculation? One member of her staff said it was briefly discussed, but with Bush always ahead, it never had to be seriously considered.

What would Bush have done? Jim Baker insisted later that the candidate would have accepted a certification in Gore's favor. "He would have conceded right then and there," Baker says. Part of that was political realism, according to Baker, because Bush would've been behind not just in Florida and the Electoral College, but also in the national popular vote. But it went beyond calculation, Baker says. "He felt very strongly that this couldn't go on forever and would do the right thing if he had to." We'll never know.

Bush was now the declared winner of the presidency. Yet Election 2000, on Day 20, was hardly over.

With all the theatricality of a kitchen-appliance store reopening for the fifth time, ABC (alone among the networks) painted Florida red on its electronic map, though refrained from designating Bush as the president-elect. "For the record," smirked Bill Carter in the *New York Times*, with ABC putting Florida in the Bush column, "the state has been white, then blue, then white again, then red, then white again, then red again." Whoever said the networks weren't patriotic? Most newspapers and magazines went out of their way not to call Bush the "forty-third president of the United States." The more popular numeral in story leads was 537, with asterisks for the more clever headline writers, as in "537*"—the cover line for *Newsweek*.

Had Bush prevailed? It was true that what Gore had fought to prevent from happening had in fact happened. And Bush took advantage of it in a prime-time speech, proclaiming two hours after the certification that he'd won the election. An early draft of the speech was militant, its second line reading, "This is now the *fourth* vote that [Dick] Cheney and I have won." In a markup, Baker noted it was "too arrogant," suggesting "softer" language. With chants of "Hail to the chief!" outside the governor's offices in Austin, Bush said he was "honored and humbled" to be awarded Florida, and he called on Gore's lawyers to pack it in. But Gore had already made clear that he was going to proceed to the contest phase, and he went on TV the next night—this time, with only twelve American flags around him—to plead for continuing patience. Just as important, Bush himself had already asked the U.S. Supreme Court to intervene, and the justices in Washington, forty-eight hours before certification, had unexpectedly agreed to take Bush's appeal.

What of that case, now that Bush had been certified? Why did it matter anymore that the Florida Supreme Court had extended the certification deadline? The case seemed moot. On the other hand, the contest phase was about to begin, at the end of which hovered the Florida Supreme Court again—and who could predict what havoc the justices would unleash the next time? How to proceed would be a fundamental strategic call for Bush, one that would shape the remaining seventeen days of the struggle.

As he did at other crucial moments, Baker prepared a step-by-step memo for the candidate. The issue, as Baker explained it, was whether to go forward with the oral argument in Washington set for Friday, five days hence, or drop the case. Putting the appeal on hold wasn't an option.

The arguments for dropping the case were straightforward enough. Bush could take the high ground, as well as deny Gore another week or two to claim the race couldn't be over if the U.S. Supreme Court was still looking at it. "Our prospects," the two-page confidential memo argued, "while better than even, are highly uncertain. If we lose the case after eking out a narrow win in the vote count, Gore will be seen as scoring a big victory, which he will use to lend momentum and legitimacy to his contest challenges in Florida courts." Moreover, dropping out now "would remove a Gore excuse for continuing to litigate and would reinforce a GWB call to rely on the numerous counts of the voting results rather than litigation." And what about a possible loss at the U.S. Supreme Court, where any litigation is a "roll of the dice"? "That could backfire on us by posing major political/legal impediments to any action by the Florida Legislature to overturn Florida court decisions for Gore in the contest proceedings." Right—because it might look like the legislature was countermanding not the justices of Florida but those of the United States.

But there were reasons to march on to the highest court in the land. "A win," read the memo, "might remove the basis for Gore's election contest. At a minimum, it would create enormous public pressure for Gore to drop his contest." PR psychology had to affect Bush as well. "It would look bad to drop the case now," Baker advised. Plus, "as long as the case is pending, the Florida Supreme Court is likely to be more careful in ruling on contest proceedings." There was also the Florida legislature, which Baker was uncertain would rescue Bush if it came to that. "Our supporters [there] would probably not look kindly on dropping the case." And in any event, "it makes more sense to maintain the Supreme Court route, if we are not absolutely determined to use the legislative route."

Baker prepared three "Sunday Night Options (if ahead)" for Bush, in easy checklist format: withdraw from the case, continue it, or "offer to drop [it] and all litigation if Gore drops all litigation," which Baker acknowledged the public would recognize as "really a rhetorical tactic, because if Gore accepts, he loses." All Bush had to do among the choices was pick 1, 2, or 3—what could be easier than a simple ballot, as it were?

Bush considered the options in a fifteen- to twenty-minute conference call with Baker, Cheney, a few political advisers, and the GOP's constitutional lawyers. Having convinced the U.S. Supreme Court to hear the case, the lawyers didn't want to back out now. But two others articulated the arguments against continuing the appeal. Josh Bolten, the policy czar who was quietly organizing transition plans for an administration, was concerned about the great risk posed by a Supreme Court defeat. Bob Zoellick, one of Baker's lieutenants and a nonpracticing attorney like Bolten, said withdrawing the appeal was the clearer path to ultimate victory on the one hand, even if it meant less public acceptance on the other.

After asking a series of questions—the public's image of him as disengaged was often unfair—Bush wasted no time making a decision. "We're going ahead with the appeal," he directed his troops. "I understand it poses a number of risks." But as much as he realized the political benefits of standing down, he worried that winning by way of the Florida legislature would appear "illegitimate." Some victories, he said, were "not worth having." The U.S. Supreme Court offered an imprimatur that no other branch of government could bestow.

Bush clearly wanted the blessing of the justices. The fact that Jim Baker earlier that day had said once again, "I don't think the American people want their election turned over to lawyers and court contests," apparently didn't strike the campaign as ironic.

Realpolitik

I t *made strange* sense that Cynthia Rapp would be the bureaucrat at the U.S. Supreme Court assigned to the presidential dispute when it blew northward from Florida. The thirty-seven-year-old Rapp had been one of the deputies to the clerk of the Court since the early 1990s and had a specialty: She was the "emergency applications clerk," whose unique job it was to track last-second appeals of all condemned inmates in the United States. On the wall of her cubicle at the Court, she liked to post *Far Side* cartoons, including the one about "Electric Chair Operators Night School," in which teacher tells pupil, "Sorry, Loman, down and up real fast is *incorrect.*" When an execution was imminent, Rapp was the woman to call. In the American capital punishment industry, she was the "death clerk."

Because the time pressure and torrent of briefs coming in made the Bush appeal analogous to a capital case, Rapp was the obvious deputy clerk to track the paperwork, organize files for the justices, and communicate with counsel. But apart from the logic, it also seemed an omen to one of Al Gore's lawyers. "It could have been a coincidence and, yeah, maybe the Court had a sense of humor," said the lawyer later on, with a wince. "But in retrospect, we should've known right at that point, things weren't looking good."

As Jim Baker had mentioned to Bush himself, the chances of the U.S. Supreme Court taking their case hadn't been much better than 50–50. Larry Tribe, the Democrats' top constitutional lawyer, thought the odds way less, as did Ted Olson, his counterpart for the GOP. For what it was worth, the press agreed. "If past cases are a guide," declared Joan Biskupic, *USA Today*'s respected Court correspondent, "the black-robed nine in Washington will beg off." Ken Starr—Bill Clinton's old nemesis, a former solicitor general, and a GOP loyalist—gave a private talk at a Washington law firm in which he, too, said there was no chance the Supreme Nine would intervene in Florida's electoral quagmire.

It wasn't that justices would view a presidential election as inconsequential, but that the main legal issues were about state prerogatives. For a generation now, since Ronald Reagan was able to put three conservatives on the high bench, as well as elevate William Rehnquist to chief justice, there had been a fair amount of lip service to the cause of "states' rights"—or, as it increasingly became known, "federalism," denoting the proper relationship between states and the federal government. In the absence of clear constitutional instructions to the contrary, states would be left to their own legislative and judicial devices, whether wise or foolish. It didn't always play out that way. In matters ranging from civil rights to, of course, abortion, the justices were willing to pay little deference to the states. But these were the exceptions, especially in comparison to prior judicial eras—most notoriously, the Court of the 1960s, led by Earl Warren and William Brennan.

The contours of the Supreme Court facing Bush and Gore were fairly predictable. While "conservative" and "liberal" labels are always simplifications, they do allow for apt categorizations of overall philosophies and voting dispositions. "Conservative" meant the justice usually voted for the government in civil-liberties cases brought by individuals; for property and corporate rights that were competing with individual freedoms; and for state interests against federal ones. "Liberals" tended to favor individuals and the federal regime.

Once upon a time, "conservative" also meant a humble view of the judiciary—not its intellect or stature, but its role. Judges tried hard to avoid deciding cases they didn't have to. Instead, they understood the virtue of deferring to the elected branches of government—legislative and executive—whether at the federal or state level. It was the view espoused most splendidly by a federal judge who never even made it to the U.S. Supreme Court, Learned Hand, who in 1944 noted, "The spirit of liberty is the spirit which is not sure it is right." But that view of judging no longer held sway for conservatives or liberals. In the six years leading up to the Court's consideration of the presidential election case, the justices had struck down more than twenty-five federal statutes—including the Brady Handgun Bill and the Violence Against Women Act—as violations of the Constitution, usually on grounds that the congressional legislation intruded on areas that should be left up to the states. In the Capitol Hill neighborhood of Washington, the Supreme Court is just across the street from Congress. Yet it's really in another orbit—the Court looks down upon its co-equal branch.

On the hard right of the 2000 Court were the seventy-six-year-old Rehnquist and Justices Antonin Scalia and Clarence Thomas—though, even at their extremes, the three were regarded more as ideologues than partisans. Rehnquist had been on the Court since 1971, plucked from relative insignificance at the Justice Department and appointed at the age of forty-seven by Richard Nixon; fifteen years later, Reagan made him chief justice. As the remaining member of the Court from the four that Nixon named, he was, as predicted at his Senate confirmation hearings, truly Nixon's Revenge, wreaking vengeance on liberal talismans for nearly thirty years. Anyone who doubted that Supreme Court appointments had the ability to shape the nation's law and culture well beyond the tenure of a presidential patron needed only to remember Rehnquist's Gilbert-and-Sullivan stripes up there on the bench eons after Tricky Dick had departed the scene.

The sixty-four-year-old Scalia, a longtime academic before becoming a federal appeals court judge in Washington, was named to the Supreme Court by Reagan in 1986 and became the most conservative justice since the early part of the twentieth century. When he was asked at his confirmation hearings if he agreed with *Marbury v. Madison*, the 1803 ruling that established the Court as the last word on all matters constitutional, he balked. Without Marbury, the Court would be a paper tiger; the last time anyone seriously questioned the decision, baseball hadn't yet been invented. Would Scalia at least acknowledge that it was correctly decided, lest he throw into question every constitutional ruling since? No, he testified, "I do not want to be in a position of saying as to any case that I wouldn't overrule it." That was tough talk, but senators, kowtowed by his relentless charm and unchallenged brains, confirmed him 98–0, even though a year later they rejected Robert Bork for a constitutional outlook no more conservative. For liberals, Scalia's only saving grace was that he had no interest in building coalitions on the Court—that was beneath his intellect and beyond his duties, which he saw as getting it precisely right, even if that meant being unable to command a majority of the Court. Given a choice between doctrinal purity and winning, Scalia picked the former every time.

In that philosophical way, as well as in ideology, he was the antithesis of Bill Brennan, the deity for the liberals, who served on the Court for thirty-four years until 1990. Brennan was as smart as Scalia, but he cared about carrying the day. More than any theory of constitutional law, Brennan used to tell law clerks, the most important principle around the Court was not a principle at all. What governed the justices was the "Rule of Five." "If you have five votes," he'd say, brandishing a big smile and five fingers on one hand, "you can do anything." Brennan was the paragon of counting votes on the Court. It made him the most powerful justice of the twentieth century, even if that candid view ratified cynicism that the Court was about nothing more than realpolitik. The Rule of Five seemed inconsistent with the rule of law.

The fifty-two-year-old Thomas, the second black justice (replacing Thurgood Marshall, the first), was, of course, the subject of tempestuous hearings in 1991 when he was nominated by George W. Bush's father. Anita Hill accused him of sexual harassment at the hearings, which Thomas assailed as a "high-tech lynching." Confirmed by only a 52-to-48 vote, he turned out to be every bit as conservative as Scalia, and his harshest critics called him a water carrier for Scalia. During the 2000 campaign, George W. Bush described Scalia and Thomas as his ideal justices. With the two of them and Rehnquist, conservatives could claim three votes for most causes.

And yet, in the Florida election cases—if one put purely partisan considerations aside—conservative principles cut in favor of leaving the state on its own. If there was hope for Bush, it was that the three justices weren't in the habit of citing Learned Hand. Theirs was a smug self-assurance—like that of their brethren on the left—that they generally knew best and, in spite of their unelected status, were happy to step into any raw political fray. If Rehnquist, Scalia, and Thomas were at all bothered by what they regarded as a judicial circus in Florida, they'd have no principled objection to meddling. And it didn't hurt that you could wager the national debt that none of them voted for Al Gore on Election Day.

The left flank of the Court—or what passed for it these days, after the retirements a decade before of liberal lions like Brennan and Marshall—consisted of Stephen Breyer, Ruth Bader Ginsburg, John Paul Stevens, and David Souter. Breyer, sixty-two, and Ginsburg, sixty-seven, were nominated by Bill Clinton in his first term and were the Court's only current members appointed by a Democratic president. Both voted reliably liberal—he was a former aide to Senator Ted Kennedy, she was one of the early courtroom champions of women's rights—but in the Brennan-Marshall era they would have been called moderates, and correctly so. Theirs was a style based on compromise, not boldness. That's one of the reasons both sailed through their confirmation hearings.

The bow-tied Stevens—at eighty, the oldest justice—had been on the Court since 1975 and was Gerald Ford's sole appointment. He succeeded William O. Douglas, perhaps the most liberal justice ever, and could only have moved the Court to the center. Yet he turned out to be surprisingly in sync with much liberal jurisprudence, sometimes more so than Ginsburg and Breyer. Stevens was quirky and independent—he's the only justice who criticized the current fashion of swearing in new Court members at the White House—and tended to write more lone dissents than his colleagues. Souter, a sixty-one-year-old lifelong Republican, was put on the Court in 1990 by Bush's father, advertised as a "home run" for such constitutional crusades as overturning *Roe v. Wade*. Instead, he turned out to be a moderate, nondoctrinaire jurist who typically sided with the liberal justices. It didn't make him a liberal—this was a passionately modest man in matters of law as well as life—as much as it reflected how far the rest of the Court had yawed starboard.

In the middle of the Court—or what passed for it—were Sandra Day O'Connor and Anthony Kennedy. Just as Stevens and Souter were called liberals on the continuum of the current Court, O'Connor and Kennedy were called moderates. But that label had everything to do with who sat to their right. Given the division of the rest of the justices, how these two went often determined the Court's pronouncements. Selected by Reagan, the seventy-year-old O'Connor was the first woman on the Court. She sided with Scalia more than she did with Ginsburg, but she was never as pure as the GOP right wing had hoped for, particularly on abortion. Because so many of her opinions appeared to be ad hoc and because she had been in a state legislature herself—the Arizona Senate, as majority leader—Bush lawyers worried she might be sympathetic to letting the Florida Supreme Court and legislature duke out their intramural squabble themselves.

In fact, O'Connor was the only current justice who had ever held elective office. Whereas prior eras of the Court included former senators, governors, attorneys general, and others from outside the cocoon of judicial life, the Rehnquist regime was dominated by former law professors and lower-court judges. As such, the Court of 2000 had justices who were personally unfamiliar with the vicissitudes of politics and who could bring no appreciation of public life to bear on the work of constitutional judging. That deficiency proved to be critical later on when the Court had to decide if it or Congress would be the branch of the federal government to consider the Florida turmoil.

The sixty-four-year-old Kennedy, as the justice charged with receiving emergency requests from Florida, knew even better than the others what was percolating up to the High Court. Another Reagan appointee—he got the seat that Bork lost—Kennedy seemed to play the part of Court sad sack. It wasn't so much his droopy demeanor on the bench as that privately he bristled that it was O'Connor who was always described as "the Court's most influential member." In a 5-to-4 ruling, as so many were, why wasn't he just as decisive? The Rehnquist-Scalia-Thomas troika was an ideological given—you could often predict their votes the minute the Court accepted a highly charged case—but you needed two more votes to get a majority. So why did O'Connor get the credit as the fulcrum?

He had a fair point. The answer is that Kennedy's centrism got tangled up with his penchant for indecisiveness. Shakespeare had Kennedy pegged when he wrote "Let 'I dare not' wait upon 'I would'"; it's little wonder Kennedy was a fan of the Bard. Kennedy's brethren sometimes thought he could be flipped, as he had been in the landmark 1992 abortion ruling that refused to reverse *Roe v. Wade.* So wobbly was he perceived that inside the Court he'd long had the unkind nickname "Flipper." One year, at the annual private revue put on by law clerks to celebrate the end of the Court's calendar, they lampooned Kennedy with the theme song from the old TV show about a fun-loving dolphin. "They call him Flipper, Flipper . . ." went the tune. Scalia, so Court lore goes, was quite amused.

Despite the prognostications, the Supreme Court agreed to take the appeal from Florida just forty-eight hours after the Bush request was filed on Thanksgiving Eve. Without comment—and, curiously, without stopping the ongoing recounts in south Florida that could have put Gore into the lead—the justices scheduled oral argument for a week later, December 1. In Court time, that was extremely swift—the briefing schedule typically took months—but come the next and final round in the presidential dispute, it would seem leisurely.

The only ruling under review would be the certification extension by the Florida justices, rather than the equal-protection claim Bush had unsuccessfully put forward in two lower federal courts. While it wasn't that big a deal—the Court had latitude to consider virtually anything a lower court had looked at—it appeared at least to Gore's lawyers to show a lack of interest in equal protection. When Bush's lawyers submitted their list of three proposed questions for the Court to examine, the justices accepted the first two—dealing with a state court's authority to change electoral rules after Election Day and a state court's power in relation to a state legislature—but they specifically declined to include the equal-protection question. Although they never said why they took some questions but not others, some of the justices would later explain privately that all they were doing was giving a lower federal court—the

11th U.S. Circuit Court of Appeals in Atlanta—the opportunity to develop it first. But this explanation rang hollow, given the time crunch.

More likely, the Court skirted the equal-protection issue because it was so contentious. Indeed, when the justices returned from Thanksgiving to decide whether to take Bush's appeal, the conservative wing already had the votes, with no debate required. The only matter to discuss was which of the legal questions suggested by the parties should be briefed. It was clear even at this early juncture that equal protection would be a source of division, and the last thing the Court wanted was a 5-to-4 split. In momentous cases of the past, like school desegregation or the Nixon tapes, the Court had often figured out how to speak with a unanimous voice. If it could avoid fracturing over a presidential election, it might save itself from the howls of partisanship.

However, ducking equal protection and then taking it up in the endgame in mid-December—and then ruling that Electoral College deadlines left *no more time* for recounts to be conducted in such a way that satisfied equal protection—was either bad planning or exquisite cunning. The Court was praying it wouldn't see the case again, that the dispute would somehow resolve itself on the legal return trip to Florida that the justices would soon order. But the Court had to have known there was a substantial chance its prayers wouldn't be answered.

With the ideologies of the justices in mind—and the possibility of a 5-to-4 schism—the Bush and Gore legal teams tried to game the Court. In their three rounds of briefs, both sides repeated much of what they'd argued before. Bush especially played to the Court's arrogant view of itself as the nation's final arbiter of any legal question; Gore appealed to the Court's regard for federalism and deference to state processes that had been "applied throughout this country for centuries."

Bush described a scene of "striking chaos" in Florida, of which, the brief stated, "this Court is undoubtedly aware." (Justices have TV sets, too.) The varying standards of the recounts showed their "absurdity"; and counties were engaged in a "blatantly arbitrary, subjective, and standardless process . . . in an effort to divine the intent of the voters." In short, Bush argued, Florida had become a big top, and it was time to take the tent down and declare an end to the show.

Who was to blame for the chaos, according to Bush? He said it was the Florida justices, who had "embarked on [a] lawless exercise of judicial power." All the while, "the nation's citizens . . . anxiously await a resolution of the election outcome," their "angst" prolonged by a rogue state supreme court. How could the U.S. justices not decide it? This was strong language about the highest court of a state—the kind of thing not seen since the days of the segregation cases. But Bush's lawyers calculated that this was the best way to get the U.S. Supreme Court's attention. "This is precisely the type of question that the nation justifiably expects this Court to decide," read the brief. Failure to do so could result in "the ascension of a president of questionable legitimacy, or a constitutional crisis." Bush compared the case's magnitude to that of *United States v. Nixon* in 1974, where the president was ordered to turn over subpoenaed tapes to the Watergate special prosecutor. (Until the year 2000, no other case had so thrust the Court into determining who would become or remain king.)

Gore's lawyers tried to dial down the constitutional volume, rebuking Bush's petition for being so "intemperate" in the highest court in the land, while they counterpunched with their own rhetorical warnings. Even with the presidency in dispute, they wrote, Bush's appeal was essentially a "garden-variety" disagreement over state law that he was attempting to "federalize." Bush hadn't won in the state forum, so he was taking another shot before a different set of referees. "At bottom," the brief stated, all that Bush "can really claim is that, in his view, the Florida Supreme Court got Florida law wrong." But the selection of presidential electors "is both fundamental to state sovereignty and constitutionally reserved to the states." Besides, Gore contended, whatever else the Florida Supreme Court had done, it hadn't changed any law, but had only engaged in the routine resolution of a statute's ambiguities and conflicting provisions, which all courts indisputably do. Permitting hand recounts to be given effect wasn't "like changing the rules after the game had been played," but was "like using a more powerful photo-finish camera . . . already mandated by the legislature . . . to determine the winner of the race more accurately."

Far from adding a sheen of "legitimacy" to the outcome of the election, as Bush had argued in his brief, involvement by the Supreme Court "in still-ongoing state proceedings" would "deflect and derail the elec-

tion process in untoward and unprecedented directions." And beyond
the presidential race, it would subject federal courts to "promiscuous
charges of usurpation," an "onslaught" of claims by "losing parties in
state courts alleging that the decisions in their cases constituted an
unconstitutional departure from pre-existing law." Much of Gore's
powder seemed aimed at Scalia; the brief was sprinkled with references
to both his Court opinions and extra-judicial writing. (It wound up
being a wasted effort—pissing in the juridical wind—as Scalia never
showed any reluctance to second-guess the Florida Supreme Court.)

Among all the flourishes in Gore's legal papers, one might've
thought he'd at least present the case for judicial restraint—something
more than mere federalism. The latter was about the constitutional division of power between the federal government and the states. The former was an all-embracing philosophy about how "activist" judges
should be or, conversely, deferential to the political branches of government. Judicial restraint was a style of judging generally—an instinct—
that could be applied toward any legal question, including (but not
limited to) the proper boundaries between federal and state power.
Alexis de Tocqueville was wise in the 1830s to write of the High Court
that "a more imposing judicial power was never constituted by any people." This didn't mean, however, that the judicial cudgel always had to
be swung.

Should not Gore have offered some invocation of Learned Hand or
Professor Alex Bickel, or former justices Felix Frankfurter or John Marshall Harlan? These were the apostles of restraint, revered for their
recognition of what courts should and should not do. They sometimes
failed to practice what they preached—restraint is in the eyes of the
beholder—but they got it right more often than not. In Gore's briefs,
there was mention of some of these leading lights, but only for unrelated
scholarship. Perhaps it was a sign that a Democrat who worshiped an
extravagant ruling like *Roe v. Wade*—or his bold counsel, Larry Tribe—
realized that calling for institutional restraint might elicit snickers, especially because it was the action of Florida *judges*, after all, that was under
review. (But there was a distinction: Florida election law specifically
contemplated a role for the courts; it wasn't so easy to cook up a rationale for federal intervention.)

More likely, however, it never seriously occurred to Gore's lawyers to call for restraint. Tribe, their intellectual warlord, had long dismissed it. "Judicial restraint," he wrote in the introduction to his consummate treatise on American constitutional law, "is but another form of judicial activism." The "highest mission" of the Supreme Court, he advocated in 1977, "is not to conserve judicial credibility, but in the Constitution's own phrase, 'to form a more perfect Union' between right and rights within that charter's necessarily evolutionary design." Though Tribe would heartily disagree, the Court of this generation in many ways represented the ascendance of his view. The Court did as it pleased and dispensed with the niceties of even discussing restraint. Such was the disrepute into which judicial humility had fallen. Such was the triumph of the judiciary—not necessarily "the least dangerous branch" at all.

Every trade has its favorite in-house gags, the ones that always get trotted out on the golf course or in keynote speeches by dinner speakers. Everyone's heard the joke, but everyone delights in retelling it and applying it to new circumstances. It's sort of like scripture. In the fraternity of state court judges, everybody loves the one about the doctors.

One afternoon, Saint Peter is administering business at the Pearly Gates when three men in coats and ties come walking up. "What's your story?" Saint Peter asks the first.

"I was a dermatologist," he replies.

"Too many of them here already. You're out of here." And Saint Peter points him away from heaven. Turning to the next guy in line, he asks, "And you?"

"Orthopedic surgeon."

"Sorry, no room for you either."

With that, the third man starts walking off even before Saint Peter says a word. "Where are *you* going?" Saint Peter asks.

"I'm a psychiatrist. You surely don't want me."

"Actually," says Saint Peter, "we could use you. We need someone to talk to God—he thinks he's a Supreme Court justice."

Despite the Florida certification by Katherine Harris, some of Gore's field operatives were nothing if not optimistic after Thanksgiving. Assuming their candidate ultimately won a recount ratified by the Florida Supreme Court, the Gore slate of electors would have to meet somewhere on December 18 to formally cast their votes. But it was a good bet that Bush would continue to fight and would have the Florida legislature name *his* slate of electors. The legislature had been making noises of calling a special session ever since the state supreme court intervened. A Bush slate would obviously meet at the capitol. So where were the Gore electors supposed to go—the Doubletree?

Nick Baldick, the campaign's chief field person in Tallahassee, thought of the *Old* State Capitol Building, just across the plaza from the new one. It was the one with the distinctive red-and-white awnings over the windows, as well as the rich political tradition. The old capitol, dating to 1839, was now a museum, also used for private receptions. What could be a better venue to name the forty-third president? Baldick couldn't very well try to reserve it in his own name. He'd risk the campaign getting caught. So in late November, a Broward fund-raiser signed the place up for a party she claimed to be throwing. It would've made for a great stunt.

Gore himself was showing signs of lost optimism. On the Saturday after Thanksgiving, Walter Dellinger paid a visit to the vice president at his residence. Dellinger, a past solicitor general in the Clinton administration, was close to Gore's brother-in-law, Frank Hunger, as well as a confidant of Klain and other guns in the Gore campaign. Gore and family wanted Dellinger's take on the litigation. Things weren't looking up for the candidate. Just the day before, the U.S. Supreme Court had decided to hear Bush's appeal. Tomorrow, Harris was expected to certify Bush the winner of Florida's electoral votes. Hunger picked Dellinger up and they headed for the Naval Observatory.

The meeting with Gore, Tipper, and two of their daughters, along with Bill Daley, was uneventful and Dellinger was on his way to leave when Tipper stopped him at the door. She had heard from and about Democrats who thought it was time for her husband to be exiting the stage. She could read the newspaper editorials and hear the incessant chanting from protesters across the street from the residence, "Get out of Cheney's house!" The catcalls unnerved some of Gore's children, who sometimes felt like prisoners in their own home.

"Do you think we're doing the right thing in pursuing this?" she asked Dellinger, according to someone else in the room. "Should Al be staying in?"

The vice president, who had been talking to someone else nearby, overheard the exchange and wandered over. "What do you think, Walter?"

"I think the presidency is not yours to give away."

"That is a very powerful thought," Gore said.

"Just because it might be better for you or the party—it's not something you own. A hundred million people voted in this election, and I don't think you have the right to give the presidency to someone else just because this is a difficult process."

"When does it end?" asked Tipper. "When do we end it?"

At the earliest of two moments, Dellinger advised: when Gore became convinced he had not won or when he wouldn't be able to prevail even if he had won. "That," Dellinger said, "is when you ought to bring it to an end."

Dellinger says he didn't have the impression that Gore was on the brink of pulling out, but was thinking through choices—a contrast to the public view of a candidate obsessed only with winning. "I was impressed throughout the process that he was showing his skills as a leader," Dellinger says. "It was crisis management in the best sense."

If Gore had been able to get across those abilities during the general campaign, he might not have been behind by 537 votes in Florida.

Here's where Gore stood on November 27, the Monday after Thanksgiving. The strikes against him were accumulating. Even with the extra time to count votes, he'd lost the election, according to Harris's certification. He, too, was staring at an impending U.S. Supreme Court argument from which he had nothing to gain except not losing. And there were only fifteen days until December 12, the date that David Boies had told the Florida Supreme Court was the deadline of deadlines. Above all else, Gore had to get the recounts going again, and the only way to do that was to file his much-discussed contest action.

Boies, along with Ron Klain—monitored from afar by Bill Daley and Warren Christopher (who had returned to California for personal reasons)—had to select from a range of complaints: recounts that didn't happen; recounts that did but used the wrong chad standards and then were ignored by the secretary of state because they came in a couple of hours late; recounts that happened properly and on time, but were nonetheless ignored by canvassing board officials; the confusing butter-fly and caterpillar ballots; overseas absentee ballots that shouldn't have been tallied because of technical flaws; black voters who'd been wrongly turned back at the polls because their names had been purged from voting rolls based on alleged felonies; and minority voters who'd been scared away from voting by the presence of police roadblocks and other intimidation tactics.

The list was a veritable indictment of Florida election procedures, though many of the problems existed in other states as well. Nobody other than an incumbent elections commissioner ever claimed elections were perfect—but they were good enough to get the job done most of the time. That's one of the reasons why Florida's presidential travails seemed so exaggerated. Because few elections are ever that close, no one bothers to spend precious local money on updating equipment, training polling personnel, or educating first-time voters. It's not a plot, just a fact of bureaucratic life. A mistake here, an oversight there—but it's almost never enough to swing an election, because there are sufficient voters to overwhelm the margin of error. However, if you ignore the problems long enough and believe in the laws of bad luck, one day the defects will conspire into disaster, magnified by the fact it's the presidency at stake. Such is what electoral accidents are made of.

There were a handful in the Gore camp who wanted to present the full indictment to a Florida court. But with time short, and with the likelihood that the Florida Supreme Court would get the last word in the state anyway, there was little purpose in a prolonged contest at the trial level. So Gore decided to include only a few parts to his lawsuit challenging Bush's certified 537-margin victory. (If Gore lost at the U.S. Supreme Court, it was probable the number would revert to the 930-vote lead Bush had on Saturday, November 18.)

Whittling that down was the whole ballgame—and doing it in a way that stayed in harmony with the PR tune that Al Gore only wanted to "count all the votes." Once Gore looked like he was trying to exclude votes, like the suspect OABs, the consensus was that he'd be regressing to the day when Tim Russert pasted Joe Lieberman on Sunday-morning

TV. Michael Whouley, the political maven, had tried to challenge that internal view, but he lost. It wasn't a bad argument, for Bush's lawyers themselves would have had to explain in one formal judicial setting how they could support "hyper-technical" rules when it came to Democratic counties but an anything-goes standard for Our Men and Women in the Military. Yet even if those subtleties played in a courtroom, Gore concluded they'd fall flat in the arena of public opinion. As to the butterflies and caterpillars, there were still no realistic remedies available. Say good-bye to the bug references.

Thus, Gore's thirty-four-page complaint demanded that the ne'er-do-well counties of Palm Beach and Miami-Dade be put back into the mix, using Broward as the model. That meant including Palm Beach's 174 net Gore votes (or 215, if you believed the numbers proffered by Gore rather than by the county itself) in the certified totals. And it dictated that Miami-Dade return to the counting tables, in order to "transcend mob action" there; the county already had shown a net pickup of 157 for Gore, with most of the 10,750 undervotes yet to be inspected. Gore also asked that Nassau County be forced to go with the results of its automatic recount, rather than its Election Night count, which would net him 51 more votes.

If Gore could put all those numbers on the board — 174, 157, and 51 — he'd be 155 dimples short of the presidency. In a Miami-Dade recount of undervotes, that would be all he'd need to harvest. Plus, Gore maintained, if the judge in the contest would review some 3,300 disputed ballots from Palm Beach that weren't converted into legal votes, Gore would pick up some more — 800 or so net, according to Gore's court papers. (This was the one part of Gore's claim that highlighted his desperation, as well as lent credence to the Republican cry that he would seek recount after recount until he won. The Palm Beach board had put a good-faith effort into its recount and attempted to come up with a standard that reflected voter intent. Dimples and other ballot indentations were murky at best and it was hard to see how their conservative evaluation of them was anything but reasonable. Others could decide differently, and Broward County had. But Gore's choice to contest Palm Beach's rejection of the 3,300 disputed ballots seems to have been based on nothing other than the hope that the next decision maker in line might see it his way. It smelled bad. If the strict Palm Beach standard had put Gore in the lead and then Bush pleaded for dimples, would Gore have joined him in the court case?)

All this, Gore's lawyers believed, met the legal standard to win a contest—that sufficient "legal votes" had been rejected "to change or place in doubt the results" of the election. Moreover, Florida law gave vast power to the court in a contest proceeding. To the vanquished candidate, winning seemed reasonable and doable, notwithstanding the courage it would take of a single trial-level judge to undo a certified election.

It surely didn't help Gore's cause that the contest was assigned to Norman Sanders Sauls, the one judge on the Leon County Circuit whom the vice president's lawyers dreaded. Dexter Douglass, the Tallahassee legal whip who knew the bench as well as anyone, believed Sauls embodied the worst-case scenario. "We're gonna lose," he told Boies. Gore's lawyers tried to consolidate the contest with the earlier case before Terry Lewis, the judge who had upheld Harris's discretion to reject late returns and was subsequently reversed by the Florida Supreme Court. Bush objected and Sauls denied the motion, after consulting privately with Lewis, who thought it "smacked" of shopping around, which the random-assignment system was designed to prevent.

On the spectrum of styles on the Leon County bench, the fifty-nine-year-old Sauls sat in contrast to Lewis. While Lewis was regarded as evenhanded and open-minded, Sauls was considered stern, crusty, autocratic, and, above all, stubborn. As a younger man he fought in divorce court with his first wife over fifty dollars; after all, he argued, she had violated their divorce agreement by keeping a saddle from a horse they owned together. It wasn't that Sauls wasn't capable or lacked personality—he was the model of the stogie-chomping, aphorism-speaking, bourbon-drinking Panhandle native who loved to play up his Southern drawl to folks without one. But of all the trial-level judges in Leon (and the state), Gore had the one who'd gotten into an impressive pissing contest with the Florida Supreme Court. This was just perfect, lamented the Gore lawyers.

Sauls had taken over as chief judge in Leon County in 1996. But two years later, he became entangled in a personnel struggle with a court administrator. Despite a search committee recommending one candidate for a court position, Sauls went with his own choice, who had been recommended by a hunting crony. The court administrator protested. Sauls then skewered him for disloyalty, which led to a courtwide fracas over the appointment and Sauls's conduct. The Florida Supreme Court, as overseer of the entire state court system, hauled him in and dressed him down, ordering his removal as chief judge for "the continuing disruption in the administration of justice." Sauls returned to the trial bench, but apparently never forgot his public mortification.

Two days after the election-contest lawsuit ended, while he sat in his living room, Sauls's wife stood outside their home in Tallahassee and lit into the state supreme court. In a memorable front-page article in the *New York Times*, Cindy Sauls said her husband had told her that the justices "of all people were not interested in the facts" and that he'd been demoted because "he wouldn't bend over and kiss their boots." Nobody suggested that Sauls would rule against Gore because he despised the court, or that the court would eventually override him based on personality, but those factors didn't help their respective credibilities, and it was a good bet that Sauls and the justices didn't share any Happy Meals.

Sandy Sauls was assigned the presidential case because the other judges already had other election matters before them. It didn't have to work that way. Leon County divvied up its civil caseload at random, but not completely. Cases were separated into such broad categories as "negligence," "contractual," and "equitable." The latter was a catch-all, including, say, an injunction to prevent construction of a fence, a request to partition real estate, or a demand to throw out the results of an American presidential election. The computer kept track of the number of cases each judge had within a category; the more he or she had, the lesser the odds of getting a similarly designated case. The jurisdiction's current chief judge asked his colleagues early on if it might be better to consolidate election cases before one or two judges. The other judges wanted to adhere to the regular protocol. When the wheel spun for Gore's contest, Sauls was the odds-on favorite—he had nothing on his docket from the election.

To the extent that Sauls was a lost cause and that the Florida justices were the real audience, David Boies figured the game was to put in just enough evidence to be credible and create a record sufficient for appeal. The Florida Supreme Court, in the case of the aborted Miami-Dade recount, had shown itself to be persnickety on procedure, and the last thing Boies needed in a fifteen-day sprint was to be told to return to the starting line. On the other hand, the longer the hearing before Sauls went, the more chances Bush would have to stall, preventing Gore from ever reaching the finish. Boies had to find the right balance.

On the Monday the contest was filed, at a scheduling hearing, Sauls looked out over his courtroom and beheld the most ridiculous scene he'd ever seen. "Let's see now," he noted, "more lawyers than specta-tors." The septuagenarian Douglass couldn't even get a seat. Sauls ruled that he'd start taking evidence on Saturday, five days away. In an ordi-nary trial, even without a jury, that would be whiplash-quick; but in this proceeding, letting that much time elapse eliminated a third of the period before which Florida had to name its presidential electors.

Sauls also turned down Boies's motion to have Miami-Dade and Palm Beach immediately go back to counting. The theory had been to preserve Gore's rights while Sauls considered their legal relevance. Barry Richard, Bush's lawyer, well recognized the same old Gore ploy to get more votes on the board, since any further counting would be in press accounts forthwith. Richard did what any defendant's lawyer does: delay, delay, then delay some more. If Gore was awarded recounts in Miami-Dade and Palm Beach, Bush wanted some as well, in other coun-ties. The closer December 12 got with Bush ahead, the more of Gore's options evaporated. Reasonable people could differ on the fairness of the legal system, but everybody agreed it was slow. Trying to adapt the system to the demands of a political and constitutional calendar was absurd.

Sauls sided with Bush's request—why should he give Gore anything until he'd heard some testimony, all the more so when enough vote tal-lies in Gore's favor would put diabolical pressure on Sauls to accept them regardless of the legal merits? Boies went to the Florida Supreme Court and asked it to order immediate recounts in the two counties, but the justices denied the request summarily (on the same day they rejected the challenge to the butterfly ballot—the earliest of the lawsuits filed after the election).

While Sauls's dry demeanor did little for cable ratings, he did unintendedly manage to produce one of TV's lasting images of the carnival. Both sides had agreed that ballots from Miami-Dade and Palm Beach should be brought to Tallahassee. Gore wanted just the undervotes, a total of about 14,000. Bush wanted them all—more than a million. Sauls ruled for Bush. The ballots would be delivered by the two counties separately. On Thursday, a yellow Ryder rental truck journeyed north from Palm Beach to Tallahassee under armed guard and escorted by police cruisers. TV helicopters hovered along, covering the nonevent live. Spectators waved from highway overpasses. Ryder executives giggled the whole day as a nation watched the truck—which screamed "Rent me" on its side, with Ryder's toll-free number and Web address helpfully provided—make the eight-hour trip.

Florida resident O. J. Simpson offered that his 1994 nationally televised low-speed police chase in a white Bronco was more suspenseful. "Here," he cogently explained to the Associated Press, "they know the ballots are going to get to Tallahassee."

eight

Groundhog Days

L*arry Tribe and* Ted Olson didn't have time to enjoy Ryder's Ride of the Century. They were preparing to argue on behalf of the presidential candidates before the U.S. Supreme Court the next morning, December 1. In contrast to Olson, who liked to practice his presentation before colleagues posing as justices, Tribe frowned on moot-court preparation, preferring instead to play out exchanges in his mathematical mind.

The argument was the biggest show in town that Friday. All four of Gore's kids were there, squired by Thurgood Marshall Jr., son of the late justice and a former Gore aide. The packed audience of 475 also included members of Dick Cheney's family, former Justice Byron White, Caroline Kennedy Schlossberg, Judge Charles Burton from the Palm Beach canvassing board, Warren Christopher and Bill Daley, and the columnist George Will, who hit the daily double by landing top tickets for both this argument and the World Series in New York City a month earlier. More than two dozen members of Congress attended, including John Ashcroft, Orrin Hatch, Patrick Leahy, Arlen Specter, John Kerry, and John Edwards. Strom Thurmond was a no-show. Olson's wife, Barbara, was in between Senators Ted Kennedy and Fred

Thompson. Olson saw them. "What fun they must be having," he thought, as he recalled it afterward. "This is never going to happen like this again."

Most of these folks were Washington regulars, and their appearances turned heads at the Court more for their aggregation. But Judge Burton was a fish out of Florida water. His fame had been made complete the night before at a Capitol Hill café, the *Palm Beach Post* whimsically reported, when a passerby asked if he was really Charles Burton. "Would it help you if I assumed the position?" he asked, whereupon he held an imaginary ballot to the light above his head.

For the marshal's office of the Supreme Court, the crush of VIPs made the morning an adventure. "Each of them squeezed ahead of the others," recalls one usher. "*Everybody* was a VIP, so nobody was a VIP. The point of being a VIP is you're V.I.—in this argument, it didn't matter. We didn't have front-row seats for everybody, not that they accepted this fact so quickly."

Ted Koppel couldn't even get one of the 122 seats reserved for press. (Correspondent Jackie Judd got the assigned spot.) Instead, he recruited an ABC courier to hold a place in the all-night line for the general public gathering outside the Court. Demonstrators dressed as Darth Vader and a Florida ballot box were told that decorum dictated they'd get no seats in costume. (Best protest sign: "Even Milosevic conceded!") After doing *Nightline* and getting a little sleep, Koppel arrived in the autumn drizzle at 5:30 A.M., four and a half hours before the oral argument. The riffraff in line were impressed and gladly let him take the courier's spot. Grateful Ted bought everyone a round of muffins and joe, then posed for pictures. The clerk of the Court, William Suter, wanted to meet Koppel. Suter, whose job it was to supervise the logistics of the docket, knew the magnitude of the election cases: He would later ask the attorneys for both sides to autograph the Court's official call sheet, which formally lists counsel for each day's arguments.

The courtroom of the U.S. Supreme Court is as glorious a setting as there is in government, a testament to the splendor of marble and congressional appropriations. The courtroom of the Florida Supreme Court could easily fit inside of it. Even the Oval Office in the White House, when one actually goes in it, is a relatively small room, spartanly decorated with the furniture arranged on a human scale. By contrast, the

Supreme Chamber is a tableau of ornate grandiosity—measuring eighty-two feet long by ninety-one feet wide, flanked by twenty-four columns and massive windows, with richly colored coffers in the soaring four-story-high ceiling. Above the columns are sculpted panels depicting lawgivers such as Moses and Confucius and legal themes such as the "Majesty of the Law." The elevated, curved bench—where the chief justice sits in the middle, with the eight associate justices alternating by seniority on both sides—is all mahogany. Above the bench is a big hanging clock; behind are heavy velvet drapes through which the magnificent nine appeared precisely when the marshal chanted, "Oyez! Oyez! Oyez!" and brought the Court to order at the stroke of 10 A.M. Someone once said of the chamber that if God had an office, it would look like this.

Even getting to the courtroom from outside the building is an exercise in monumental intimidation. Consecrated in 1935, the marble temple was designed on a grand scale, according to planners, to symbolize "the national ideal of justice in the highest sphere of activity." For its first 146 years, the Court never had its own structure, forced to meet in the Republic's early days in the Merchants Exchange Building in Manhattan, then in Independence Hall in Philadelphia, and finally in six different locations within the Capitol. With its classic Corinthian architecture and adornments—the evocations of mythology, ancient Rome, the Magna Carta—the new building left no doubt of its lofty intentions.

You enter the building by walking up the forty-five exterior steps and passing through the thirteen-ton twin sliding bronze doors. The main corridor, at the end of which is the courtroom, is the Great Hall. Busts of all former chief justices are displayed on each side, set on pedestals. Visitors instinctively know to whisper; only the cads don't take out their chewing gum. Said Chief Justice Charles Evans Hughes upon groundbreaking for the courthouse: "The Republic endures—and this is the symbol of its faith." Who could not be awed by the setting? If the trappings ever went to the justices' heads, who could blame them?

The media often criticized the justices for shrouding themselves in anonymity. On the ground that showing "frailties" wasn't something judges should do, Scalia wouldn't permit even C-SPAN to tape his innocuous speeches at such open venues as universities or bar association meetings.* But, still, it was hard to dispute that their very inaccessibility enhanced their mystique, and their headquarters certainly didn't hurt the image. As it was, the Court only reluctantly broke with its policy on recordings and agreed to release an audiotape of the oral argument immediately after the session. While this wasn't the same as letting TV cameras or broadcast microphones under the tent, it had never happened before at the Court and reflected the justices' acknowledgment that they were at the center of the storm now—even they could be buffeted by the PR winds. (The Court was well behind other courts in opening its processes to public inspection. Before the fall of 2000, it posted no briefs or other filings online.)

Clips from the audiotape were played on all the networks; five cable outlets—CNN, MSNBC, C-SPAN, CNBC, and the Fox News Channel—broadcast the entire tape. As TV went, it was bland stuff. The tapes, after all, were ideally suited for radio. News directors tried to jazz up the screen with still photos of the justices accompanied by biographical factoids, along with dancing flags and 3-D renderings of the chamber that suggested it might be the setting for a new Game Boy cartridge. But computer animation just didn't do justice to all that marble.

When the hearing got going, the justices were locked and loaded. Over the course of ninety minutes, they asked 175 questions (that was a lot). Only Clarence Thomas, as was his habit, said nothing. The other eight obviously had read the briefs and thought through the issues. (This wasn't universally so with some of the dull cases the Court wound up with every term—the so-called "dogs," involving ERISA or some other piece of legislative arcana.) It was a far intellectual cry from the bloviating, sloganeering slop elsewhere in Washington and the precincts of Florida.

---

*The justices' fixation with anonymity notwithstanding, one of the ironies of their involvement in the 2000 presidential dispute was how the popular culture began to take more notice of them. In early 2002, two different networks will broadcast prime-time soap operas set at the Court. The 1980s had *Dallas* and the 1990s had *E.R.*—now we'll get *The Court*, starring Sally Field, and *First Monday*, with James Garner and Joe Mantegna.

Many of the exchanges between bench and counsel echoed what had already been well presented in the briefs: What made this a federal case? Given the strange time frames set out in Florida election law, how could recounts ever be done in populous counties? Who had the final say in the Sunshine State—its legislators or its justices? Was the Florida Supreme Court's reliance on its *state* constitution a pivotal mistake, to the extent that Article II, Section 1, of the federal Constitution gave a state *legislature* the power to determine how presidential electors were selected? What about the "safe harbor" created by federal law—was that a sword that George W. Bush could use to override the Florida Supreme Court, or was it merely a benefit a state could claim if it fulfilled certain conditions? And just why was it that the U.S. Supreme Court was resolving any of this, considering that the Constitution made Congress the headmaster of the Electoral College, the last arbiter in close presidential elections? Could not—*should not*—Congress sort it all out, if the Florida authorities didn't?

Reading the justices based on oral argument was a perilous game. Rather than being advocates for an outcome, they sometimes were just thinking out loud—more for the benefit of their brethren than counsel—or even having sport. Antonin Scalia, for example, was legendary for making cracks only to show how much smarter he was than his colleagues or any of the lawyers at the lectern. Yet the questions in Case No. 00-836 broke pretty much the way that students of the Court had predicted. The conservatives, led by Scalia and William Rehnquist, thought the Florida Supreme Court had strayed far off the constitutional reservation; the liberals wanted to know why this became a federal case to begin with. In the middle, Sandra Day O'Connor and Anthony Kennedy tried to dance on both sides. In short, it could safely be surmised, the justices were neatly divided.

But the tenor of some of the justices' questions seemed to raise another way out. It would be more in the nature of an escape than a compromise—inaction to preserve the Court's treasured reputation for neutrality. A 5-to-4 rift would expose the justices to attack that they were no more than nine partisans cloaked in black robes—the fact of the split going Bush's way was beside the point. So how to avoid the controversy?

The Court's docket was discretionary: Just as it could take any appeal presented to it, so, too, could the Court get rid of a case it no longer wanted to decide, all without explanation. There were different mechanisms by which to duck. The Court could say Bush's complaint was moot because, after all, the extension of the certification deadline by the Florida justices hadn't cost him victory. "Is there any respect in which this really makes a difference?" Breyer asked, leaning forward from his high, leather-backed chair. The answer was 393 votes—the difference between the 537-vote margin when Katherine Harris certified and the 930 she could've used had the Florida Supreme Court not enjoined her. But Bush was ahead anyway, so unless the contest proceeding that was getting under way in Tallahassee threw out the election returns, the margin of victory didn't matter.

Mootness wasn't the only escape valve for a seething Court. It could also pull the procedural trick of dismissing the appeal as "improvidently granted"—which was Courtspeak for "Oops, on second thought, we shouldn't have taken this case." And there was one other choice, mentioned in passing by Ginsburg. Instead of slapping down the Florida justices, she wondered aloud to Tribe, "I suppose there would be a possibility for this Court to remand for clarification." The tool of "vacate-and-remand" was rarely used. Ordinarily, the law permits no replays. If a lower court was wrong, it got reversed and that was it. But in unusual instances, the offending court could be given another swing, all the more so when it was a state supreme court and the U.S. Supreme Court wanted to show what deference it could. "Vacate" meant the lower-court decision was tossed, but "remand" meant the lower court could rewrite its decision in the hope of passing constitutional muster. Ginsburg thought her suggestion might be able to command a unanimous decision: It would satisfy the conservatives' desire to send Florida a message, but it would appease the liberals and at least postpone an institutional reckoning for the Court. Tribe immediately tried to latch onto the Ginsburg lifebuoy—it would represent a defeat, but only a minor one—though Scalia interrupted to press the argument against allowing any appellate do-over.

The Supreme Court argument ended as all do. When the small red light on the lectern came on, signaling that the last lawyer's time was up—regardless of whether he was in mid-sentence or -syllable—Rehnquist said simply, "The case is submitted." Bad use of passive voice, Mr. Chief Justice. Get that man a grammarian!

■ ■ ■

The day after the big Friday argument in Washington, the legal action bounced back to the televised Tallahassee courtroom of Sanders Sauls. Cramped, austere, and bathed in fluorescence, it didn't exactly conjure up the majesty of the U.S. Supreme Court.

Contests were usually long affairs in Florida. The legal proceeding over the mayoralty in Miami back in 1997 went on for months, resulting in the removal of a mayor who had already taken office. That couldn't happen with the presidency. Whatever was going to take place had until December 12 to play out. From behind the reading glasses that rarely left his nose, Sauls had spent the week leading up to the contest trial presiding over motions, schedules, seating arrangements, ballot storage, and everything but listening to testimony. He likened the experience to being "nibbled to death by a duck"—raising the question of how he'd know, but it was probably just Southern humor or that he couldn't imagine a worse fate than having eighteen top-gun lawyers in his courtroom all trying to talk at once.

While Bush's lawyers talked of calling ninety-one witnesses to the stand, Al Gore had decided to put on only two, in an attempt to show Sauls that fresh hand counting was needed in Miami-Dade and Palm Beach; for a time, David Boies considered having no witnesses at all. This was a trial all right—with testimony, exhibits, evidentiary standards, objections, and burdens of proof. Yet even though the protocol and vocabulary of the law applied, there was a certain sense of charade in the room. Sandy Sauls wasn't likely to render the final verdict on Bush and Gore. Did it really pay to exhaust precious time putting on a case that was as much political as legal?

In the prior twenty-five days, the judge could read the newspapers and watch the TV coverage that had been as boundless as the sea. Was there that much more he was going to learn from a few more witnesses? No one would suggest a judge make rulings based on press accounts and film clips, but the two-day proceeding in Sauls's courtroom raised the question whether a lot of trees were being studied to the exclusion of the forest. The one item of evidence that Sauls should have looked at—the one item that no trial judge during the entire Florida siege ever examined—never made it to his bench. All those ballots shipped up from south Florida remained in a vault. Rather than merely introduce the disputed ballots as evidence, Gore should've insisted that Sauls get a firsthand sense of them, and Sauls, the fact-finder, should've had the judgment to inspect some of the ballots.

Gore's two witnesses on Saturday, December 2, were a voting-machine expert and a Yale statistician. The first, Kimball Brace, described how improperly maintained punch-card equipment, like in Palm Beach, could lead to undervotes. The county's machines, he said, hadn't been cleaned in two years. The accumulation of old chads might not allow a chad poke to fully punch out a hole in the ballot. This, rather than voter incompetence, is what gave birth to dimples, according to Brace, whose testimony lasted almost four hours. A week of trial preparation had come down to this: Was stubborn "chad buildup" going to be responsible for putting George W. Bush in the White House? Under cross-examination, Brace did acknowledge that a recount in all sixty-seven Florida counties was preferable to selective counts—a concession Gore didn't need.

After lunch, Gore's legal team put on its second witness, statistician Nicolas Hengartner. At this pace, even if Bush called only a fifth of his witnesses, the trial would last into January. Hengartner, whom Boies kept calling "Hangarden," argued that punch-card counties had a higher percentage of undervotes than optical-scan counties only because of the technology. The odds that the order-of-magnitude difference—five to eight times, depending on the county—was coincidental, Hengartner testified, were "less than winning the lottery." Statisticians always make for enticing subjects of cross-examination—Hengartner was derisively asked about any correlation between storks in Great Britain and the birth rate there—but he held his ground and managed to finish before dinner. The two witnesses, along with a parade of exhibits, including canvassing board transcripts, constituted the entirety of Gore's contest. Boies had wisely strategized that testimonial set-tos weren't going to win it for his client—only the ballots could. But even though they were technically in evidence, the punch cards never made an appearance in the courtroom and were never perused by Sauls. The omission might not have made a difference, but whatever drama Gore hoped to stage for Sauls's benefit was lost without it.

Bush's nine witnesses appeared late Saturday and into Sunday. First was Charles Burton, from the Palm Beach canvassing board, who explained that dimpled ballots had been given due consideration and that he had no partisan agenda. After Gore's lawyers went after him, Sauls offered his condolences and acclaimed him a "great American." Next on the stand, to rebut Gore's voting-machine expert, came a professor of rubber and plastics from the University of Wisconsin. (In yesteryears, Lincoln and Douglas debated "a house divided." In 2000, the candidates brabbled over material science.) On Sunday, Bush's witnesses included his own statistician (he had a nice French accent), his own recount witnesses, a Fort Lauderdale voter who voted but specifically chose not to select anyone for president, and his own machine expert, John Ahmann, who turned out to make *Gore's* best case.

Now a Napa Valley rancher—he took the stand in a bolo tie— Ahmann used to be a mechanical engineer for IBM and had helped design Votomatic punch-card equipment in the 1960s. His message for Sauls: The machine didn't need to be cleaned for five *decades* before chads would clog it. But a Gore lawyer, working the Web from Miami Beach, had miraculously tracked down one of Ahmann's patent applications, from back in 1980: an application for improvements to the Votomatic. It was right there on the site of the U.S. Patents and Trademark Office and admitted the flaws of punch-card technology, given "clogs" and "incompletely punched cards." In the courtroom, Ahmann acknowledged the language was his and further conceded that hand counts might be necessary in "very close" elections that utilized punch cards. After all the tedious testimony leading up to this, finally there was something out of *Perry Mason*. But would Sauls buy into it?

The judge finished taking evidence after nightfall and announced he'd rule the next day.

On that next day—Monday, December 4—the U.S. Supreme Court was in session, as usual, at 10 A.M. Halfway through the morning session, Rehnquist suddenly stood up and departed behind the crimson curtains. Regular observers of the Court knew the chief justice was just stretching his back, as he did at routine intervals. Even out of sight, he could still hear the proceedings. But today he didn't return after his customary minute or two.

There was a good reason. A staffer of the Court urgently needed to consult with him because the justices' pending ruling in the presidential election had prematurely, and accidentally, been posted online for law schools and other subscribers to the Court's opinions-delivery service. That was supposed to happen only after the Court announced from the bench that it had a decision and then released a hard copy of its opinion manually to the press through the public-information office. This time, there was a glitch. Nobody had seen the online opinion, so far as Court staff could tell, but in theory the cat was out. What did the chief justice want to do? Rehnquist ordered the opinion released forthwith.

Word spread right away in the Court's press gallery, just off to the left of the bench. The rows emptied as print reporters dashed to the press room downstairs and their TV counterparts headed to the plaza outside (even as an important case was being argued about a Texas mother who was handcuffed and jailed for not wearing a seat belt). The media game was to instantaneously read all seven pages of the Court ruling and assess their impact on the presidential standoff—and, especially on the tube, to do it at least seconds before your journalistic compatriots. "I can Name that Ruling in thirty seconds!" "No, I can do it in twenty!" But it's not so easy—opinions don't come with headlines and, sometimes, their legalese makes them impenetrable.

"The United States Supreme Court has struck down the Florida Supreme Court ruling in favor of Vice President Gore!" announced Dan Rather, as CBS cut in on *The Price Is Right* just when a contestant was about to claim a lovely dinette set. "It's a Bush win!"

CBS was relying on an AP bulletin, the first report out of the box, but the wire service within minutes amended its story. That was because AP now had actually *read the ruling*. The story was corrected to say that the justices had only sent the case back to the Florida Supreme Court for clarification, and CBS figured it out soon enough. To its credit, ABC was duly cautious from the outset. But given what happened on Election Night barely a month before, one might've thought all the networks would be more careful about bold pronouncements. Such was the media race to be first, if not also right.

The confusion surrounding release of the Court's opinion, both in the courtroom and on the news, contrasted with what had happened at the Florida Supreme Court. Rehnquist had seen that tribunal send a spokesman, Craig Waters, out on the courthouse steps. That, he thought, was tackier than allowing TV cameras at court proceedings. He'd sooner allow beer and popcorn to be sold in the gallery than have his Court's decisions disseminated by a flack, whether it was one resembling Secret Squirrel, Edward R. Murrow, or anyone else. In Rehnquist's view, oracles didn't do spin—and that's what he believed (wrongly) had happened in Florida. It was okay for justices themselves to give occasional professional talks, attend conventions in faraway, exotic locales, and even to chat up their own books now and then (at least if they were the chief justice and had an abiding interest in obscure historical subjects). But interaction with the media was just not done. Rehnquist made his wishes perfectly clear to his own press staff after Waters's performance. The chief justice should have learned a very different lesson from it.

What the Court had done in the presidential election case was to punt. This was the vacate-and-remand that Ruth Bader Ginsburg had recommended during oral argument and then urged in the justices' formal, private discussions afterward—"the conference," as it's known at the Court. The conference was truly the inner sanctum, held in a grand room near the chief justice's chambers that was routinely swept for surveillance bugs. No one other than the Supreme Nine was allowed in. The gofer within the conference—the one who answered any knocks on the door and who brought in coffee and tea—was the most junior justice, Stephen Breyer, who'd been in the position since 1994. At the conference following the election case, the justices had indeed expressed misgivings, however muted, about the Florida Supreme Court ruling, but they wanted to give that lower court another chance. This was the appellate equivalent of a shot across the bow or, as a law clerk put it, "across the distinctly port side of a lower court."

More significant, the justices simply wanted to get out from under without having to issue a split opinion and in hopes of the mess never returning. "We are unclear as to the extent to which the Florida Supreme Court saw the Florida constitution as circumscribing the legislature's authority" under Article II of the U.S. Constitution, the justices wrote in a unanimous, unsigned opinion—the same kind of device the Florida

Supreme Court had used the week earlier. "We are also unclear as to the consideration the Florida Supreme Court accorded" the Electoral Count Act, which was the nineteenth-century federal statute establishing a safe harbor for states that put their electoral slates in order by December 12. Bottom line: The justices wanted two issues clarified—one constitutional and one statutory, and both related to the arcana of presidential election law. There was not a word mentioned about anything dealing with equal protection, or the inherent fairness or unfairness of hand recounts.

Rarely does a Supreme Court opinion state "We are unclear." The justices may be, but rarely do they say it—the better to convey an aura of omniscience. Yet the Court used the phrase twice in one paragraph. They were sending a message of maximum displeasure to their brethren below: Your judicial handiwork is an embarrassment. Fix it. Of course, having provided a lay of the land for the Florida justices, it shouldn't have been that hard the second interpretative voyage through.

Bush's official margin of victory in Florida remained at 537, but there was a strong argument that it went back up to 930—or would do so if state election officials took the ministerial steps—now that the state supreme court's certification extension had been erased. If, on the other hand, the Tallahassee Seven got their language and doctrine right the second time, their decision could stand and so, too, could the 537. While Gore had won nothing other than the opportunity to carry on with his fight, Bush hadn't won much either. What had taken place in Washington was basically a draw. For now, but not for long, the Supreme Court of the United States had walked away from the institutional abyss.

Exactly five hours after the ruling in Washington, Sauls came out with his ruling in the contest. If the U.S. Supreme Court had been merely suspicious, the Tallahassee judge was repelled. After working deep into the night that the trial had ended, putting his opinion down by hand on a legal pad, he'd decided to throw Gore out on his ear. Claim by claim, in a curt, dismissive tone, Sauls cast aside the vice president's arguments and rejected the facts he'd asserted. Though there had been "less than total accuracy" in the voting machines of Miami-Dade and Palm Beach, Sauls said, Gore hadn't demonstrated the high degree of "probability" that further recounts would "place in doubt" the results of the election. "In this case, there is no credible statistical evidence and no other competent substantial evidence" to suggest a different outcome, he said. Nor did the evidence "establish any illegality, dishonesty, gross negligence, improper influence, coercion or fraud, in the balloting or counting processes."

Besides, even if there should be more counts, Sauls concluded, they would have to include all ballots, not just the 14,000 undervotes Gore proposed—in this observation, he was noting the fundamental equal-protection problem that all courts had so far dodged, as well as presaging what was about to happen in a higher court. In this regard, he cleverly cited the advisory opinion by Florida's Democratic attorney general, Bob Butterworth, written soon after Election Day. That document warned of a "two-tiered" system for recounts, with voters treated differently depending on what county they lived in; voters in a hand-recounted county had a better chance of having their votes counted. This, Butterworth had prophesied, risked "legal jeopardy." Sauls was now calling him on it; Gore hadn't even addressed the topic during the hearings. As for the two-hour-late returns from Palm Beach, the judge sided with Katherine Harris.

"They won, we lost," Boies put it afterward, at a press conference.

It was true enough that Boies hadn't put on a powerful evidentiary case before Sauls—how could he in two days?—yet this was the dilemma posed by expecting a political battle over the presidency to be mediated according to the rules of a courtroom. For his part, beyond conducting the trial at breakneck speed, Sauls did little to consider his ruling in light of the calendar that federal law drew for presidential elections. What kind of "competent substantial evidence" did he want Gore to put on, especially if Sauls wasn't going to examine any contested ballots in the first place—of which only 538 or 931 were needed to undo the official certification? The ballots, Boies kept insisting, were the "best evidence." There was no way out of the conundrum for Boies or his client. Sauls was doing his best imitation of Joseph Heller.

Gore was home for the televised Sauls ruling. As he always did at critical times, he got on the phone to talk with advisers; conference calls were as much a part of the day as mealtime and turning on MSNBC and

CNN. He could still show gallows humor. After watching Sauls knock him down pin by pin, Gore called Bill Daley. "That went well, didn't it?" cracked the vice president.

But Sauls obviously would not have the last word. Long before he finished delivering his ruling from the bench, both legal teams had begun preparing for a trip to the Florida Supreme Court. And before he had uttered the formal "plaintiffs will take nothing by this action," David Boies had passed along a message to a junior staffer to file the formal instrument of appeal by closing time that day. It would be the campaign's fourth petition in a month to the Florida justices. For everybody, it seemed like a scene out of the comedy *Groundhog Day*, where the protagonist kept reliving the same events and knew it as he did so, as if observer and observed became one.

Sauls had consciously tried to make his opinion as fact-based as possible. A trial judge was the master of facts—he'd seen the witnesses, looked at the exhibits, weighed the cross-examinations. Appellate courts were typically reluctant to overturn factual findings unless they were "clearly erroneous"; it was mistakes of law that an appeal was supposed to concern. There were legal aspects to Sauls's decision, about partial recounts and the discretion of canvassing boards, but most of his ruling was based on not believing Gore's only two witnesses. This is what Boies had to confront.

Still, a few in the Gore camp believed it was precisely the sweep of Sauls's ruling that would be its undoing. The forty-eight hours following it were among the lowest in the thirty-seven days of the campaign. The twinkling lights of Christmas had bedecked Tallahassee by now, but there was only gloom at the Gore outposts in town. "We all were convinced we were dead at this point," is how Nick Baldick remembered it. "But Michael Whouley was totally optimistic. He was the one keeping everyone else up."

"It set us up perfectly," Whouley recalled. "Sauls denied us everything, he wouldn't even look at the ballots that he had brought to Tallahassee. I told our people this was going to be completely reversed by the Florida Supreme Court. They'll count the ballots. We'll get this done."

The consensus among Whouley's platoon of recount observers

around the state was that he was nuts. "We all started saying, 'Michael has drunk the Kool-Aid,'" Baldick says. But others started to drink it, too. Baldick and Whouley's other gladiators went out to buy containers of powdered Kool-Aid for their desks. In his honor, they kept the Kool-Aid as souvenirs.

The Bush and Gore legal teams had less than two days to get their briefs into the Florida Supreme Court, even as they were also filing responses on the appeal that the U.S. Supreme Court had remanded back to Florida. Both sides had become brief-writing assembly lines—Gore in the squeezed storefront adjacent to Dexter Douglass's offices, Bush in the state GOP headquarters. At this point, it wasn't clear whether the remanded case from the U.S. Supreme Court would be combined with the Sauls contest, or whether the justices would even have a new round of oral argument on it. But the Florida Supreme Court had agreed to consider the contest—that Thursday morning, five days before the December 12 safe harbor closed. It was yet another example of a court moving far more swiftly than it was used to, placing itself under logistical and intellectual constraints for which the task of judging was especially ill suited.

Gore's brief on the contest was nearly apoplectic. "The issues presented are matters of national importance," it beseeched the Florida justices. "Time is extraordinarily short because of the schedule imposed by federal law. . . . The Florida Supreme Court must immediately and finally resolve the issues." Gore gave Sauls virtually no credit, perhaps knowing that five of the seven justices had been part of the court when it humiliated Sauls in 1998. The cornerstone of the appeal was that Sauls never gave Gore the opportunity to prevail. "It simply cannot be the case that a candidate must prove his or her claim in order to get access to the very evidence needed to prove that case," the brief stated. Surely, the two witnesses Boies put on, together with the razor-close margin for Bush, established the real possibility that recounts could change the election's outcome. Gore's lawyers even seemed to get in a dig at Bush's constant refrain about changing-the-rules-in-the-middle-of-the-game: Had not Sauls done just that by "dramatically" gutting the role a trial judge was supposed to play in an election contest—a role "enacted by the state legislature"?

There was also the frontal attack on Bush's game plan of the past month. "[We] have striven mightily to expedite this proceeding," the brief argued. Bush "had engaged in a legal strategy aimed at delay. . . . In but a few more days, only the judgment of history will be left to fall upon a system where deliberate obstruction has succeeded in achieving delay." Gore demanded that the Florida Supreme Court take over a manual recount of the 14,000 disputed undervotes in Miami-Dade and Palm Beach. The vice president claimed he would trail Bush by only 103 votes if the court included results from Miami-Dade's aborted recount, Palm Beach's late results, and Nassau's newer tabulation. (The counties subsequently showed Gore's numbers were off by around 50 votes. The would-be margin was never as low as 103.)

In his answer to Gore's papers, Bush preached finality, for the sake of averting the "massive uncertainty and discord" that would come with further recounting. "The best exercise of this court's judgment," his brief read, "would be to decline to hear this appeal" at all. Time was up. "To resolve the legal issues in this appeal and in the [U.S. Supreme Court] remand, to gather the ballots in question, to segregate any sub-sets to be counted, to determine who should conduct a recount, to ascertain what standards govern the count, and to ensure fairness, open-ness and regularity—all before December 12 comes and goes—is all but entirely unfeasible. And even then, no doubt, the litigation would continue, key federal questions would be unresolved and subject to appeal, and the public's distrust in the ultimate outcome would grow." The analysis was correct, but it was based on a veiled threat: If Gore kept going, Bush would do everything to drag things out past December 12.

Bush's brief spent most of its time buttressing Sauls's ruling on vari-ous grounds of state law, but threw in a few mentions of the U.S. Con-stitution and federal law. It was an important inclusion, addressed not so much at the Florida justices—though perhaps they had in fact been chastened by the U.S. Supreme Court vacate-and-remand now back in their laps—but to an ultimate audience in Washington. The U.S. Supreme Court has vast discretion, but not unlimited jurisdiction. It cannot hear appeals based solely on state law, because that's not its turf. Nor can a litigant decide to raise the requisite federal issues *after* losing in state court. That's a rule grounded on efficiency and common sense— the Supremes didn't very well want to take on an issue that hadn't played out in a lower court, and it wouldn't be fair to victorious parties to have that surprise thrust upon them.

So Ted Olson—the man litigating Bush's federal claims—had made certain that Barry Richard, who had supplanted Michael Carvin in the state case, raised the constitutional challenge based on equal protection. Because of the equal-protection clause of the Fourteenth Amendment, Bush's brief insisted that any recount in the contest had to be statewide; it even cited Butterworth, the democratic attorney general, just as Sauls had. Lo and behold, at this late date, the GOP now was daring a court to order a statewide recount—not a statewide recount of undervotes only, but one of "*all* votes cast in the state." The demand was meant to make a point, as well as to throw yet another temporal monkey wrench into Gore's plans—but there was great irony nevertheless in Bush even bringing up the statewide recount he had steadfastly resisted to this point. Gore didn't even address the equal-protection issue in his main brief. Why should he? The U.S. Supreme Court hadn't just two days earlier.

Bush had been forging ahead with his equal-protection argument in the federal courts, separate and apart from Gore's lawsuits. The governor's federal case was the very first either party had filed. Both a federal judge in Miami and the 11th U.S. Circuit Court of Appeals in Atlanta had declined to intervene for Bush, at least at these stages of the litigation, especially with Florida state courts handling related cases. This was judicial restraint and federal deference in action. But now the 11th Circuit was back in the mix, after Bush renewed his request to have hand recounts declared unconstitutional. On the same day that Gore and Bush had filed their contest briefs in the Florida Supreme Court, the 11th Circuit had ruled 8–4 to stay above the fray, for the moment. Despite four vigorous dissents (from judges all nominated by Republicans) that the recounts were indeed unconstitutional, because they only were in Democratic counties and used inconsistent standards, the majority found it was premature to rule on the constitutional questions. Perhaps there would be no more recounts, perhaps Gore would fail anyway, perhaps the state courts would resolve things—in any event, it behooved the federal court to abstain. If things all went in Gore's favor, the 11th Circuit said Bush could come right back with his appeal.

Once more, Olson, who had argued before the 11th Circuit, had two jurisdictional fairways on which to play. He could try to advance Bush's federal case to the U.S. Supreme Court or appeal any adverse ruling that Bush got from the Florida Supreme Court, or maybe try to do both and let the U.S. Supremes choose. Given the U.S. justices' evident scorn for the Gang of Seven, it made complete sense for the Bush legal team to set up their Florida Supreme Court argument accordingly. That way, if the decision went bad, their nine brethren in Washington could tee it up.

Charlie Wells knew a scene from *Groundhog Day* when he saw it. The chief justice of Florida had an eye for the wry. "Good morning," he announced to a full chamber on Thursday, December 7, "and welcome once again to the Florida Supreme Court." He could've been hosting a Seminoles-Gators game. But any levity promptly disappeared, as the most important oral argument in the history of the state got under way.

David Boies barely got his own name out when Wells pounced. "Mr. Boies, let me start right out," said the chief, cutting off the lawyer. Wells wanted to know about *McPherson v. Blacker*, an 1892 decision of the U.S. Supreme Court that had occupied much of the colloquy six days earlier at the High Court; indeed, it was the one part of the oral argument in Washington that experienced lawyers said had flustered the unflusterable Larry Tribe. The 108-year-old McPherson decision—the only case cited by the U.S. Supreme Court in its vacate-and-remand opinion—was obscure and obtusely written, but it suggested that state legislatures had full dominion over presidential electors, no matter what any other branch of state government might believe. Did that not mean, Wells demanded, that the Florida legislature had "full power," which could not be "eroded even by the state constitution" or any state court invoking that constitution? The legislature had passed a statute vesting the *trial* court on which Sauls sat with the power to hear election contests. But "where do we get our right to . . . appellate review?" Wells asked. That, he seemed to be insinuating, was coming more from judicial usurpation than legislative grant.

This was oral argument and the standard rules applied—Boies couldn't know for sure whether Wells was just playing devil's advocate or, in light of the volley by the U.S. Supreme Court, had now switched away from his support of judicially sponsored recounts. But either way, Wells was adamant for a response to McPherson. If he didn't get it, Boies thought at the time, there would be at least one fewer judge for Gore.

Boies offered a nervous smile and a pause. Both sides had pretty much acknowledged the court's right to review Sauls's ruling; the main Bush brief didn't even mention *McPherson v. Blacker*. Yet Wells had opened the argument fixated on it. Boies calmly tried to explain that what the Florida Supreme Court had done, and was being asked to do again, was what it always did: "interpret" the "statutes of the state." The legislature knew that full well when it created election-contest proceedings, Boies said. "Whenever the legislature passes a law, [it knows the law is] going to be interpreted by the courts." That was true of contests, for which Boies noted there obviously was no exception for presidential elections.

Wells kept revisiting the jurisdictional question, even with the lawyers for Bush and Katherine Harris. But the other members of the court chose to move beyond it. In this abbreviated argument—half the time the lawyers had in the first oral argument seventeen days before—these six justices wanted to discuss the merits: Had Sauls been wrong and, if so, what was the solution? Could anything be done within five days, by December 12—the date Boies, in the first argument, had foolishly conceded was determinative? If recounts were to begin yet again at this late date, which ballots would be examined and must any counting be statewide? "If we're looking for accuracy, which is what has been the statement from day one," asked Justice Peggy Quince, why did Boies want renewed counting in only Miami-Dade and Palm Beach? "Why wouldn't it be proper for a court, if they're going to order any relief, to count the undervotes in all of the counties where, at the very least, punch-card systems were operating?"

Boies gave the party line the campaign had adopted early on. State law provided for both candidates to seek recounts where they chose and Bush had turned down the chance to ask for any. It didn't really answer Quince's question—the mere fact the statute allowed something didn't make it a good idea, let alone constitutional. As much as Wells's point about the court lacking power to get involved at all, there was now a second issue simmering about the fairness of allowing cherry-picked hand counts. Yet some other members of the court, as well as Boies, thought this equal-protection concern was wasted energy. After all, hadn't the U.S. Supreme Court declined even to hear about equal protection? The High Court engaged in a lot of hand-wringing over changing the rules and the authority of the Florida legislature, but there were no caution flags posted about equality.

From the outset, Larry Tribe had tried to get David Boies and Ron Klain to spend more time on the equal-protection issue in the various briefs before the Florida Supreme Court. But Tribe was unsuccessful. Part of the reason was logistics and the crunch of time: Tribe was never in Tallahassee and always had to get in his two cents by phone. More important, though, Boies and Klain had decided that, strategically, they needed to concentrate on state law; getting into federal matters, statutory or constitutional, only made the litigation more appealing to federal judges.

Sandy Sauls seemed to be the subtext of many of the questions from the Florida Supreme Court. One of his glaring omissions troubled both Justices Harry Lee Anstead and Barbara Pariente. Why hadn't Sauls bothered to inspect any punch cards? Wasn't that what fact-finding was all about? "Isn't it highly unusual for a trial court to admit into evidence certain documents that one party claims will be controlling," Anstead asked Barry Richard, "and yet never examine those documents before making its decision?" Pariente cited the election code's provision that the trial judge "do whatever is necessary to ensure" that any complaint in a challenge is investigated. That, she said, was "rather unusual language to use in a statute"; how could Sauls ignore it?

There wasn't enough basis to act, Richard argued. "The only thing [Boies] did was put two witnesses on the stand to say that they were speculating that Votomatic machines are inherently unreliable." But this didn't answer the question—because the ballots, rather than the witnesses, constituted the main evidence for Gore.

Among the lawyers on both sides, there was peculiar agreement that the case would be decided 4–3. There had just been too many different, passionate views expressed by the justices to expect unanimity anymore. In both the earlier Florida Supreme Court case and at the U.S.

Supreme Court, the respective justices had managed to paper over any differences and speak with a single voice. But that was then. The trouble with the predictions of a 4-to-3 outcome was that the lawyers didn't agree whether Bush or Gore would come out victorious.

It took little more than a day to find out. Craig Waters, the court's reluctant celebrity, was told about the decision an hour ahead of time and sequestered himself in his office to prepare for another appearance in front of the TV spotlights, which included having to write a brief statement that the justices had to approve. Waters closed his door, turned off his cell, and ignored the flashing lights on his telephone, lest he talk to anyone and accidentally tip off the ruling. He was obsessed with appearing "utterly neutral" and used a podium to conceal body language. "It also concealed how nervous I was when I had to announce this decision," Waters says. "Even then, one network reported that my hands were visibly shaking, which they were. I did smile briefly at the end because I was so glad I had made it through and because a reporter gave me a thumbs-up. But when I got back to my office, I had several dozen e-mails telling me to quit smirking. The experience was surreal. Every little thing I did, or did not do, was subjected to an absurd level of analysis."

Just before he went out on the courthouse steps that afternoon, Waters was offered a bulletproof vest by one of the marshals. He turned it down, worried that the press would notice. But the offer rattled him. There were, he remembered, those old bullets still lodged in the building's giant aluminum doors.

Just after four, before the firing squad of TV cameras, Waters read his statement. The operative phrase was "manual recount," which elicited cries of "Treason!" and cheers of "Yes!" from the different camps of protesters near the courthouse. The justices had in fact ruled 4–3 for Gore, with Chief Justice Wells administering a tongue-lashing dissent to his colleagues that left some of them privately stunned. Unanimity among the justices was common, and even dissents were usually measured. But Wells was irate and his concerns would soon prove to be providential.

The majority opinion for the court was unsigned, though the four justices who joined it were Anstead, Pariente, Quince, and Fred Lewis—the newest jurists, who generally skewed toward the left.

Among them, Pariente was the most likely intellectual leader. The forty-page opinion was more utilitarian than doctrinaire; stylistic elegance was secondary, all the more so since it was written overnight. Its essence was Gore's mantra about the "will of the people." Wrote the four justices: "The legislature has expressly recognized the will of the people of Florida as the guiding principle for the selection of all elected officials in the state of Florida, whether they be county commissioners or presidential electors." The court directed that a recount of undervotes begin immediately—not just in Miami-Dade, but *statewide* and regardless of whether counties used punch-card or optical-scan voting systems. It wasn't necessary to manually count every single vote in the state, the four justices found, but it was "absolutely essential" to count any ballot where a presidential vote was not recorded. The court set no deadline for the counting of what amounted to between 40,000 and 45,000 ballots.

According to the court, converting even some of these thousands of undervotes into actual votes would "place the results of this election in doubt," which is exactly what contest proceedings were about under state law. And while the justices rejected Gore's claims that the Palm Beach canvassing board erred in rejecting 3,300 questionable ballots and that Nassau County was wrong in using its older tabulation, which negated a Gore gain of 51 votes, the justices did order that Miami-Dade's partial numbers, as well as the late votes from Palm Beach rejected by Katherine Harris, be included in any certified total. So, Gore remained in the hunt—now down by around 200 or fewer votes (for those scoring at home, the number was 154, 165, 193, or 204, depending on who you believed knew how to count), unless the true certified margin had gone back up to 930, in which case Gore's deficit was between 583 and 633.

Though he had been upheld on the Nassau and Palm Beach–3,300 findings, Judge Sauls got the brunt of the blame from the state supreme court. "Without ever examining or investigating the ballots that the machines failed to register as a vote," noted the majority, Sauls "concluded that there was no probability of a different result" in the presidential election. Gore was therefore "denied the very evidence" he was relying on to gain relief. Sneering at Sauls, the court said he had "presented [Gore] with a Catch-22—acceptance of the only evidence that will resolve the issue but refusal to examine such evidence." All Sauls had done was "summarily state" that "Gore failed to meet [his] burden of proof." This was the equivalent of calling Sauls derelict in how he handled a two-day evidentiary hearing.

Could recounting be completed, and legal challenges resolved, in the remaining 104 hours before midnight, December 12? Even the Will of the People might not be enough to overcome the exigencies of time, but the court wanted to try. "While we agree that practical difficulties may well end up controlling the outcome of the election, we vigorously disagree that we should therefore abandon our responsibility to resolve this election dispute under the rule of law," the majority declared. "We can only do the best we can to carry out our sworn responsibilities to the justice system and its role in this process." Put forth as an assumption, the last nine words were really the *question*. Was fidelity to the *justice* system, rather than the admittedly messier political system, the way to choose the president of the United States? And was it the "role" of judges to be in the maelstrom?

And what of *McPherson v. Blacker* and the U.S. Supreme Court's vacate-and-remand? Four days after being rebuked, the Florida court had yet to issue a new opinion in that first election case, suggesting they didn't fully gauge the High Court's annoyance. If Mom and Dad go off the deep end telling Junior to clean his room, most Juniors would not ignore the command for a week, particularly when they're in the process of setting up toys in another room in the house. Some of the justices explained later that they weren't stupid, just busy. Between the time the U.S. Supreme Court had ruled on Monday and now, on Friday, the Florida justices had to consider whether to take the Gore appeal, read hundreds of pages of briefs, conduct regular business, *and* contend with an impending execution. Were you really supposed to drop all that and deal with the U.S. Supreme Court? (Yep.)

At any rate, in this current appeal from Sauls's courtroom, the Florida majority dealt with the vacate-and-remand only elliptically, tendering its assurance that "statutes established by the legislature govern our decision today." Gone were the references to the Florida Constitution; statutes were now the sole basis of the decision. It was an effort by the court to insulate itself from reproach by the U.S. Supreme Court; indeed, the Florida justices cited the Electoral Count Act of 1887 at the beginning of their analysis, looking to show they had gotten religion on sticking with rules that existed before Election Day. But the effort was feeble; the justices didn't bother to explicitly acknowledge they'd just been scolded by the U.S. Supreme Court. It wasn't until the High Court was reviewing their judgment again that the Florida justices formally disposed of the vacate-and-remand. Their neglect in dealing with the U.S. Supreme Court more punctually and seriously would wind up costing them.

What was also striking about the Florida court's decision was its disregard for the equal-protection problem set up by the manual counts it had just ordered—sixty-four of them. (Palm Beach, Broward, and Volusia Counties, having already inspected undervotes, were off the hook.) It was true the counts would be supervised by a single judge—and not Sauls anymore, because he recused himself, telling others he wanted nothing more to do with the case. (Asked at a gathering months after about his withdrawal, he snapped, "My book publisher doesn't want me to comment.") But in the first instance, the recounts would still be the responsibility of sixty-four canvassing boards. The matter of chads that had surfaced in the prior four weeks was rearing up again: What standards should govern recounts and who should decide? How could various counting boards and the volunteer counters assisting them possibly act consistently?

And even the notion of a single judge imposing uniformity on the counts was flawed. Because the Florida Supreme Court had just ordered ballots from Miami-Dade and Palm Beach included in the newest statewide tally, it had eliminated any chance of one standard applying to the contest; those ballots were now beyond the reach of any trial judge. When Ron Klain read the ruling, he was delighted to still be in the game, but anxious about the court's rationale. "I was taken aback by the new and not-asked-for remedy that the court had imposed," he says. "How would we implement a sixty-four-county recount and what new legal issues would such a count raise?"

Three days later, Justice John Paul Stevens of the U.S. Supreme Court, who resolutely supported the Florida justices' authority to do what they pleased, nonetheless observed that their actions raised concerns not just about equal protection, but about "rationality." In reaching out to be fair, why had the Florida Supreme Court ordered that just undervotes be counted statewide? It was no answer that they were the only ballots Gore had contested. He'd done so for two counties, yet the court chose to go statewide on its own. The justices could have done the same thing for *overvotes*, even though they weren't part of the contest. Overvotes could show voter intent as well. (In fact, the focus on undervotes, to the exclusion of what were more than 100,000 overvotes, turned out to be misguided. As an *Orlando Sentinel* story demonstrated the following month, there were many ballots in optical-scan counties that had been disqualified because people penciled in the oval for a candidate and then wrote in the same name in the "write-in" slot. These became known as "Gore-Gore" and "Bush-Bush" votes. There couldn't be any doubt which candidate a voter intended in those cases.)

The Florida majority never discussed chads and provided scant guidance on how to count. "In making a determination of what is a 'legal' vote," they wrote almost as an afterthought in the last paragraph of their opinion, "the standard to be employed is that established by the legislature in our election code, which is that the vote shall be counted as a 'legal' vote if there is 'clear indication of the intent of the voter.' "

This, of course, begged the question. Recapitulating a vague statutory standard was worthless to the canvassing boards that would be counting that weekend. Did a dimple constitute a legal vote, or didn't it? Need chads be "tri," or was a mere swinger or hanger-on enough? The court was silent, totally dodging the quandary. They had calculated it was better to say nothing and let the decisions be decentralized—as the Florida election code seemed to contemplate—rather than create a standard that risked being "new" post-election law that would violate federal strictures. The court might've tried to say that any standards it came up with were only technical implementations of long-standing Florida law, as in: "We simply hold that swinging chads should count as votes and any dimples should not, because we find this to best reflect the 'clear indication of the intent of the voter.' "

But at best, that would be a stretch. Because of the poorly drafted election code, and because the U.S. Supreme Court had chosen to accept this as a federal case, the Florida justices were in a box. Still, it might've been smarter to admit the problem and especially advisable to address the equal-protection predicament that the decentralized, standardless recounts presented. "Equal protection" wasn't even discussed in the opinion; it might have been implicit in the idea of the court-created *statewide* recount, instead of only one in Miami-Dade, but by omitting any standard, the court was undoing what it shrewdly thought it had done. Why would they omit a standard? The justices just didn't believe it was possible that the U.S. Supremes would ever go down that road.

Wells felt otherwise, much as he had intimated in oral argument the day before. In a withering twenty-one-page dissent, more vividly presented than the majority opinion, the chief justice said he was not unsympathetic to the plight of Al Gore, who might be "ordinarily entitled" to the remedy he sought. But in this particular case, Wells said, quoting a Florida justice writing in 1936, the fix would "result in confusion and disorder," and "produce an injury to the public which outweighs the individual right of the complainant." The fact that the "individual right" here involved the presidency didn't matter. Indeed, Wells wondered whether the crazy quilt of Florida election-law clauses and federal requirements, both statutory and constitutional, precluded "any practical way" to litigate "a presidential election in Florida in the year 2000." "This contest," Wells said, "simply must end."

The chief was counseling institutional restraint, in part because of what the U.S. Supreme Court had done, but also because he seemed to have little patience for "confusion and disorder," so much so that it's curious he'd been convinced to be part of the unanimous opinion in the first case. The extension of the certification deadline right before Thanksgiving, against the order of Katherine Harris, certainly had led to "confusion and disorder." Perhaps Wells had given his court a chance to get it right and had come to realize that politics was beyond its reach. "I have a deep and abiding concern that the prolonging of judicial process in this counting contest propels this country and this state into an unprecedented and unnecessary constitutional crisis," he wrote. "I have to conclude that there is a real and present likelihood that this constitutional crisis will do substantial damage to our country, our state and to this court as an institution."

The specter of crisis was vastly overstated, but more than any of the other justices, Wells saw the ripening equal-protection problem—though he could just as easily have discovered it ten days earlier when he agreed to let selective recounts proceed. He now wrote: "There is no doubt that every vote should be counted where there is a 'clear indication of the intent of the voter.' The problem is how a county canvassing board translates that directive to these punch cards. Should [it] count or not count a 'dimpled chad'? Here the [boards] disagree. Apparently, some do and some do not. Continuation of this system of county-by-county decisions . . . is fraught with equal protection concerns which will eventually cause the election results in Florida to be stricken by the federal courts or Congress." He did not distinguish between the courts and Congress—a vital distinction that any separation-of-powers aficionado like himself should have recognized—but Wells brilliantly foretold what was coming. "The majority ignores the magnitude of its decision," he warned. Its ruling "cannot withstand the scrutiny which will certainly immediately follow under the United States Constitution." What his colleagues had done, in short, was to hang a giant "Kick Me" sign around the neck of the Florida Supreme Court.

And then, despite the invitation he'd just extended to Rehnquist & Co. in Washington, came a two-line observation about his *own* court that would haunt the Supreme Nine: "Judicial restraint in respect to elections is absolutely necessary because the health of our democracy depends on elections being decided by voters—not by judges. We must have the self-discipline not to become embroiled in political contests whenever a judicial majority subjectively concludes to do so because the majority perceives it is 'the right thing to do.' "

Wells's dissent also furnished a telling snapshot of what a divided appellate court looked and sounded like. That wasn't his fault; he was entitled to his convictions no less than the four justices in the majority. But there was a good institutional reason that supreme courts strive to speak with unanimity in special cases. Days earlier, the U.S. Supreme Court had effectively punted the presidential election case to conceal discord. Now, the Florida court couldn't avoid a split, and at least the rhetorical consequences were foul. It portended a similar picture at the highest court in the land.

The two other dissenters, Major Harding and Leander Shaw—both former chief justices themselves and, as such, the veterans of the court—agreed with much of what Wells had written about such matters as evidentiary burdens of proof, the discretion to be given canvassing boards, and the role of a trial judge. But their primary objection to the majority's decision was that it provided "a remedy which is impossible to achieve." Even if the statewide recount could be finished in a few days, "speed would come at the expense of accuracy, and it would be difficult to put any faith or credibility in a vote total achieved under such chaotic conditions," Harding and Shaw wrote. "The uncertainty of the outcome of this election" would be greater in those circumstances "than the uncertainty that now exists." Theirs was a complaint more about realities than principle. Quoting the great football coach Vince Lombardi, they said, "We didn't lose the game, we just ran out of time." Shaw's dissent was surprising because he was usually the most liberal justice and would've been expected to join the majority; the fact he didn't was just another sign of the wound the presidential case had opened.

The war councils reacted predictably. Gore, who would've had to concede if the Florida ruling went the other way—appealing to the U.S. Supreme Court would have been ridiculous—was euphoric, a phoenix risen again. Bill Daley, the campaign chairman, emerged from the Gore residence in Washington and, to the extent that someone in the middle of this ordeal for so long could, he beamed. "This decision is not just a victory for Al Gore and his millions of supporters. It is a victory for fairness and accountability in our democracy itself."

Democracy itself. Yet thirty seconds later, Daley proclaimed, "All of these matters should be resolved by the Florida judiciary—not by the politicians." From the Gore campaign—from the son of the boss of political bosses, Mayor Daley—it was the crowning confirmation of how much politics had become judicialized; why trust the political system when the system of *justice* would make everything right in the end? The judgeoisie ruled the Republic. Would Thomas Jefferson ever have imagined that a disputed race for the presidency would come down to a duel not between a state legislature and Congress, but two supreme courts?

In Washington, Representative Tom DeLay, the militant House majority whip who had pushed to impeach President Clinton in 1998, called the Florida ruling "judicial aggression [that] must not stand." Jack Kemp, the GOP vice presidential candidate in 1996, said, "America has witnessed a judicial coup d'état." On behalf of the Bush campaign, Jim Baker professed resignation as much as indignation. "It is very sad," he said at a press conference after the Florida Supreme Court ruled. "It is sad for Florida. It is sad for the nation. And it is sad for our democracy." He invoked the language from Wells's dissent about the ruling not being able to "withstand the scrutiny which will certainly immediately follow."

Baker well knew where it might be coming from. By the time he was talking, Bush's lawyers were already in a taxi in Washington on the way to the U.S. Supreme Court, where the nine justices thought they had just begun a four-week holiday recess. Right after the Florida defeat, the Bush legal team had pumped out forty-two pages in under an hour, a testament to adrenaline, caffeine, and the ability to cut and paste from previous federal filings. In this round, on this Friday evening, the lawyers would ask not only for the justices to take on the presidential case and reverse the Florida Supreme Court as expeditiously as possible, but for them to halt the recounts right away.

This was a request for immediate relief—the proverbial stay of execution—the kind that the U.S. Supreme Court almost never gives, except when there's going to be an execution of a prisoner who might not deserve it. When Bush's lawyers went upstairs last time, after the Florida Supreme Court had extended Katherine Harris's certification deadline, they didn't ask to stop the counting pending a decision. It may have been an oversight or the recognition that such extraordinary relief—blocking three south Florida canvassing boards from counting ballots—would never have been granted that early in the litigation. Now, though, the endgame loomed, and the U.S. Supreme Court had already demonstrated that it would poke its nose in. If the justices were predisposed to settling things once and for all, the Bush lawyers guessed, then putting an immediate stop to the counting seemed perfectly plausible.

In Tallahassee, both houses of the Republican-controlled state legislature had spent part of the day gearing up for a special session the following week that would award Florida's electors to Bush. Those efforts had been in the works for weeks and the state supreme court ruling only increased the chance the deed would have to be done. If Gore pulled ahead in the recounts, the Florida justices might direct Harris to certify him the winner and then order the governor, Jeb Bush, to sign the requisite formal documents for transmittal to the Electoral College. If both state executives refused, the court might itself name the Gore slate the winner. Jeb Bush, in fact, had previously stated that "no judicial power exists" to compel him to send along a Gore electoral slate. It was the only time in the thirty-seven days that a major player suggested he or she would defy a court order, which was a remarkable indication of the judiciary's primacy. People made a living disobeying executive edicts and legislative proscriptions, but the courts were off limits, which was just another reason for them to conserve their power by leaving political disputes to the two political branches.

Whatever the Florida Supreme Court did, the legislature might pay no attention and go ahead with the Bush slate. That would mean two slates of electors going to the Electoral College, just as in 1876, and more gridlock, ultimately requiring Congress to sort it out and declare a winner in January 2001, presumably in time for Inauguration Day.

Such pathology among the three branches of government in Florida— and the chance it would metastasize to Congress—terrified most of the participants. In the battle of sound bites, "constitutional crisis" competed with "counting all the votes" and "stealing the presidency." But the fear was exaggerated. It would have been sloppy, it would've been nasty, it might have taken a while. But it would have been "We the People." The question was: Did "we" need to be saved from ourselves?

nine

"Nine Scorpions in a Bottle"

*A*nd *the recounts* came.

Again.

The four-justice majority of the Florida Supreme Court had said to start counting immediately, which didn't mean waiting for morning or Monday or until the U.S. Supreme Court decided if it would intervene. Two hours after the Florida justices ruled on Friday, December 8, Al Gore's weary brigade of lawyers were back up the street in circuit court with motion papers to get the recounts rolling. Because Sanders Sauls had stalked out of the process, a new judge was needed to oversee this final stage of the contest. Enter Terry Lewis, who three weeks earlier had thought his moment in the media sun was over, when he twice ruled for Katherine Harris in the certification matter and was soon reversed by the Florida Supreme Court. "Every time we thought he'd done his thing, the dispute came back to him," says his wife, Fran. "It was like a bad penny."

This time, it was up to Lewis to mold the vagaries of that court's latest order into rules and procedures—and to do so on the fly. Out of what could only be described as a mammoth logistical undertaking, born of a hastily written court decision, Lewis was supposed to create order and make everything right. Over the course of several weeks, Palm Beach hadn't managed to get its recount completed on time, due to indecision and litigation and Thanksgiving dinner. And Miami-Dade never got it done at all, because of indecision and litigation and a mob scene. But now one judge was expected to preside over the actions of sixty-four county canvassing boards. And the judge had to do it as the electoral clock ticked down to zero. Who knew if board members could even be found and brought together on no notice? The admonition of the Florida chief justice, Charles Wells, about "confusion and disorder" had a certain ring to it.

At a televised hearing after dinner, George W. Bush's team of lawyers did their best to make that point and to delay what appeared to be the inevitable restart of the recount. They complained to Lewis about dimples and chad standards, how the thousands of undervotes might be segregated from the rest of the ballots (since many counties lacked the technology to automatically sift out undervotes), and what official record would be made of the proceedings. "We're going to end up with a horrible mess," said Phil Beck, the Chicago lawyer who had helped Barry Richard around the state in the various election lawsuits.

A better way to go, Beck recommended, might be for Judge Lewis to count all six million Florida ballots himself. At, say, thirty seconds a ballot, that would take ... only fifty thousand hours. Assuming Lewis counted round the clock every day, including Christmas and Easter, he could be done by August 23, 2006—halfway into the *second* term of a Bush presidency.

"What would be your Plan B?" asked Judge Lewis, sarcastically.

Richard's no-show was one of the more intriguing byplays of the litigation. He had anticipated a 4-to-3 decision from the Florida Supreme Court in Bush's favor and says he was "demoralized" it went the other way: "I'd run the decathlon and then they moved the finish line." But that wasn't the reason he declined to argue before Lewis. That was a subtle tactical call. "We had to demand specific standards," Richard says, "but we also realized our best chance in the U.S. Supreme Court was if there were no uniform standards. We decided to ask for them, but not too vigorously." Beck had already prepared a detailed outline of the hoops that Lewis would have to go through to properly adopt standards, and Richard thought Beck was better suited to deal with—and obfuscate—those issues, to the extent they arose.

The judicial audience for the Bush team wasn't only Lewis in person. In and around Washington, several of the justices of the U.S. Supreme Court learned of the hearing and watched the show on TV (which was rather ironic in light of what they thought about cameras in court-rooms). The justices didn't like what they were seeing.

More than Bush's lawyers, it was David Boies who wanted to talk about standards—the broader, the better. He believed that was why the Florida Supreme Court had talked about "intent of the voter" so much. Boies asked that counting begin early the next day, Saturday.

Near midnight, after more than an hour of argument, Lewis ruled that counts would start at eight in the morning and all tallies were due in by two on Sunday afternoon. That meant thirty total hours for the task. "I'm very concerned with the perception of these votes and whether they are going to be done accurately and fairly," said the judge. But, just as Richard had hoped, he declined to spell out chad standards, explain-ing that the Florida justices had twice refused to do so. Instead, he would leave dimple analysis up to the canvassing boards in each county, two-thirds of which were controlled by Democrats.

Here was another key moment: Had Lewis stepped into the breach that the Florida Supreme Court had left—if he set forth uniform rules for the recount, which he alone was supervising in the first instance—he might have partially sabotaged the appeal Bush was making right then to the U.S. Supreme Court. The equal-protection challenge would've dis-solved, even as the changing-of-the-rules problem might have been resuscitated. Lewis said later he thought he had no discretion to act where the Florida justices had consciously decided not to. Moreover, he didn't think it was his place to act, given the state election code. "In Texas, they had established specific criteria on ballots," he says. "But in Florida, they didn't, just like they didn't establish a mechanism for a statewide recount. If you really believe in the 'rule of law,' there's not much a judge can do with that."

Lewis decided that he would supervise the counting of the con-troversial Miami-Dade undervotes, which were still in Tallahassee. Although representatives of both campaigns could be present to observe the twenty-eight two-person counting teams actually inspecting ballots, there would be no objections allowed until the end. More than one-fifth of the undervotes had already been counted in the aborted effort by the Miami-Dade canvassing board; Lewis would oversee the rest, but it produced the situation where a *single* county's ballots now wouldn't be judged by the same arbiter. This was the epitome of an equal-protection violation, according to Bush's lawyers.

The discussions in Lewis's courtroom were orderly and calm. The judge didn't think there would be that much "confusion and disorder" at all. "I thought the Florida Supreme Court had its doubts," he recalled later, "but I was going to do the best I could to fashion a method that would accomplish the count as the court had instructed." And he would try to do so "in sufficient time to allow for resolution of disputes and appellate review of my decision," including, he guessed, by the U.S. Supreme Court. Lewis believed he could complete Miami-Dade by Sunday, and all the other sixty-three counties (except Duval) reported to him they thought they could meet his deadline as well. Duval couldn't figure how to sort the undervotes from the other votes, and they obviously didn't have time to wade through all 260,000 ballots in the county.

Lewis had only read through the Florida Supreme Court decision quickly before the hearing began. "I concentrated on the directive language, not the merits," he says. In fact, his view was mixed—that both the majority and dissenting opinions made fair points. "I don't know where I would've come down on the issues had I reviewed the trial record and been privy to the conference among the justices." Unlike four justices on the state supreme court, Lewis at least would've contemplated restraint. "Nobody who drafted the Florida statutes thought of an election like this," he says. "It's something for which the judicial branch just wasn't suited. Maybe the courts should've just left it up to the Electoral College."

But apart from the principle of the thing—*whether* the recounts should be done—he believed the logistics were pretty straightforward. "We would have gotten it done," Terry Lewis says.

To monitor the recounts, both sides had to remobilize the hundreds of troops who a month earlier had gathered from near and far. Some of the volunteers and lawyers were still in the Sunshine State; others rushed to airports to fly down Friday night or Saturday morning. And then there was the tale of young Marie Therese Dominguez.

A longtime Gore supporter, she had been a senior attorney at the Federal Aviation Administration and the Department of the Army, and had come to Florida in October to organize the get-out-the-vote effort around Orlando. Then, after Election Day, Dominguez returned to help during the initial recounts. On December 8, that last Friday of the thirty-seven days, she had to go back home to Washington for a long-standing personal appointment. No one knew when or how the Florida Supremes would rule, so at 4 P.M. she boarded Amtrak's Auto-Train in Orlando, along with her twenty-year-old sedan loaded with suitcases. She took her seat, opened up *Angela's Ashes*, and promptly fell asleep. Twenty minutes later, her cell phone went off. "Did you hear? Did you hear?" a friend squealed. "The Florida Supreme Court ruled for Gore."

Nick Baldick, the campaign's chief field operative, reached Dominguez minutes later. "We need you to stay in Florida," he told her. "We need you right now."

Trouble was, she was on a train that made two stops—the first in South Carolina the next day and the last at its final destination in the D.C. area. She told the conductors she absolutely needed to get off the train *right away*, though she couldn't say why—what if the train employees were Bush loyalists? They laughed her off. "The train stops tomorrow morning and not before," Dominguez was told.

"Who else can I talk to?" she asked. The sandwich jockey in the club car jingled the engineer on the radio and he came to see her. He wanted to know if Dominguez had a medical emergency.

"No, no, but it's *imperative* I get off this train."

For some reason, he bought it, without getting any details, but knowing that his passengers rarely used the word "imperative." The next city along the way was Jacksonville. "Lady, we can't stop the train completely, because passengers will wonder why," the engineer said. But he'd arrange to slow down just outside Amtrak's Jacksonville station and she could jump off. Her car, though, would have to remain.

And so it happened. She threw her carry-on bag, containing only a phone, toothbrush, cosmetics, book, and sweatshirt, off the side of the train, and then leaped herself. She even managed to land on her feet. An Amtrak employee working on a nearby track saw it all and put her on one of those hand-pump-propelled carts last seen in Road Runner cartoons. "We don't get many Auto-Train passengers here," the man deadpanned.

Dominguez made her way into Jacksonville, found a Wal-Mart to buy underwear and a Kinko's to print instructions for recount observers, and the next day coordinated the Gore effort for Duval and some of the smaller neighboring counties. Her story became one of the legends of devotion in the vice president's camp: Throw Marie from the Train!

In Bush's inner circle, in Tallahassee and Austin, the candidate and his commanders couldn't believe that the campaign now faced a recount that could leave them behind in votes as December 12 approached. Unless and until the U.S. Supreme Court moved in, their hopes rested with the luck of the numbers and, beyond that, the Florida legislature and the Congress.

In Washington, Joe Lieberman received a call from Gore right after the Florida Supreme Court ruling. Gore wanted to issue a press statement and, as Lieberman remembered it, "to exult together." And why not? Only minutes earlier Gore was getting his concession plans in order, in case the Florida court decided against him.

"Why don't you both come over for dinner and stay the night if you want?" Gore asked Lieberman. "Tipper and I have bought the wine and challah."

Friday night, of course, was the start of the Jewish Sabbath—a day of rest and, fittingly in this thirty-seven-day struggle, rebirth. Lieberman and his wife, Hadassah, strictly observed the rituals, and didn't drive or otherwise engage in workaday activities for the twenty-four-hour period commencing at sundown. It was a strange scene as they arrived at Gore's residence. The Naval Observatory was aglow in holiday lights, and here the Liebermans walked in with their ceremonial wineglass, bread cover, and other accouterments of Judaism. They spent a few minutes praying in private. "It was the first time I davened in a room with *a Christmas tree*," he says. It was a major ecumenical moment.

The evening was the best of the recount period for the two couples, as satisfying as the early morning of November 8, when the campaign ticket came back from the dead. When evening turned to night, Tipper and Al walked the Liebermans the thirty-five minutes home along Wisconsin Avenue and down near Georgetown Hospital, with two Secret Service contingents in tow. "It was a glorious evening," Lieberman says.

It would be the last one for a while.

Apart from a little luck, winning an emergency stay from the U.S. Supreme Court required litigants to prove two things. First, they had to show the "likelihood" they'd win on the actual merits once a case was briefed and argued. But that wasn't enough, since the justices frequently knew how some appeals were likely to come out when they decided to take them in the first place (though under Court rules it took only four votes, not five, to accept a case). The second thing litigants needed was to demonstrate they'd suffer "irreparable harm" without a stay.

The former requirement wasn't that tough for Bush. The Court knew its internal scorecard from the first case. Behind the scenes, the discussion among the justices in the conference after the first argument left no doubt there was a 5-to-4 majority in reserve, assuming the constitutional and statutory issues remained roughly the same. It was the latter requirement—proving "irreparable harm"—that worried Bush's lawyers, and rightly so. Just why was it, other than in a public-relations sense, that converting undervotes to legal votes posed any injury to Bush? It might be politically damaging, even devastating, but was that the Court's problem, such that it should in effect prejudge a case? A stay was meant to preserve the status quo. If you let the condemned inmate go to the chair or permit the two companies to merge, there's no way to undo the deed. Was the possibility of a small lead for George W. Bush morphing into a small lead for Al Gore the equivalent?

In his papers late Friday to the U.S. Supreme Court on Bush's behalf, Ted Olson offered roughly the same points he'd made to the justices in November—the Florida court had usurped power belonging to the Florida legislature under both the U.S. Constitution and the Electoral Count Act of 1887; the Florida court had changed the rules in the middle of the game; and recounts were "capricious." "More than one month after November 7," the brief read, the events in Florida had thrown the presidential election into "intense turmoil and controversy." Unless the justices stepped in now, "the integrity of the electoral process" for the two highest offices in the country would be imperiled. Without a stay, there would be irreparable harm to that process, to the GOP candidate, and "to the nation." But just what was the harm?

According to Bush, the harm was any chance that Florida's twenty-five electoral votes—certified twelve days earlier to him and Dick Cheney—might now be "called into doubt" by the Florida Supreme Court's action. The supposed December 12 deadline drew near, after which Bush might be "precluded" from "seeking meaningful relief by this Court." And beyond merely Florida, the brief warned, "the entire electoral process under our federal/state dual scheme" was threatened, thereby "undermining the national interest." The last point was overkill, because the constitutional and statutory scheme allowed for the very possibility of a state's electoral votes *not* being considered. But in any event, the argument about December 12—whether it was that date rather than December 18 or January 6 that was determinative—was being made three days too early. If that was the very essence of harm, it was in no way "irreparable."

But in a subsequent petition to the Court—short and not very sweet, filed early Saturday morning—Olson pleaded again for a stay by trotting out the parade of horribles that Bush's lawyers had just witnessed in Lewis's courtroom: sixty-four separate recounts, conducted by canvassing boards and volunteer counters who weren't parties to the litigation, of undervotes segregated from other votes by no reliable process, with "no guidance whatsoever" about chad standards, with no opportunity for observers to object—all to be miraculously completed in thirty hours, "in manifest disregard" for the role of the secretary of state, "the chief election officer" of Florida. "This is but a first glance at the imponderable problems the [Florida Supreme Court] creates," Olson wrote, quoting Charlie Wells's dissent for the ninth time in his stay papers.

And then came the kicker, in which Olson finally came clean on the harm the Bush campaign feared. "Whatever tabulations" ensued from this "indisputably inconsistent and unprecedented process" would be "incurable in the public *consciousness* and, once announced, cannot be retracted." In short, "irreparable harm" was about bad PR.

The betting on the Bush team was that, unlike in the first appeal to the High Court, it couldn't hurt to ask for a stay, but that it was far from certain the justices would oblige.

On Saturday afternoon, the Court did just that. Next to Election Night, when Gore pulled back his concession, it was the most jaw-dropping instant of the thirty-seven days. At 2:52 P.M., after they had met in conference—and without any oral arguments by the lawyers—the Supreme Nine ordered the Florida recounts to stop at once. It was only about seven hours after the counting had resumed. "The mandate of the Florida Supreme Court is hereby stayed," stated the one-paragraph order that, looking back, was the effective denouement of the presidential drama.

The justices didn't just grant a stay. They agreed to take jurisdiction over the case, which Bush had yet to formally request. It was a good sign they were loaded for bear—and piqued over what several of them, none more than Sandra Day O'Connor, regarded as insurrection by the Florida Supreme Court.

Briefs were due the next day (neither side would have the opportunity to respond to the other) and oral argument was set for Monday morning—an unprecedented schedule for the Court, but one that nonetheless precluded any possibility of continuing the counts. Even if the justices ruled the same day, there would barely be twenty-four hours before midnight struck on December 12.

The vote of the Court was 5–4. The deceiving unanimity of the prior Monday had vanished and the fissure between the justices—speculated on by pundits but previously known only to themselves and their law clerks—was exposed for the nation to see. The justices were divided down the center, no different from the rest of their countrymen. In *Bush v. Gore*, aptly named, the Court would be selecting the forty-third president. Bush against Gore—once upon a time, it was a battle the voters were supposed to settle. The 5-to-4 vote was the beginning of the end for Gore—and for any chance the Court would escape with its prestige intact. Perhaps the emperor had no clothes indeed.

The four liberals laid bare the breach at the Court. Justice John Paul Stevens—joined by Stephen Breyer, Ruth Bader Ginsburg, and David

Souter—took the uncustomary step of writing a dissent to the stay. It was extraordinary enough for the Court to declare ahead of time where it stood on an appeal—*pre*judging, as it were—but publishing a dissent at this preliminary stage manifested a depth of anger seldom heard at this, the most dignified institution in the land, where every private conference among the justices begins with handshakes all around, thirty-six of them.

This was the singular moment during the presidential dispute when the Court's legitimacy—built up and nurtured over the ages, through such lows as the Dred Scott slavery case in 1857, the approval of segregation in 1896, and the upholding of Japanese internment during World War II—perished, at least for our times.

"To stop the legal counting of votes," Stevens wrote in a four-paragraph lament, "the majority today departs from three venerable rules of judicial restraint that have guided the Court throughout its history. On questions of state law, we have consistently respected the opinions of the highest courts of the states. On questions whose resolution is committed at least in large measure to another branch of the federal government, we have construed our own jurisdiction narrowly and exercised it cautiously. On federal constitutional questions that were not fairly presented to the court whose judgment is being reviewed, we have prudently declined to express an opinion. The majority has acted unwisely."

It was more than a little hilarious to hear the liberals complaining about judicial restraint—just as it was to see the conservatives trampling over the prerogatives of states—but Stevens was correct. What could justify intervention at this juncture—where was the irreparable harm? Echoing the Gore brief, Stevens said, "Counting every legally cast vote cannot constitute irreparable harm. On the other hand, there is a danger that a stay may cause irreparable harm to [Gore]—and, more importantly, the public at large—because of the risk that the entry of the stay would be tantamount" to deciding on the merits for Bush. "Preventing the recount from being completed," Stevens advised, "will inevitably cast a cloud on the legitimacy of the election."

This was too much for Justice Antonin Scalia to bear. If dissents to a stay were rare, concurrences to them were unheard of—something

Scalia himself noted. Stay orders were administrative instruments rather than carefully rendered opinions that would be studied by future generations; a stay order typically was a single sentence with *no* explanation appended. A short dissent was in the nature of saying, "I just want to note here for the record," even though a longer, comprehensive dissent on the merits would be forthcoming, assuming the Court lineup didn't change. But writing a *defense* of a stay smacked of gloating. What Scalia possessed in doctrinal smarts and ebullient wit he lacked in discretion. He'd shown that before. In a case that declared prayer at high school graduations unconstitutional because of latent social pressure, Scalia taunted the majority: "Interior decorating is a rock-hard science compared to psychology practiced by amateurs"; in an abortion dissent, he said simply that his colleagues' approach "cannot be taken seriously." If Scalia had ever been wrong in his life, he hadn't told anybody.

For Scalia, confrontation was a sport, and a smirk was as good as a smile. He never tired of being an intellectual show-off, even when it was best to lie low. Stevens knew this and baited him into penning his emotions. While none of the other justices in the majority signed Scalia's concurrence, they presumably were not so troubled by it to issue their own defenses for the stay. On a less expedited calendar, they might've been able to talk Scalia down a bit, but in this case there was no time for such deliberation.

"I believe a brief response is necessary to Justice Stevens' dissent," Scalia explained. "The counting of votes that are of questionable legality does in my view threaten irreparable harm to [Bush], and to the country, by casting a cloud upon what he claims to be the legitimacy of his election. Count first, and rule upon legality afterwards, is not a recipe for producing election results that have the public acceptance democratic stability requires."

The job of justice was fantastic, certainly the best the legal profession offered. It provided power, life tenure, princely office space, rank when you wanted it but anonymity at the grocery store, summers away from the Potomac swelter, and all the intellectual benefits of law practice without the hassle of clients. Yet life within the cloistered institution could be trying. Notwithstanding that most of the justices got along personally, the vitriol of *Bush v. Gore* called to mind the line attributed to Justice Oliver Wendell Holmes Jr. three generations earlier. Reflecting on how they served together for years at a time and had to deal with each other every day and in close proximity, Holmes likened the justices to "nine scorpions in a bottle."

Both sides, then, could agree that *any* ruling by the Supreme Court was going to cast a cloud on legitimacy—it just depended on whose parade the rain would fall. Stevens said that failure to recount would cast the cloud; Scalia said that failure to halt the counts would do so. Shouldn't that have caused the rest of the justices in the majority—William Rehnquist, Clarence Thomas, Sandra Day O'Connor, and Anthony Kennedy—to wonder why the Court was mixed up in this to begin with? It was O'Connor and Kennedy, who passed for the Court's center, who represented Gore's last chance to win. Picking off either one from the hard-liners, unlikely as that seemed, could still yield a victory, though perhaps Pyrrhic, given the late date.

Scalia's defense of the stay was not the finest piece of persuasion he'd ever authored. Why, for example, was *Bush's* claim on legitimacy more relevant than Gore's? Wasn't it the job of the arbiter to be neutral? And what of Scalia's reference to *"his* election"? Wasn't the whole point of this post–November 7 exercise to determine who had won?

The subtext of what Scalia wrote was that the justices granted the stay not out of concern for injury to Bush, the public, or the electoral system, but fear for their own hides. The country had done just fine watching an unbelievable process unfold in Florida from Election Day to Thanksgiving and now approaching Christmas. Even with all the fulminations and artifice, even with the real chance that the candidate who lost the popular vote nationally would become president for only the fourth time in history, polls still indicated the American people were altogether confident that life would go on. This wasn't out of any particular fondness for either candidate—far from it—but the confidence, if also smugness, that we'd endured far worse.

No, the "irreparable harm" that filled the majority with dread was the possibility that it might have to confront a vote count with Al Gore in the lead—that the last image the public might see on TV was the vice president mulling over carpet swatches in the Oval Office. Assuming the Bush-leaning Court was going to invalidate the process by which Gore pulled ahead, that would put the justices in the embarrassing position of snatching away a victory. In fact, there wouldn't have been that big a problem. The Court routinely reversed the status quo, most dramatically when it reinstated death sentences that had been thrown out by lower courts. The inmates involved were often then executed. The only difference was that heinous killers had no constituency to offend. Gore had more support than that.

Bush had argued in his brief that "irreparable harm" came down to a public-relations blow in a presidential race. By Scalia's own words, the majority seemed to agree that PR was the issue—but its own. The Court was flexing its equitable muscles not to shield liberty but as an exercise in self-defense. But granting the stay would hardly prove to enhance the Court's credibility.

Around the state of Florida, nine counties had already completed their recounts, netting Gore ten votes. Four more were proceeding apace, on schedule to finish by Terry Lewis's Sunday deadline; they included the Miami-Dade recount under way at the Leon County Public Library, which was showing an early net gain for Bush of forty-two votes. But the other fifty-one counties were in various stages of disorganization. Some were still trying to sort ballots, using software that arrived from the manufacturer hours before counting was supposed to begin. Bradford County complained of trying to find "40 needles among 21 haystacks." Others were able to isolate the undervotes from the rest of the ballots, but the pile included all races for which no candidate had been selected; from this stack, the presidential undervotes had to be sifted out.

Still other officials got nowhere, unsure how to proceed except to keep consulting with lawyers, which was now a fairly typical way to spend a Saturday morning; in one county they debated whether Pepsi would be allowed at the counting tables. Duval County reported in to Judge Lewis with a fax that acknowledged their counting was going to be "tantamount to a guess." Clay County was having trouble rounding up volunteers because, as the *Florida Times-Union* of Jacksonville put it, "most were at the grand opening of the BJ's Wholesale Club in Orange Park." Bay County was considering ignoring the court order entirely.

While Lewis may have been optimistic about finishing the statewide efforts—and however noble the intentions of the Florida justices who birthed this process—the mounting anecdotal evidence from canvassing boards suggested that "confusion and disorder" were widespread. And they were being aired coast-to-coast, as television stations hopped between counties as if they were covering a big hurricane. At the U.S. Supreme Court, the TVs were on in chambers, as they often had been since the presidential mess first landed at the Court. If any justices wanted confirmation of chaos, all they had to do was turn up the volume.

In Tallahassee, Judge Lewis was rather disappointed. "I didn't see the harm in counting," he said later. "And it was frustrating in the sense that when you watch a movie on TV and then have to go out and never see the ending, you want to know what happened." It was the only expression of sentiment from the one judge during the thirty-seven days who best understood his role.

When the stay order flashed across CNN at the Hillsborough County elections center near Tampa, the chairman of its canvassing board proclaimed: "The monkey is dead. The circus is over."

Since the canvassing boards weren't parties to the litigation at the Florida Supreme Court, it could be argued that they were counting not under court mandate, but merely at the *request* of the court. Technically, the Florida justices may not have had jurisdiction over them. If this were so, then the boards were also not subject to any order of the U.S. Supreme Court. Indeed, all the U.S. justices did in their stay was to block any legal effect of the Florida ruling; the stay order didn't even *mention* the recounts.

In short, there was nothing to prevent canvassing boards from continuing to count—for the record, as it were—just as there had been nothing to prevent them from counting prior to when the Florida Supreme Court got involved. If the U.S. justices subsequently overturned their own stay, there would be no impediment to including results from recounts conducted under those post-stay circumstances; if the justices upheld the stay, any tabulations by the canvassing boards would just be legal nullities. Why did none of the canvassing boards consider continuing? Outraged as some of them were, they probably were intimidated by the specter of flouting the U.S. Supreme Court and the Republican cries that would have followed. But imagine a different scenario, in which the U.S. justices had ruled that recounts were the brightest beacon for democracy since John Hancock took out his quill pen and that, as a result, Gore picked up enough votes to pass Bush in the Florida tally. What would the GOP-controlled Florida legislature have done? It likely would've selected a slate of Bush electors. And that would have been perfectly legal—no more in defiance of the judiciary than canvassing boards choosing to count votes, even if the Florida Supreme Court wasn't allowed to order them to. In either case, it simply would have been other duly constituted branches of government—one legislative, one executive—exercising their powers.

Nearby in Tallahassee, Jim Baker spoke for Bush and couldn't restrain his glee; he had hardly been certain the recounts would be stopped cold. Baker reiterated his belief that the Florida Supreme Court had changed the rules. But he also repeated how "sad" he thought it was that "we seem to be deciding a national election for president of the United States in lawsuits and in courthouses." It would have been a nice note to end on. Instead, referring to his legal team, Baker announced, "Our folks are ready to go!" Apparently, lawsuits and courthouses weren't that bad, after all. David Boies and Ron Klain did their best to put on a good face at a press briefing, but they knew the stay was the tolling of the knell. Nick Baldick later referred to December 9 as "that glorious Saturday that turned into the worst day of the Florida experience."

At the Naval Observatory, Gore was astonished by the ruling. Bill Daley told him the game was over. Gore insisted that O'Connor or Kennedy might still be reeled in and that a 5-to-4 loss could be converted into a 5-to-4 win. Daley told him the game was over. Maybe Gore's campaign chairman was right, but for both tactical and genuine reasons, the vice president didn't want his representatives tearing into the judiciary, a branch of the national government he'd always associated with protecting individual rights. He had watched as Jim Baker and other Republicans did that to the Florida Supremes, and that wasn't for him. Flipping on his ever-present BlackBerry, Gore sent an e-mail to his spokesmen, Mark Fabiani and Chris Lehane, less than half an hour after the stay was issued.

"Please make sure that no one trashes the Supreme Court," it read. The message was signed "Robert Stone," the online pseudonym that Gore used throughout the campaign, though nobody knew if he was a fan of the novelist.

Over the prior two decades, Larry Tribe had argued thirty cases at the U.S. Supreme Court, including the first presidential election case the week earlier. He assumed *Bush v. Gore* would be No. 31. Tribe had been handling the ongoing federal litigation at the 11th U.S. Circuit Court of Appeals out of Atlanta. Just fifteen minutes before the U.S. Supreme Court issued its stay in the state litigation, the 11th Circuit had declined to block the nascent recounts. But now Tribe was back at Harvard to teach two makeup sessions. Because of the December 1 oral argument at the U.S. Supreme Court, he had been forced for the first time to cancel classes other than for illness. As he summed up to his 125 students on the afternoon of December 8, and waxed on about the nobility of the law and who-knew-what-the-future-would-hold, someone interrupted him.

As Tribe recalls it, "A kid in the last row says, 'Oh, I thought you knew—the Florida Supreme Court ruled for Gore, 4–3. We heard it twenty minutes ago during our break.'

"I nearly fell over." And then Tribe told the class, "I guess I'm going to be busy."

When he got back to his office, Klain reached him. Bush would obviously be appealing the Florida ruling. "The vice president wants to make sure you're still available to write the opposition brief and argue it if the Court takes the case," Klain said. The two had talked the day before about this possibility.

Tribe agreed and began working out of his study in the old Philip Johnson house on Ash Street. Once the 11th Circuit refused to stop the recounts, Tribe was certain that, while the U.S. Supreme Court was likely to take jurisdiction, there was "no way" the justices would grant a stay. Within fifteen minutes, he was proven wrong and, as he described it afterward, was "completely deflated." He talked both to Klain and Tommy Goldstein, a young Washington lawyer who in recent years had carved out a nice piece of Supreme Court practice for himself. They both asked Tribe if he thought the stay meant they were cooked. "It's very uphill," Tribe told them, but, as he put it later, "it wasn't over until Justice Scalia sings." Tribe said they had to proceed as if they still had a chance.

He caught the 5 P.M. shuttle to Washington to work out of a riverview suite at the Watergate, his usual hotel. The oral argument was thirty hours away—what was he going to *wear*? Tribe said he owned only two good suits, and the dark blue that was best for the Court was in Miami Beach at Michael Tilson Thomas's house, which Tribe was using for a month. He had taken along his brown suit to D.C., but that just wouldn't be right for the most important argument of his career. So his wife, still at the vacation home, arranged to FedEx the other one up to arrive just before the argument. It wound up being the worst-spent $150 of Tribe's professional life.

Brief-writing is an art form—high stakes, limited space, transforming dry doctrine into something that will keep judges from nodding off. For a U.S. Supreme Court case, preparing the filings that form the core of the case takes weeks and sometimes months, and only after the arguments have been fully refined in and by lower courts. For many appellate litigators, a brief to the Supreme Nine is the most important document they'll ever author. In *Bush v. Gore*, the challenge over a twenty-four-hour period was to make sure the briefs were in English, with the paragraphs in the proper order. Tribe, with Goldstein and a fax machine set up by the hotel, would coordinate the Gore effort out of the Watergate, but much of the drafting was done by committee elsewhere in Washington, as well as in Tallahassee, Atlanta, and Palo Alto. For Bush, Olson also got material from lawyers scattered about, including Michael Carvin and Barry Richard. It was no way for either side to conduct an appeal—though the briefs would turn out to be remarkably well done, particularly in comparison to what the Court itself would eventually produce. The briefs from both litigants essentially reprised the positions they'd articulated in the papers filed on the stay motion, and Olson managed to lard in twenty more citations to Wells's Florida dissent. The chief justice should've demanded royalties.

Other interested parties, including the Florida legislature, filed "friend of the Court" briefs. This was typical in appellate litigation. What was unusual was that the U.S. Congress stood silent. In the ultimate case about its supremacy—implicating one of its fundamental roles under the Constitution—Congress spit the bit. Some members of the Senate and House even proclaimed they were pleased that the Supreme Court would take the election into its own hands, because it was the one institution the American people respected enough to deliver a fair result. This abdication of responsibility, of course, was less about faith in the justices than the legislators' fears that, heaven forbid, they might have to act decisively. The Court might have observed this reluctance and concluded that it obliged the Court to intervene. Instead, it was really the best reason for the justices to keep their distance. The fact that Congress wanted no part of the election—because it was so politically hot—was the most exquisite evidence that it *was* the ideal institution to weather the storm.

As Tribe tried to gear up for what would be an all-nighter, the phone rang. Warren Christopher, having returned to Gore's command group, wanted to stop by to see him. Tribe had no idea why—others in the campaign knew, but didn't want to be the bearers. Around 8 P.M., Christopher arrived in a grave suit and topcoat that Tribe later said made him look like, well, a secretary of state. The two had never met. "I guess you're busy," Christopher noted.

"Yes."

They sat down and Christopher got to it. "I've learned when you have bad news, it's best to deliver it right away."

Unless Christopher had new information that the Supreme Court had decided the case without hearing oral argument, Tribe surmised what was coming. "Go ahead," he said.

"The vice president has decided that David should argue the case."

Why Boies over Tribe? "The vice president thinks you're the best advocate in the Supreme Court," Christopher explained, "but the best way to present this case is being about the specifics of Florida law, and that is what David's been doing."

"I'll certainly help David in any way I can," Tribe replied, biting his tongue.

Christopher seemed to be expecting a protest, so he quickly added, "The vice president is very decisive and, when he makes a decision, he sticks with it."

While that was true enough, he was also a details freak, a political lumberjack who didn't always see the forest. During the recount period, Gore liked to personally orchestrate which of his minions would do the *Today* show or *Good Morning America*. (It was creepily reminiscent of how Jimmy Carter controlled the sign-up sheet for the White House tennis court.) An event during the New Hampshire primary that became campaign lore illustrated the tendency especially well. Gore was flying in for a rally and was told there would be supporters there to greet him.

"How many will there be?" Gore asked. Aides advised him it would be between one hundred and three hundred.

"But how many *exactly*?"

Who argued Bush v. Gore on the vice president's behalf was surely a more important question, but swapping horses so late in the game reflected a fundamentally different management style than his GOP counterpart's—as well as, perhaps, a lack of loyalty to those who sweated blood for him. George W. Bush did not lie awake at night wondering if Ted Olson was still the right man; at this point, Bush might not have been able to pick Ted Olson's face out of a lineup. When Richard replaced Carvin for the second Florida Supreme Court argument, Bush wasn't even consulted on it. But Bush was known in his world as intensely loyal to his troops. (It was a contrast of reputations that Gore's image police sought to dispel—or hide. In the reportage of Boies's ascension as chief advocate, an anonymous Gore aide was quoted the next day saying the Supreme Court appeal "belonged to Boies all along," which was untrue.)

As Tribe sat with Christopher, assuring him that he'd complete the brief and meet with Boies, he couldn't help but register a dissent. "This isn't an attempt to change anyone's mind, but I hope you realize this doesn't make a great deal of sense," Tribe said. "I don't really see how the U.S. Supreme Court could be interested primarily in Florida law rather than the federal constitutional issues here."

Christopher was a diplomat. He thanked Tribe for his understanding and they parted cordially. Tribe bristled, speaking with his wife in Florida and several others, among them Bob Shrum, his old friend and an ancient consultant for the Democrats, including Gore this round. Shrum told Tribe that he and Carter Eskew, another of the consultants, thought Gore had made a mistake. But Tribe knew there was little to be gained by venting and that it was, at the end of the day, up to a client to choose his own champion. "If Gore really believed that his chances of winning were a little better doing it this way," Tribe said later, his disappointment still evident, "he was right to do it. I had no entitlement." And since five members of the Court had pretty much made up their minds for Bush anyway, it wasn't like any lawyer selected by Gore had much of a chance. Boies put the odds at "not much better than 5 percent," and while Tribe wouldn't quantify Gore's prospects, he wasn't exactly an optimist.

Soon after Christopher left his suite, Tribe got a call from the vice president, who wanted him to know this was about appellate strategy and wasn't personal. But it was. What neither Gore nor Christopher shared with Tribe was that his fate had been hanging in the balance all afternoon. Shortly after the stay was granted, Gore phoned Klain in Tallahassee. "Are you really sure Larry should be arguing this case?" Gore asked.

"No doubt in my mind."

"Why not David?"

"Larry's the best advocate of our time, period. David's argued one case before the Supreme Court."

The case was *Pennzoil v. Texas*, back in 1987, after Texaco and Pennzoil had gone to war over Getty Oil. The issue was whether federal courts could meddle in Texas state court proceedings—Pennzoil had won a ten-billion-dollar verdict against Texaco that would send it into bankruptcy. Boies defended Texaco on appeal and lost at the Supreme Court, 9–0—to a Harvard law professor named Larry Tribe. Boies's losing argument? Of course federal judges had to save the day when a state court behaved egregiously! Lawyers are perfectly allowed to argue for one client today that the earth is round and for another client tomorrow that it's flat (as long as each puts down a retainer), but there was a certain poetic justice in Boies getting hoisted with his own conceptual petard.

Gore called back in half an hour and said he "really" preferred to go with Boies. Klain walked him through the choice and urged a broader discussion with Daley, Christopher, and anyone else Gore wanted to bring in.

The vice president wanted to switch to Boies because there had been ongoing chatter that Tribe was lackluster in his first argument before the High Court, the one in which the justices vacated and remanded the ruling by the Florida Supreme Court. Within Washington legal parlors, as well as among Capitol Hill Democrats who fancied themselves legal beagles, some blamed Tribe for seeming arrogant and not anticipating some of the justices' questions about the primacy of state legislatures in determining presidential electors. "I know Larry," Lieberman recalled. "He didn't have the fire I expected, or the effect we wanted. I wouldn't have initiated the change, but I supported it. We needed to strike at their hearts more." Tribe later acknowledged it wasn't his best performance, but, then again, he had so many to choose from.

The larger conversation suggested by Klain took place after dinner—a conference call between Gore, Lieberman, Christopher, Daley, Walter Dellinger, and Klain. Tribe wasn't told of the meeting; in politics, the condemned man gets no hearing. Everyone agreed that choosing between Tribe and Boies was like wondering whether you wanted Magic Johnson or Larry Bird to take your last shot.

Gore made the case for Boies, which was simple enough, strategically. First, his presence would signal the Court that Gore thought this was an appeal about state law rather than constitutional theory. Second, the *absence* of Tribe served to soften some of the political overtones of the case; Tribe was red meat for the three hard-right justices and might obscure the underlying issues. And third, any equal-protection violation was going to be a factual inquiry and Boies really had been on the ground with the recounts in Florida; he could distinguish a hanging chad from a swinger in an instant.

Nobody except Klain spoke up for Tribe, his mentor. Boies was in, Tribe was out.

Boies and Tribe got together at the hotel on Sunday. The new man felt bad for the legend he was replacing. "I don't know what to say," Boies said. But a scorer wants the ball when the clock says ":02" and, besides, it wasn't for him to second-guess the client. The two lawyers worked to get the final brief in order, with Goldstein sitting between them and manning the word processor. Goldstein raced off to the Court to file the papers by the 4 P.M. deadline. TV cameras had staked out the building; Goldstein managed to walk in unbothered, because he stuffed the *Bush v. Gore* brief in the back of his pants and pretended to be a lost tourist.

Goldstein almost missed the deadline. Twenty minutes before, his cell phone had rung. He'd used it all weekend to receive last-minute comments from various lawyers, and it was also the best way for others to track down Boies and Tribe, with whom Goldstein was spending most of his time.

"This is Al Gore," the caller said. Goldstein chuckled at what he assumed was a prank by one of his overtired colleagues.

"I'm trying to reach David Boies on a land line," the caller continued. "Is he there?"

Goldstein knew nobody other than Gore could do the voice *that* well. It *was* the vice president. And this was Goldstein's only conversation with him.

After the brief was filed, Boies and Tribe war-gamed questions the justices might ask. By nightfall, Tribe was on a plane out of town. At the argument Monday morning, it was Goldstein, not Tribe, sitting next to Boies at counsels' table down in front of the justices. Tribe would listen to the audio version of the argument on TV.

Tribe had received much laudatory coverage throughout, but the press sometimes indulged in a little teasing. In a particularly merciless bit a few days after the Supreme Court argument from which he'd been unceremoniously dumped, the *Washington Post* gossip page reported about Tribe's personal Web site, which had earlier been the subject of an online riff by journalist Mickey Kaus.

"What can you say about Laurence Tribe?—as his fellow Harvardian Erich Segal might ask," wrote the *Post* under the headline "Self-Love Story." "Quite a lot, if you happen to be Laurence Tribe and writing about yourself." For two paragraphs it quoted the professor. "Hi, I'm Larry. . . . I've written about, taught, and practiced constitutional law for many years. . . . In a future life, I think I might try astronomy or astrophysics, or maybe even pure math, which was my favorite subject in college and grad school. . . . I love brilliant magenta sunsets, unagi, Martin Amis' 'Time's Arrow,' the fish tank at [Mass. General], T. S. Eliot's 'Love Song of J. Alfred Prufrock,' eating, my Stairmaster, looking at the ocean, dreaming about impossible things, New Yorker cartoons. . . . I'm something of a political news junkie, but I am fairly disillusioned with politics in the 1990s."

Commented the snarky *Post:* "We can only imagine how he feels about politics in the year 2000."

Tribe soon took down the Web page.

The scene at the Supreme Court building Monday morning, December 11, was even more absurd than it had been for the initial case ten days before. The first time, Court personnel had a week to prepare for the crush of demands from senators and other Washington celebrities. But since the Court this round took the case on a Saturday, and scheduled it to be argued Monday, any idea of planning was a joke. The line for the public started forming Saturday night, and the phones in the marshal's office were jammed beginning early Monday morning. Ted Koppel stayed away. The usual suspects got in. Karl Rove, Bush's political man and a student of American history, made a special trip up from Austin to hear the argument. He sat right behind Karenna Gore. "This was the last chapter and, win or lose, I wanted to see the grenades go off and feel the blast of the shells hit me," Rove says. And, to make everybody's day a little bit cheerier, there was Geraldo Rivera.

Rivera, a longtime attorney, just happened to be getting his Court hunting license that morning. The Court has its own roster of sworn-in lawyers. Any lawyer arguing a case has to be on it, recommended by other members of the exclusive club, but for the most part, admission is just an honor and the chance to get an impressive certificate for your wall. The regular swearing-in ceremony was scheduled for Monday morning, right before *Bush v. Gore.* Rivera was to be one of 137 new members of the Supreme Court Bar. He came in stage makeup, to be ready to go on TV afterward.

After the swearing-in, the courtroom had to be cleared of the new lawyers and their guests; even the rest rooms were checked. Rivera, however, wanted to stick around. After all, the Court had a special section of the gallery set aside for members of its bar. He was told that other lawyers had already spent hours in line for those seats and he couldn't in effect jump the line. Rivera pleaded for an exception, to no avail, and had to leave. But he then mysteriously appeared halfway through the argument—in the lawyers' section. Jesse Jackson did even better. He didn't have one of the reserved seats (as, say, a guest of one of the justices or litigants), nor did he wait in any line. He just showed up, walked into the building and courtroom unchallenged, and waited for someone to volunteer a seat, which took but a few minutes.

Ted Olson had to wait in front with everybody else until the building opened at 9 A.M. But David Boies had a secret weapon—thirty-year-old Tommy Goldstein, who knew more about the way the place worked than some Court employees (and actually once worked for the D.C. office of Boies's law firm). One of the ways he'd been able to cook up business was by reviewing the Court's petitions list more aggressively than any lawyer in town. In that way, he could identify the cases he thought the justices were most likely to take and then offer up his esteemed appellate services to the out-of-town attorneys unfamiliar with the byways of the Court. Goldstein had the Red Top Car Service pick up Boies at the Mayflower—any time he was in D.C., Boies liked to stay at the same hotel and order the same meals—and drive right into the underground garage where the justices and clerks got to park.

They may have been arguing the Case of the Century, but Olson couldn't help but notice how Boies had chosen to dress for it. It was the standard Boies outfit—off-the-rack navy-blue Lands' End suit, blue knit tie, button-down shirt, and those ubiquitous black leather sneakers. When you appeared before the Supreme Court, you were supposed to wear what you'd be buried in (at a later date, not at argument). But Boies always wore the same clothes to work because, as he says, "it goes with everything I have" and because he believed it prevented distractions. The only exception he made was that in long jury trials he'd go through various ties. "Twenty years ago," he says, "I found that juries would fix-ate on the fact I was not changing my tie. They notice everything. And they'd tell me afterward they'd have long debates about why I didn't. In one case there was a faction that thought, 'Well, Mr. Boies is just so ded-icated to the law that he doesn't care about his wardrobe.' But you had the other faction that said, 'Oh no, big corporations don't hire anybody except very fancy lawyers—and he's just putting that tie on to make us think he's an ordinary person.' So I decided ever since that the more conservative approach was to take the issue out of the jury's hands and wear not just different-colored knit ties, but different ties altogether."

Regular-guy David. If only those juries knew about his climate-controlled, fully alarmed wine cellars at home, lined with meticulously organized rows of Lafite Rothschild and thousands of other bottles. During the thirty-seven days of Florida, Boies dined frequently at the Silver Slipper in Tallahassee. The restaurant delighted in him ordering the most expensive red on the menu. "When's that guy coming back?" the waiters ask even now.

For most Boies watchers, it was the shoes that were most out of place in the wing-tipped universe of the courtroom. But Olson couldn't believe the button-down collar — he had even wondered at five that morning, as he prepared for argument, if Boies would alter his attire. "The thought crossed my mind," Olson remembers. "I don't know why." There was a reason it was a bugaboo. In the early 1980s, when Olson was a lawyer in the Justice Department, he was asked one day by Rex Lee, the solicitor general, to lend him his shirt. Lee had received a call from Chief Justice Warren Burger mentioning that a lawyer from the solicitor general's office had argued in Court in a *button-down* shirt. That was unacceptable to the chief justice, no different than if a man from the SG's office appeared without a morning coat. Lee figured out that *he* was the lawyer in question. On that day, he had worn a button-down to work and had to argue later that morning in Court. Olson gave Lee the straight-collared shirt off his back.

As they waited for the justices to enter the courtroom and for argument to begin, Olson asked Boies what the story was with the clothes. Did he worry it drew too much attention? Or was that the point?

"David was coy about it," Olson says. "Smart lawyer."

ten

The Justice Who Picked
the President

With an air of inevitability hanging over it, *Bush v. Gore*, Case No. 00-949, commenced promptly at 11 A.M. The marshal had done his "Oyez!" three times, which was the federal equivalent of the Florida court's "Hear ye!" (except a little funnier for those spectators who thought the marshal was chanting "Oy vay.") Ted Olson opened just as he had in his brief—by ridiculing the decision now under review. "Just four days" after the Court's vacate-and-remand of the first ruling by the Florida Supreme Court, Olson said, the Florida justices, *"without a single reference"* to the vacate-and-remand, "issued a new, wholesale post-election revision of Florida's election law." The new ruling "not only changed Florida's election law again, it also referred to, relied upon, and expanded its November 21 judgment that this Court made into a nullity."

It was a powerful way to start, focusing the justices not so much on the sticky political matter, but on the presumed insolence of the Florida Supreme Court, which still had not formally dealt with instructions to clarify its previous opinion. Later on in the argument, Justice Sandra Day O'Connor would chide David Boies about the apparent willingness of Florida justices to "bypass" her Court's unanimous order and "assume that all those changes and deadlines" it had made on November 21 "were just fine." That kind of attitude was "troublesome," according to O'Connor. From Antonin Scalia, that would've been unusually tactful; from O'Connor, it was trash talk and Boies knew it.

Anthony Kennedy asked the first question, not a minute into Olson's argument. He was eager to test out ideas—"trying them on like hats," as various clerks of his liked to say—for reasons that would emerge later when the justices privately discussed the case. For Kennedy, who was so often a swing vote on the Court, oral argument was the time when he might come to grips with his own ambivalence and indecision. That was especially true this morning, because there had been so little time to reflect on the constitutional issues and institutional consequences. O'Connor, too, could be a swing vote, but by this point she was sufficiently disgusted with the Florida Supreme Court that the chances of her bolting the five-justice majority from Saturday were slim. Those chances seemed to dwindle further when she was later dismissive of the whole concept of manual recounts based on voter mistakes, be they insufficient marks on a ballot or voting for too many candidates. Forget chads and butterflies—an exasperated O'Connor asked Boies, "Well, why isn't the standard the one that voters are *instructed* to follow, for goodness' sake?" As for Rehnquist, Scalia, and Clarence Thomas, there wasn't a chance—this oral argument was for show only. They were ready to send Al Gore on his way.

Kennedy wanted to know why the Court had jurisdiction. There were five reasons, of course, and Kennedy was one of them—this was Bill Brennan's "Rule of Five" in action. It was a little late on Monday to be wondering aloud whether the stay of the prior Saturday was properly granted. Justices risked nothing from devil's advocacy (other than Scalian abuse), but Kennedy's question, which he later asked Boies as well, suggested he might be wavering. There was a reason law clerks called him Flipper, Flipper . . .

There was also a reason they regarded Kennedy as the most pompous of the justices. David Souter, by contrast, exuded humility. William Rehnquist wanted to run a tight ship; Thomas sat stone-faced. But Kennedy, personally as easygoing a justice as there was, viewed his official role as Zeus did his. Even in chambers, he was incapable of beginning a sentence with "I believe" when he was explaining his own views on a case. It was always: "The law says," with an occasional "History will judge us" thrown in. Tony Kennedy was nothing less than a lawgiver.

In a bizarre and memorable profile of the justice in *California Lawyer* magazine back in 1992, Kennedy had self-promotionally agreed to let the writer into chambers just before he went into the courtroom to announce a major abortion ruling in which he'd been a key vote. "Sometimes you don't know if you're Caesar about to cross the Rubicon or Captain Queeg cutting your own tow-line," Kennedy ruminated to his listener. Then the justice self-consciously asked for solitude. "I need to brood," Kennedy said. "I generally brood, as all of us do on the bench, just before we go on." It was just that most of them didn't do it on cue.

If Olson had any early reason for concern—if Boies was looking for a sliver of hope—it was hearing Kennedy's first question about jurisdiction. Olson answered briefly: There were palpable federal questions involved because of both Article II of the Constitution and the Electoral Count Act. But implicit in that view—that in the matter of presidential electors, a state legislature had absolute authority—was a correspondingly low view of state judicial power. Didn't the idea that the Florida legislature was immune from the commands of the Florida Supreme Court have "grave implications for our republican theory of government?" Kennedy demanded.

"It may not be the most powerful argument we bring to this Court," Olson admitted.

"I think that's right," Kennedy responded, peering down through his professorial, rimless glasses. He got the gallery's first big chortle of the morning.

Olson couldn't wait to get on to his other points. Such were the challenges of being in an argument with nine lawyers, with all the annoying questions thrown at just you.

Kennedy gave way to the liberal members on the Court, first John Paul Stevens and Ruth Bader Ginsburg, then Souter and Stephen Breyer. Their written opinion on Saturday, too, had clearly indicated how they were going to vote in *Bush v. Gore*. Their agenda in quizzing Olson wasn't so much to get answers to lingering questions as to score points with Kennedy, who they knew was the game. Souter and Breyer, more than Stevens and Ginsburg, shared some unease with the five-justice majority over how the recounts were being conducted—not enough to have halted them and maybe not enough even for the Court to meddle. But Souter and Breyer hoped to use the oral argument to point to a middle ground they might share with Kennedy.

As Olson talked on about how the statewide recount ordered by the Florida Supreme Court couldn't be done, Souter asked, "Well, if your concern was with impossibility, why didn't you let the process run, instead of asking for a stay?" It was more a rhetorical note than a question and Souter looked in Kennedy's direction when he made it.

Breyer then at long last got to the core issue: equal protection. It was now twenty minutes into the hearing. The constitutional and statutory questions about changing the Florida election rules had never seemed to gain traction, even among the conservative justices back in the first oral argument. It was a difficult point to win, since the line between rewriting law and merely interpreting it was fuzzy. Moreover, the safe-harbor provision created by Congress was hardly of constitutional dimension; at worst, Florida's failure to sail in under the deadline just denied its electoral slate immunity from congressional examination. No, Breyer believed, the conservatives were likely to rule for George W. Bush because of the "confusion and disorder" on display during the recounts. But what if that could be remedied—and a little time added to the clock?

"If [the recounts] were to start up again," Breyer asked, "I understand that you think that the system that's set up now is very unfair because it's different standards in different places. What in your opinion would be a fair standard—on the assumption that it starts up missing the [December] twelfth deadline, but before the eighteenth?"

Here was Breyer's offer to Kennedy and, for whatever it was worth, to the other four conservatives: I'll join you in finding a violation of equal-protection rights, but why don't we send it back to the Florida Supreme Court and let the counts resume with a uniform standard? Using the date on which the Electoral College gathered, rather than the safe-harbor date, there might even be enough time.

Olson allowed that "penetration of the ballot card" would be a "minimum"—he wanted nothing of dimpled chads. But Olson knew that being drawn into a discussion of standards risked creating the orderliness that had conveniently remained out of the process. He said he really hadn't thought uniform standards through and that would be the job of the Florida legislature anyway; to graft them on now would be yet another change in the rules that the election code established. And whenever it seemed that Olson might concede a bit on the chance of a constitutionally acceptable recount, Scalia jumped to the rescue. One time, as Olson was being hemmed in by Souter, Scalia became coach. If would-be voters didn't follow instructions "to detach the chads entirely," then it was their own fault that machines couldn't read the ballots, Scalia said. "It's part of your submission, I think, that there is no wrong when a machine does not count those ballots that it's not supposed to count?"

Replied Olson posthaste: "That's absolutely correct, Justice Scalia."

For these colloquies on recount standards, largely led by a Souter–Breyer tag team, Kennedy sat back and listened.

Olson provided no flourishes in his allotted time, but there was no need to. He didn't have to hit any questions out of the park—he was in the lead by a run and had only to hold on. His GOP colleague, Joe Klock, arguing for several minutes on Katherine Harris's behalf, should have been so lucky. What he provided was comic relief.

Klock chimed in against undervotes with more heat than Olson. "The whole issue of what constitutes a legal vote, which the Democrats make much ado about, presumes that it's a legal vote no matter what you do with the card," he said. "You could take the card out of the polling place and not stick it in the box and they would consider that to be a legal vote. . . . The only problem we have here is created by people who did not follow instructions."

He might best have sat down then. For in response to a question by Stevens, Klock began, "Well, Justice Brennan, the difficulty is that under . . ." The audience was aghast. "I'm sorry," Klock said. "That's why they tell you not to do that."

Good point, but too late. Klock had called Stevens by a different justice's name—and one who'd been dead for three years. The Supreme Court actually has a "Guide for Counsel." In addition to instructing lawyers to use "Mr." only in addressing the chief justice, as in "Mr. Chief Justice," it suggests sticking with "Your Honor" rather than risk getting a justice's name wrong. Indeed, before the lawyers in *Bush v.*

Gore entered the courtroom, they were given that admonition by the clerk of the Court, William Suter, in his pep talk. "The safest thing is never to say a justice's name. Just preface your answer with 'Justice' or 'Your Honor' every time." Larry Tribe and Walter Dellinger themselves had mixed up O'Connor and Ginsburg in the past.

Klock apologized for addressing Stevens as Brennan, and he moved on. Twenty seconds thereafter, trying to respond to a barrage from Souter, Klock began, "Justice Breyer, what I'm saying is that—"

He got no further because the questioner playfully reminded him, "I'm Justice Souter—you'd better cut that out."

A minute later, the justice with slicked-back dark hair had a question. "Mr. Klock, I'm Scalia," he said, with exquisite timing. The house came down. The performer beamed. What a card.

Woe betide Joe Klock. The lawyer who worried he'd forever be remembered for getting punched in the nose by a colleague would now be remembered for committing the ultimate courtroom faux pas—twice and in the biggest case of his life.

Unlike Olson or Klock, Boies did have to swing for the fences—for both his client and, as Boies explained later, for posterity. Whatever else happened, he wanted future generations to hear what was going down in the election of the forty-third president of the United States.

Boies faced the same two lines of questioning the others had: Did the Florida Supreme Court change the law and, even if it didn't, was the statewide recount unfair? On the first, Kennedy led the charge. "Could the Florida Legislature have done what the [state] supreme court did?" he asked with a glower.

"I really haven't thought about that question," Boies replied. "I think they probably could not ... because it would be a legislative enactment as opposed to a judicial interpretation of an existing law."

"I'm not sure why," said Kennedy, seeing that Boies was begging the question. "If the legislature does it, it's a new law and when the supreme court does it, it isn't?" If it had been the legislature that had effectively "truncated" the contest period by nineteen days, Kennedy said, wouldn't that have occasioned squawks?

O'Connor, still stewing over the fact that the Florida justices had yet to respond to the vacate-and-remand, seconded Kennedy's point. Didn't both the U.S. Constitution and the Electoral Count Act require the state court to give "special deference" to the state legislature? "General elections" were one thing, she lectured, "but in the context of selection of presidential electors, isn't there a big red flag up there [saying] 'Watch out'?"

The challenge of oral argument, particularly before a bench of nine jurists, is to keep so many balls in the air. While Boies wanted to keep all his interrogators happy as his forty-five minutes whizzed by, he knew who was most important and who was a lost cause. As the various justices competed with each other to steer the argument, Boies had to keep weaving to take the direction he wanted. It was impossible. O'Connor wanted to hear more about being dissed by the Florida Supreme Court; Scalia professed not to understand how any further ballots could be added to Harris's initial certification now that its supposed extension had been vacated by the Court. Neither of those inquiries was going to get Boies anywhere, nor were they even close to getting to the much larger issue that Boies wanted to engage: Were any of these specific items really matters for the U.S. Supreme Court or were they best left to Florida's courts to resolve?

Kennedy wanted to go back to the equal-protection problem and prevailed in making it the center of the rest of the argument. What he demanded to know was whether Boies acknowledged that "there must be a uniform standard for counting the ballots" under the Florida Supreme Court order in the contest proceeding.

"I do, Your Honor," Boies said. "The standard is whether or not the intent of the voter is reflected by the ballot. That is the uniform standard throughout the state of Florida."

Kennedy had enough of this dodge-and-weave. "That's very general," he remonstrated Boies. "Even a dog knows the difference in being stumbled over and being kicked. . . . From the standpoint of the Equal Protection Clause, could each county give their own interpretation to what intent means?"

"It can vary from individual to individual."

"This is susceptible of a uniform standard," Kennedy asked with incredulity, "and yet you say it can vary from [recount] table to table within the same county?"

Boies was digging himself in, but not because he was a fool. If he proposed specific rules about, say, dimples or hanging chads, he'd be tacking too near the proscriptions of the Electoral Count Act and out of the December 12 safe harbor he'd long ago conceded as significant. How do you articulate the uniform standards that equal protection seemed to require, while also *not* changing the law that existed on Election Day — especially a law that was so vague about standards ("clear indication of the intent of the voter") that it amounted to no standard at all? Boies wanted it both ways and ended up satisfying nobody. There may very well have been no way out of the bind, though Boies probably should've just tried to solve the equal-protection problem — which had constitutional proportions — and taken his chances that a majority of the Court would find the counting rules hadn't been illegally changed.

Kennedy wouldn't let Boies off. "You're not just reading a person's mind," he said. "You are looking at a piece of paper." Was there not "something objective" about how to evaluate a mark on it?

Boies again proffered nothing, except to note that states like Texas, which had statutorily delineated standards, included a "catch-all provision that says, 'Look at the intent of the voter.'" How was this practically any different from Florida? he said.

Souter tried next. "I think what's bothering Justice Kennedy — and it's bothering a lot of us — is we seem to have a situation here in which there is a subcategory of ballots in which we are assuming for the sake of argument, since we know no better, that there is no genuinely subjective indication beyond what can be viewed as either a dimple or a hanging chad, and there is a general rule being applied in a given county that an objective intent, or an intent on an objective standard, will be inferred, and that objective rule varies, we are told, from county to county."

Huh? What did all *that* mean?

It was just a reflection of how confusing the facts could be to those who hadn't been following them for a month, and another indication for the Court that trying to unravel the mess swiftly wasn't a task for which justices were well suited. But Souter did figure out his point. "Why shouldn't there be one objective rule for all counties?" he asked. "And if there is not, why isn't it an equal-protection violation?" If Souter wanted to make it any clearer to Boies what might be needed to entice Kennedy (or, possibly, O'Connor), the justice would've had to get up from the bench and walk to the lectern and bonk Boies over the head with a law book.

Yet Boies wouldn't go there. "Objective criteria," he said, didn't exist in Recountland, any more than they did in other areas of the law, including how juries and public officials went about making decisions.

Did that mean the same "physical characteristic" constituted a legal vote in one county but not the next? Souter inquired. Wasn't a dimple always a dimple?

"I don't think so," Boies insisted. That was because there wasn't evidence that counties were behaving that way. "Maybe if you had specific objective criteria in one county that said we're going to count indented ballots and another county that said we're only going to count the ballot if it's punched through—if you knew you had those two objective standards and they were different, then you might have an equal-protection problem."

Hallelujah! Boies was admitting the theoretical possibility of the problem, even if he was denying the factual reality that it had to happen with sixty-four counties recounting, almost half of them using punch-card voting systems.

Souter pointed out the obvious: "We can't send this thing back for more fact-finding." So, he said, he was going to assume the counties were acting inconsistently and in violation of equal protection. With that hypothesis, "we would have a responsibility to tell the Florida courts what to do about it.

"On that assumption," Souter asked one last time, "what would you tell them to do about it?"

"Well," Boies said, "that's a very hard question."

It took an awfully long time for him to come around to that unhelpful conclusion. And despite Boies later tepidly offering up the Texas chad standards as a guide, he had largely wasted whatever slender chance there might have been to win Kennedy over. You can't replay the inning—another first baseman might've missed Mookie Wilson's grounder just the same as Bill Buckner did, and the Red Sox still would've lost the game—but Souter and Breyer knew they had given Boies a chance, relentlessly so, and he had muffed it.

Despite the rancor in the Gore camp over the Court's decision to halt the counting in Florida, Boies never brought up the stay. He might have considered doing so—not to register a protest, but to respond to Rehnquist when asked how recounts could still be completed in time and then be reviewed by Judge Lewis and, if necessary, by appellate courts. Among the tools in any court's bag of equitable tricks is something called "tolling." This allows a court to extend deadlines when litigants are unable to satisfy them because of something that court did. If December 12 was considered to be the operational deadline (however erroneously), then the justices could easily have pushed this boundary back by exactly the interval that passed between the stay on Saturday, December 9, and when the Court ruled. "Tolling" is a commonplace judicial remedy. Good litigators think of it any time they know they can't meet a time constraint created by circumstances out of their control. Once Rehnquist raised the December 12 date, Boies should've asked the Court to toll it.

The obsession with December 12 was less a function of law than public relations. Twenty states, including the largest, California, wound up not meeting the deadline. Boies had cited December 12 back during the first oral argument at the Florida Supreme Court. Bush's lawyers happily did not object. It may be that the public didn't have the patience to go deeper into December or even January; the dates of December 18 (when the Electoral College met) or January 6 (when Congress convened to tally the electoral votes) were hardly part of the national consciousness. But Boies never seemed to even try out alternative dates.

Even Inauguration Day—the only date in all this prescribed by the Constitution rather than by statute—wasn't a drop-dead date. The Twentieth Amendment to the Constitution, passed in 1933, provided that Congress could select an acting president if nobody was yet "qualified" for the job. For example, the Speaker of the House or the Senate majority leader—both Republicans—could have handled the task. Or, as a law professor, NYU's Stephen Gillers, suggested on the *New York Times* Op-Ed page, "surely Bill Clinton would be willing to stay on for a few more weeks." Were the political odds high that Congress would invoke the Twentieth Amendment? Of course not. Could Gore's representatives have presented the case palatably to any court worried about December 12? Of course. The game for Gore was always to buy more time and, given that the U.S. Supreme Court brought the hammer down because time ran out, more time would've been a big help.

■ ■ ■

At half past noon Monday, the case of *Bush v. Gore* was adjourned and the nine justices got up to go pick the president.

Tommy Goldstein had managed to get Boies into the building without having to wait in line, and now he would do so on the way out. After the justices disappeared behind the velvet drapes, Goldstein asked a member of the clerk's staff to take him and Boies out of the courtroom and then downstairs through an exit near the gift shop. This avoided the bottleneck in the Great Hall on the main floor—and let Boies get to the TV cameras first.

Walter Dellinger, the former solicitor general, listened to the argument from the SG's offices at the Court, which had the privilege of receiving live audio of proceedings. Immediately afterward, he called Gore at his residence with a full play-by-play. "He was intensely interested, to put it mildly," Dellinger recalls. Dellinger explained to him that the ray of hope was Souter and Breyer "publicly suggesting a compromise in which the Court says there has to be a standard and then lets Florida set the standard." For Kennedy to go for that, Dellinger said, Souter and Breyer might drop in a little footnote ordering that any standard be relatively stiff, to include at least some penetration of a punchcard ballot. Dellinger hypothesized that such a coalition might then attract O'Connor and Rehnquist for the purposes of avoiding a 5-to-4 rupture along what looked like partisan lines. Such a result, Dellinger further explained, would make intervention by the Florida legislature less likely, for it would not want to be viewed as going behind the back of the U.S. justices. The news could've been worse, Gore thought.

A little while later, the vice president had Boies and his wife over to the Naval Observatory for lunch, joined by Joe Lieberman, Warren Christopher, Bill Daley, Ron Klain, and Frank Hunger. After lunch, Klain boarded a plane for Tallahassee, where he hoped to be working on a resumed recount in a day or two. Gore, Lieberman, and Boies then listened to an audiotape of the oral argument. Gore wanted to keep poring over it—if not for any strategic insights, then just to pass the time. For his part, Boies ruminated that he hadn't given "more specific examples" of chad standards used by other states. He remained a pessimist. On a clean slate, he believed he could get Kennedy, and maybe O'Connor, but not after the issuance of the stay. "They had already put their foot in the concrete," Boies says.

Elsewhere in Washington, in the weirdest photo op of the day, Florida governor Jeb Bush made an appearance in the Oval Office with Bill Clinton when the president signed a $7.8 billion bill to restore the Everglades. Neither man mentioned the big event in town, up Constitution Avenue at the Court. "A senior White House official who attended," reported the *Palm Beach Post*, "likened the Oval Office ceremony to a scene from a Fellini movie."

In Austin, as the audiotapes played on TV, George W. Bush left the state capitol for the gym. "I talked to our legal team," he told a crowd outside. "They are cautiously optimistic. If they are, I am."

In Tallahassee, committees in each house of the Florida legislature passed resolutions that, if approved by the full bodies over the next two days, would appoint a Bush slate of presidential electors—regardless of the outcome of the U.S. Supreme Court case. Whether that slate would conclusively trump anything the Florida Supreme Court did was one of the pivotal unanswered questions that made nervous Nellies speak of "constitutional crises." They weren't crises at all, just freaks of a system of government of separate branches. A crisis was when one branch of government ignored the order of another co-equal branch, or when an officeholder refused to transfer the reins of power after an election. Those sorts of things didn't happen in the stable American system. The worst that could happen in a clash between state supreme court and state legislature was that the Congress might have to be the arbiter, which was hardly a constitutional crisis, but rather the Constitution properly, if not neatly, at work.

If two slates of Florida electors arrived at Congress's doorstep on January 6, the Senate and House of Representatives would each have to settle which slate would be recognized. The GOP-controlled House would presumably go for Bush. But if the new Senate were divided 50–50 between Democrats and Republicans, it would be up to the individual presiding over the body to cast the deciding vote. The Constitution made that individual the vice president—actually, it was his only constitutional role as VP. Gore would be in the unbelievable position of deciding in favor of himself.

With the House and the Senate split between electoral slates, the one that had been "ascertained" by the governor of Florida would be the winner, again according to federal statute. That meant Bush won, unless the Florida Supreme Court declared his signature a nullity and ordered another state executive to sign in his place—maybe the state attorney general, Bob Butterworth, a Democrat—or maybe under the circumstances the Florida court would just sign for the slate itself. Most assuredly, it would be great theater and uncharted political terrain, but it still wouldn't be a constitutional crisis. In any event, by getting its own Bush slate ready, the Florida legislature was at least letting all the other branches know it stood ready to play its electoral card.

In the swirl of activity on this last Monday of the thirty-seven days, the least likely participants were the justices of the Florida Supreme Court. Acting as if they wished to have been in Washington defending their honor themselves, they issued a revised opinion in the first election appeal—the ruling that the U.S. Supreme Court had vacated and remanded a week earlier and that Sandra Day O'Connor that morning had castigated them for not yet revising. Late Monday afternoon, after they had heard the argument at the High Court, the Florida justices, by a 6-to-1 vote, took the cue and stated that their first ruling—extending the certification deadline—"was simply interpreting two conflicting election statutes," which, it noted, "were enacted long before the present election took place." The justices were not "making new law," they emphasized.

Unsurprisingly, they took exactly the tack that the 9-to-0 order of the U.S. Supreme Court had directed them to. It was fairly uncomplicated. So what had taken a week? In a defensively written footnote on the first page of its new opinion, the Florida Supreme Court explained that "we have issued this decision as expeditiously as possible" under the "time constraints" it then spelled out—there were the briefs in the contest appeal from Sanders Sauls's courtroom, the briefs for the vacate-and-remand, and then the oral argument and opinion in the contest. In the escalating intrajudicial feud between Washington and Tallahassee, both O'Connor's jibes and the footnote in the new state opinion seemed tonally in sync with the bickering of the presidential candidates. They were getting downright snippy about it.

Charles Wells, the Florida chief justice, dissented from his court's new opinion, even though it was essentially a restatement of the unanimous one his court issued on November 21. He chose not to explain himself, except to express his annoyance that the majority would release its opinion while the latest appeal was pending at the U.S. Supreme Court. It seemed disrespectful to him, which was especially unwise tactically, given the attitude of the Supreme Nine toward his court.

On Tuesday, everybody waited for the equivalent of white smoke to puff out of the U.S. Supreme Court. The candidates, the lawyers, the media, the Congress, the Florida legislature, the country—all assumed this would be the day, given its perceived significance on the electoral calendar, as well as the fact that last time the High Court took only one business day to rule.

In Tallahassee, the Florida Supreme Court disposed of its last election case. GOP campaign workers in Martin and Seminole Counties had been allowed by the canvassing boards before Election Day to add missing information to hundreds of preprinted voter forms for requesting absentee ballots. This violated the Florida election code. Gore supporters, though not the candidate himself, filed a contest lawsuit asking for *thousands* of absentee ballots to be disqualified; there wasn't any way to separate out ballots that had been tainted in the applications process. Two trial judges had rejected the lawsuits and, on this Tuesday, the Florida justices unanimously upheld those decisions—the fourth time they'd ruled against Gore at a critical moment. While the Martin and Seminole election officials had acted improperly, the justices said there was no evidence of fraud. Had the Florida Supreme Court gone the other way, at this late date Gore would have moved into the lead. It also might've made the impending ruling in Washington irrelevant.

At the U.S. Supreme Court, a hundred or so members of the press corps looked for any sign inside the marble temple that a decision was imminent. There's not much investigative reporting done around the place—the justices rarely give interviews, the law clerks sign in virtual blood that they'll never say a word, the Court police are trained to offer no comments on anything but Washington weather. So, when a justice

was seen departing the building, or any employee entered the courtroom, or the poinsettias were moved on the table where opinions were
usually distributed, the press room on the ground floor buzzed with
anticipation and presumed knowledge.

Around three in the afternoon, a reporter told Tommy Goldstein
that it looked like a decision was imminent, based on some scurrying-
about he'd seen among the public-information office staff. Goldstein
promptly called Boies, Tribe, and Klain to say what he'd heard, though
clearly didn't know. Within twenty minutes, the wire services and some
of the networks, citing "sources inside the Gore campaign," were
reporting that a decision was "imminent." Whoever Goldstein had told
in turn told others who leaked the "news" to the press. This was the
media cat chasing its tail—unintentionally manufacturing its own story,
which was supremely inaccurate.

In the chambers of the justices, most of the law clerks had worked all
night. Larry Kramer, a law professor at NYU, had long-standing
appointments Tuesday morning to interview clerks for teaching jobs.
They all showed, but one dozed off during the interview and the others
were zombies. Kramer, a clerk for Justice William Brennan fifteen years
earlier, couldn't help but be curious about what was going on in chambers. The various clerks—for Kennedy, O'Connor, Souter, and Ginsburg—couldn't let on anything, but Kramer knew they were under
great stress. It was a strange contrast to the festive atmosphere among
the civil servants in the Court as they put up the big Christmas tree in
the Great Hall the same day.

"Gee, you look tired," Kramer said to one of the clerks.

"I wonder why," was the dry reply.

As the campaigns and the country awaited the U.S. Supreme Court
ruling, Gore couldn't sit still. Now, into what Garrison Keillor referred
to as "the second month of Election Day," the events had just kept
building up. More than his opponent, who was laid back by nature but
who also realized he'd lucked out in Florida, Gore had been victimized
by a conspiracy of accidents in Florida. Now he needed to vent his
views and emotions, with whatever degree of optimism he could muster.

So on Tuesday afternoon, he decided to write an Op-Ed for the *New York Times*, on the assumption the Court would rule in his favor. "As I write this," it began, "I do not know what the Supreme Court will decide." Gore repeated the themes of the five-week post-election struggle: Count all the votes "so that the will of the people" was honored; work "for the agenda that Senator Lieberman and I put forward in the campaign," which fifty million Americans supported; and appreciate that history and the public trust and the "integrity" of the national government demanded he fight on after Election Day.

Gore acknowledged that "no single institution had been capable of solving" the electoral standoff and that this resulted in "continued uncertainty." But the greater good, he contended, was being served. Invoking Lincoln and Jefferson, he mused on the "consent of the governed" and the "wellspring of democracy," and how "We the People" were the very first words of the Constitution, a predicate on which other rights and responsibilities—and the institutions of government themselves—were based. Jefferson had "justified revolution" because the people of the colonies had not given their consent to be governed by George III. How could the U.S. Supreme Court justices "claim for themselves" the right to determine the presidency? It was up to the people. "Can we really give up on the 'consent of the governed'?" Gore asked. Counting the ballots was the only way to be faithful to the Constitution.

And then he concluded by quoting Lincoln's First Inaugural Address, delivered a month before Fort Sumter: "Why should there not be a patient confidence in the ultimate justice of the people? Is there any better or equal hope in the world?"

It was only a draft and Gore might have toned it down before publication, given its intimations of revolution and allusions to the Civil War. But it was strongly worded, all the more so as the justices of the U.S. Supreme Court had *Bush v. Gore* in front of them. The vice president phoned Walter Dellinger for counsel. "I've spent the last few hours writing an Op-Ed for tomorrow's *New York Times*," Gore told him. "Howell Raines [the editorial page editor] is holding space for it. I want your judgment on whether I ought to run this or not."

Dellinger liked it, suggested some changes that Gore punched into his laptop, and they were done. Gore said he would send it to Bill Daley for one last look. But he had one more question: "Is there anything else I need to think about?"

"As a lawyer, I wouldn't write an Op-Ed on a case I had argued that was pending at the Court. But, then, you're not the lawyer. You're the client, so there's no rule about keeping silent." Dellinger then added, "But still, you should be thinking about whether running this would *provoke* the Court." After all, it was Gore who'd told aides after the recounts had been halted over the weekend that no one in the campaign should "trash" the Court. Might this aggressive Op-Ed be regarded as the velvet-gloved equivalent?

"Okay, Walter, let me think about it."

Gore paused for only seconds, then made up his mind. He chuckled. Said the vice president of the United States about the Supreme Court: "—— 'em."

The few people in Goreworld who heard about his remark had the same reaction: If he'd shown that kind of animation during the campaign, he wouldn't have been in the position of having to make the remark.

The Op-Ed never ran. Before the *Times* closed the piece, it became moot. Just before 10 P.M., on December 12, the U.S. Supreme Court ruled. The justices did so not from the bench or in any other way that signified the magnitude of what they were doing. Instead, they went home beforehand, slithering out of view. They didn't even summarize their bottom line at the beginning of the ruling, as the Court almost always did in what's called a "headnote"; it wasn't that the Court aimed to be oblique, but that the whole thing was a rush job. That kind of unprecedented haste was why the Florida Supreme Court had gone about releasing its opinions differently. It knew something of stage management, if not legal logic. Whereas Craig Waters had read formal statements in Tallahassee indicating whether a lower-court decision had been upheld or overturned — and by what head count among the justices — the U.S. Supreme Court just put out stacks of the sixty-five-page ruling in the press office and left it up to the media to take it from there.

And what a job they did that night. Waving the potpourri of freshly issued opinions, TV reporters rushed out of the building to the bright lights and cameras waiting in front of the Court. The networks switched to them live, right away. Shivering in the December air, they furiously thumbed through the pages trying to decipher who won and whether it was final. It was as if the Clue board game had been adapted for play in the U.S. Supreme Court—Anthony Kennedy in chambers with a quill pen. Dan Rather, our old friend from Election Night, later explained to *USA Today* that CBS *had* to go on immediately. Sure, he'd considered waiting until the correspondent actually *read* the Court ruling, but "if you do that," he said, "competitively, you're just going to get killed."

The spectacle unfolded as some pretty smart journalists—many of them trained as lawyers—spent much of the next half hour trying to be certain what the justices had done, as the network anchors kept asking what-in-God's-name-was-going-on. Had anyone heard the phrase "confusion and disorder"? MSNBC had arranged for a staffer to be in the Court press office, ready to race any opinion out to Bob Kur on the Court plaza. "Here comes our runner!" Kur told Brian Williams back in the studio. The sacred scrolls arrived. Kur leafed through them. "Hang on, Brian! Looking for the summary!"

He never found one.

On ABC, Peter Jennings enlightened his viewers with the news that "we are in the midst of trying to sort this out." It was, he said, "quite frankly, not particularly easy." He turned to his two correspondents at the Court, Jackie Judd and Jeffrey Toobin. "Jackie," Jennings asked, "why don't you start?"

"Peter, I'm going to turn it over to Jeffrey."

To which Toobin replied, "I was hoping to turn it over to Jackie."

Very helpful. It was "like Mark Twain's famous line about wanting to write a shorter letter but not having time," wrote *USA Today*. "TV was so quick to break the news of the Court decision that it took forever to figure out what the decision was."

The vaudeville notwithstanding—a fitting last act for the media in these thirty-seven days—they did figure it out. The justices had split 5–4 for Bush, just as they had the prior Saturday when they stopped the recounts. There were to be no surprises—at least on the surface. (Jim Baker was incensed any time the media referred to *Bush v. Gore* as a 5-to-4 ruling. But even though seven justices did find an equal-protection problem, only five believed it couldn't be repaired. That disagreement over remedy was elemental and was the reason Breyer and Souter styled their opinion as full "dissents," rather than partial dissents and partial concurrences. Baker protested too much.)

Inside the Court, the law clerks were exhausted. In Souter's chambers, even though their justice had cast a mournful dissent, several clerks found a beer to share, just to celebrate the end of the ordeal. That's all they had, but it was enough to get them tipsy, given how tired they were.

One had to be a careful reader to find the ruling's essence—that the standardless recounts were an unconstitutional violation of equal protection and there was no time left for Florida to do anything about it. Not until the fourth page did the ruling even mention equal protection; not until three pages later was it discussed further. In retrospect, the best way to distill the meaning was to read not the main opinions, but the dissents. Page after page of the ruling was a rote recitation of the case history. (In the old days, even the Kremlin didn't do this good a job of burying its decisions in some long-winded edict.) There was no method to the Court's obtuseness—just proof that good writing takes time. Justices don't handle short deadlines well.

Despite its sixty-five pages, consisting of six different opinions, *Bush v. Gore* came down to another unsigned statement, just as the first election case before the High Court had. That one, however, was unanimous, as virtually all unsigned "per curiam" ("for the Court") orders were. This one, given the various signed concurrences and dissents that followed, was obviously the view of only Kennedy or O'Connor, or both, but it nonetheless represented the law of the land. Later, it became clear that Kennedy himself had drafted the opinion. The internal dynamics of the Court made sense. The four liberals wrote dissents: Breyer and Souter conceded there was an equal-protection problem (which is why a few commentators mistakenly said it was a 7-to-2 ruling), but one that should be sent back to Florida for repair; Ginsburg and Stevens argued more vociferously that the Court should have stayed out of this political thicket altogether. But how did the other five justify the result and how did they divvy up opinion writing?

In these historic cases, Rehnquist sometimes liked to write the main opinion. It wasn't merely his prerogative, but that his title alone—not chief justice of the Supreme Court, but chief justice of the United States—carried a certain imprimatur. In *Bush v. Gore*, he couldn't get it done, though for a time he thought he might. Rehnquist had circulated a draft of a majority opinion throwing out what the Florida Supreme Court had ordered. His arch-right brethren, Scalia and Thomas, agreed to sign it without hesitation. But Rehnquist would still need Kennedy and O'Connor to make five. He couldn't get them (that's why Rehnquist's opinion was only a concurrence). And, indeed, Kennedy wound up being more tempted to defect to the four dissenters than to go along with the Rehnquist trio. That reflected how intemperate the Rehnquist concurrence was in its upbraiding of the Florida justices.

Ginsburg harped on that in her dissent. She directed particular criticism at Rehnquist, citing him ten times. "I might join the chief justice were it my commission to interpret Florida law," she wrote. "But disagreement with the Florida court's interpretation of its own state's laws" was insufficient "warrant" for the U.S. Supreme Court to interfere, especially if the conservative justices' respect for "our system of dual sovereignty" was sincere. "The extraordinary setting of this case has obscured the ordinary principle that dictates its proper resolution: Federal courts defer to state high courts' interpretations of their state's own law. This principle reflects the core of federalism, on which all agree."

Rehnquist recognized he had to take that on, though he didn't mention Ginsburg by name. Along with Scalia and Thomas, he had made a living on the Supreme Court holding forth on the virtues of federalism and the rights of the states. So, at the outset, he defended his hypocritical intrusion into Florida's business. "In most cases, comity and respect for federalism compel us to defer to the decisions of state courts on issues of state law," he wrote. But this was no "ordinary election," but one for president and vice president—"the only elected officials who represent all the voters in the nation."

Under that pretext, Rehnquist ran wild over the Florida Supreme Court, whose interpretation of state election law he called "of course absurd," "distorted," "peculiar," and "perhaps delusive." The Florida justices had violated the U.S. Constitution, a federal statute, state law, and common sense. They had usurped the state legislature's authority; wrongly second-guessed Katherine Harris; "shortchanged" the contest period; and "emptied" the state's certification of Bush "of virtually all legal consequence during the contest," despite previously concluding—by extending the certification deadline—that certification was "a matter of significance." By contrast, Rehnquist wrote, the Florida legislature had "created a detailed, if not perfectly crafted, statutory scheme." And as for Harris, she was simply performing her duties as "authorized by law," compared to Bob Butterworth, the state attorney general, who "was supporting the Gore challenge."

As frequently happened at the Court, Kennedy wouldn't go as far as his strident colleagues. So he produced a separate opinion, to which O'Connor agreed not to object. But unlike the rest of the justices, and despite their assent becoming decisive, neither Kennedy's nor O'Connor's name appeared anywhere in *Bush v. Gore*. Since the Kennedy opinion reached the same conclusion as that of the three hard-liners—no more recounts—Rehnquist, Scalia, and Thomas could join it and, with O'Connor's acquiescence, it would become the "per curiam" ruling. Unfortunately, the overall effect of the fragmented majority was to prove that while they agreed on a result, they had no governing rationale. Supreme Court rulings that are edicts in search of a reason don't make for convincing reads.

The weakest part of what both the Kennedy and Rehnquist factions wrote was that they never bothered to explain *why* they were ruling in the first place. It wasn't enough to try to tell the American people what the guarantee of equal protection meant and why it was relevant to the recount—though articulating those things was a fine idea. The more crucial mission should've been to defend how it was that the justices—as opposed to Congress or the Florida legislature—were the right ones to untie the electoral knot. The fact was, *any* institution that resolved the election was going to be viewed as partisan by 50 percent of the public: Half the people will always believe that more Florida voters intended to select Gore, and half the people will always believe that more properly executed ballots recorded votes for Bush. This irreconcilable division should have given the U.S. Supreme Court all the more incentive to keep from being singed.

But the twin notions of "judicial restraint" and "separation of powers" don't even make an appearance in the Kennedy and Rehnquist opinions—the notions weren't even raised to be swatted down. Stevens, in dissent, drove home the points. The Court's ruling, he said, "can only lend credence to the most cynical appraisal of the work of judges throughout the land. It is confidence in the men and women who administer the judicial system that is the true backbone of the rule of law. . . . Although we may never know with complete certainty the identity of the winner of this year's presidential election, the identity of the loser is perfectly clear. It is the nation's confidence in the judge as an impartial guardian of the rule of law." Neither Kennedy nor Rehnquist so much as referred to Stevens.

In past crises of legitimacy, it was the failure of the justices to be persuasive about why they inserted themselves in a political dispute that imperiled them. That was the lesson of the 1876 election, when the vote cast by one justice, sitting on a special electoral commission, awarded the presidency to Rutherford B. Hayes. In a "highly politicized matter" like *Bush v. Gore*, Breyer wrote in his dissent, echoing Stevens, "the appearance of a split decision runs the risk of undermining the public's confidence in the Court itself. That confidence is a public treasure. It has been built slowly over many years, some of which were marked by a Civil War and the tragedy of segregation. It is a vitally necessary ingredient of any successful effort to protect basic liberty and, indeed, the rule of law itself." The justices needed only to look to the Florida Supreme Court to see what happened when the patina of neutrality was washed off a tribunal.

Just because you have the power doesn't mean it has to be exercised; sometimes the best use of power is not using it. Louis Brandeis, a former justice, liked to say, "The most important thing we do is not doing"—a refrain of restraint to which Breyer now added, "What the Court does today, the Court should have left undone." Over the generations, the Court's authority has been derived from its ability to explicate the foundation of its rulings based on constitutional language. It wasn't sufficient to dictate an outcome, as Congress did in legislation, or the president by executive orders or military command. The Supreme Court was the only branch of the national government expected to explain, not merely decree.

Most of us could agree on any number of political and cultural ills— an irrational tax code, the unfairness of health-care distribution, toddlers at fancy restaurants, the designated-hitter rule in baseball. We might even agree on the appropriate solutions to them. But that doesn't mean they're proper concerns for a court, let alone a federal court. Not every problem, major or minor, has in its origin—or cure—a constitutional "principle." The incredible thing about *Bush v. Gore* is that in this unique case, where the Court should have gone out of its way to say why it was intervening, the majority offered up nothing. That unexplained arrogation of power, as much as putative partisanship, was the keystone of *Bush v. Gore.*

So was its apparent disdain for the Florida justices. Underlying the U.S. Supreme Court's "entire federal assault on the Florida election procedures," Stevens wrote, "is an unstated lack of confidence in the impartiality and capacity of the state judges who would make the critical decisions if the vote count were to proceed." Outrage at supreme courts in the South was one thing in the 1950s and '60s, when rulings sometimes were blatantly designed to avoid federal civil rights laws. The U.S. Supreme Court then intervened. But, as Ginsburg noted, the Florida Supreme Court "surely should not be bracketed with state high courts of the Jim Crow South." Moreover, to the extent that any justice worried that Florida judges were outlaws, there was little to fret over. Nothing a Florida court did would be dispositive on the state's slate of electors. Congress would always have the final word.

When Kennedy, in the thirteen-page per curiam opinion, got around to discussing equal protection, he noted that an individual's right to vote for presidential electors came not from the Constitution itself, but from the eventual decisions by state legislatures to relinquish that right themselves. This was an implicit dig by Kennedy at both Gore's and the Florida Supreme Court's propensity for invoking the "will of the people." Once individuals had the privilege of picking the electors, Kennedy wrote, their respective votes had to be accorded "equal weight" and "equal dignity." Having "granted the right to vote on equal terms," he said, "the state may not, by later arbitrary and disparate treatment, value one person's vote over that of another." According to Kennedy, citing both Boies's admission at oral argument and the dissent by Florida's chief justice, the recount procedures ordered by the Florida

Supreme Court did precisely that. Palm Beach provided the best evidence, where, Kennedy said, "the process began with a 1990 guideline which precluded counting completely attached chads, switched to a rule that considered a vote to be legal if any light could be seen through a chad, changed back to the 1990 rule, and then abandoned any pretense of a *per se* rule."

The process struck Kennedy as farce. "The recount mechanisms implemented in response to the decisions of the Florida Supreme Court do not satisfy the minimum requirement for non-arbitrary treatment of voters necessary to secure the fundamental right" of voting, he wrote. The mere incantation of following the "intent of the voter" was "unobjectionable as an abstract proposition and a starting principle," but not without "specific standards to ensure" equal treatment for voters. "The formulation of uniform rules to determine intent," Kennedy concluded, was "practicable" and "necessary."

But isn't evaluating "intent" inherently subjective? Kennedy argued that assessing a witness's testimony at trial is thoroughly different from interpreting "marks or holes or scratches on an inanimate object." How so? "The fact-finder confronts a thing, not a person." It wasn't much of a distinction—and Kennedy said nothing more about it. Nor, tellingly, did he think through what he really meant by equal protection. Just what was the exact harm of, say, County A counting a dimpled chad as a legal vote and County B not doing so? The worst that could happen is that ballots in County B would remain invalid. Which candidate did that hurt, though? (Remember, it was the candidates who brought the lawsuits.) Was there not the same probability of those ballots going for either Bush or Gore? The fact is, neither would suffer more harm as a result of County B running its recount differently from County A— *unless* the greater risk was to Bush because he was the guy *ahead*. Kennedy's equal-protection logic sounded a lot like Scalia's embarrassing attempt the prior Saturday to justify halting the recounts.

Consider as well what Kennedy had as an alternative to the manual recounts: doing nothing. Was directing that all undervotes remain uncounted—though this treated *them* equally—fairer, given that nearly six million *other* voters around the state did have their ballots counted? It was only reasonable if you believed that a human mistake in punch-card voting weighed decisively against that ballot even having a chance to be manually examined. This didn't seem to comport with Kennedy's initial proclamation that the "right to vote" was "fundamental."

Furthermore, was it truly *human* error if punch-card ballots consistently registered undervotes up to eight times more often than optical-scan ballots? Didn't that sound more like a mistake born of design or technology—and, if so, why wasn't that disparity in the accuracy of voting systems *itself* a violation of equal protection that, according to Kennedy's reasoning, would require the results of the entire state to be scrapped? There was no compelling reason for different voting systems, except the indulgence of laziness and cost cutting—surely insufficient justification for effectively denying the "fundamental" right to vote. "In a system that allows counties to use different types of voting systems," Breyer wrote in dissent, "voters already arrive at the polls with an unequal chance that their votes will be counted." One could even insist that, based on Kennedy's opinion, hand recounts were constitutionally *mandated* because of the voting-rights violation inherent in voters in different counties being subjected to machines that varied in their ability to read ballots. There had never been any cases like this before—no yardsticks by which the Court could measure its instincts, which during the Rehnquist regime had been to *restrict* equal-protection rights—so Kennedy, at best, was making judgments based on his gut. It didn't say a lot for his gut.

On December 4, the U.S. Supreme Court had warned their Florida brethren not to make changes in the state's election law, but it said nothing about equal protection, even declining to accept briefs on that question. Now, a mere eight days later, with Kennedy saying the "new law" issue was beside the point, the High Court was finding equal protection to be determinative. It was no wonder many of the Florida justices felt they had been sandbagged.

If the recounts were defective only because of the absence of standards, couldn't Kennedy's objection be remedied by another remand to Florida? Would it not be possible for the state supreme court, together with Judge Terry Lewis and the canvassing boards, to cobble together enough rules to pass Kennedian muster? No time, said the justices' order. It was, lo and behold, just two hours before the December 12 safe harbor closed. But whose fault was *that*?

Twenty days earlier, in the first election case, Bush had asked the U.S.

Supreme Court to step into the presidential dispute. Yet only now were Gore or the Florida justices—or the nation—hearing anything from the Court about equal protection. Moreover, seventy-nine hours before, the Court had stopped the recounts by way of an emergency stay, robbing the canvassing board and Judge Lewis of precious time. Kennedy didn't attempt to address any of these facts; instead, he took another dig at the Florida Supreme Court. The time period for the contest proceeding before Judge Sanders Sauls was "truncated" because of the Florida justices' efforts in the first election case, he argued. By forcing Katherine Harris to extend the certification deadline—at Gore's *"own urging,"* Kennedy emphasized—the Florida justices had no one to blame but themselves for having to cut corners on the statewide recount they'd ordered up three days before the December 12 deadline. In any event, Kennedy said, "a desire for speed is not a general excuse for ignoring equal-protection guarantees."

And what of the alleged deadline? The dissents by both Breyer and Souter maintained that December 18 was fine and that Florida might get its recounting act together in a six-day period. In another dissent, Stevens pointed out that, after the 1960 presidential election, Congress had accepted a slate of electors from Hawaii on January 4, long after the safe-harbor deadline and when the Electoral College met.

Yet Kennedy scoffed. He maintained that the Florida Supreme Court itself had found that "the Florida Legislature intended to obtain the safe-harbor benefits" of the Electoral Count Act, so it was that interpretation that would govern. But the Florida justices had done nothing of the sort. At most, they had made passing reference to December 12; and the legislature itself had nothing on the books to that effect. And since when, anyway, did the Florida justices suddenly get deference from the U.S. Supreme Court? Even if it were true that the Florida justices previously had wanted to honor the safe harbor—a benefit that the state legislature had never mentioned in the election code— the circumstances had now changed. Perhaps, in balancing that presumption on one hand against a desire to "count all the votes" on the other, the Florida justices would decide the safe harbor could be ignored. At the very least, wasn't it up to them to say what they had meant? Kennedy's one-paragraph dismissal of an alternative date bordered on the mystifying or downright disingenuous.

So, too, did his remarkable disclaimer that the Court's expansive new holding about equal protection in elections was "limited to the present circumstances"—a snowflake that melted before it hit the ground. That isn't the way the Court does business. Because it is the top court in the nation and because it decides fewer than one hundred cases a year, it both has to select appeals that will have broad application to other litigation and has to write opinions to guide judges in the lower courts (as well as the Supreme Court itself). Rulings that are confined to a single moment and one set of litigants—in "the same class as a restricted railroad ticket, good for this day and train only," as Justice Owen Roberts put it in a famous 1944 dissent—not only squander the Court's time, but open it up to attack that its decision making is unprincipled and result-driven.

Scalia could have told Kennedy all that. "The Supreme Court of the United States does not sit to announce 'unique' circumstances," he thundered in a lone dissent from a ruling that made the Virginia Military Institute co-ed. "Its principal function is to establish precedent—that is, to set forth principles of law that every court in America must follow. . . . That is the principal reason we publish our opinions." Yet *Bush v. Gore*, the Court instructed, had no precedent-making, as opposed to president-making, value.

It was not surprising that the *Bush v. Gore* majority might worry about the logic of its ruling, so wholly unreceptive as the five justices had long been to expanding any voting rights under the Fourteenth Amendment. The five conservatives believed that voting disputes were the province of the elected branches. But *Bush v. Gore* seemed totally disconnected from any prior opinions. And the justices wanted to make sure it remained unmoored from anything that might follow. "The problem of equal protection in election processes generally presents many complexities," Kennedy wrote, purportedly explaining why the ruling was "limited to the present circumstances." But that was mush—generalities wrapped in platitudes inside a haze. Of course the transmogrification of electoral inequalities into constitutional violations is "complex." Carried to its extremes, the *Bush v. Gore* rationale could invalidate most statewide elections in America, run as they are at the county level. Why should recounts be treated any differently from the initial counts known as elections? Standards are standards.

States, counties, and even local communities use different voting machines, tabulation equipment, and ballot designs; lines are short in affluent neighborhoods and around the block in poorer precincts; the polls are open for twelve hours in some places, fifteen in the next; election officials have varying degrees of experience. Lurking behind many of the inequities, intentional or otherwise, is their disparate effect on blacks, which has always been the lodestar of equal-protection jurisprudence; African-Americans tend to live in poorer areas, which tend to have less reliable voting equipment. But the Court had never found that local variations in "election processes," unless specifically animated by bias, were actionable.

So, for Kennedy and the other four justices to declare a bold change in the law that worked to the *detriment* of blacks and minorities in Florida in this presidential election—and, in the next breath, to say that the revolutionary principle could never be used again—was more than ironic. It was brazen. It seemed to prove that *Bush v. Gore* wasn't about "equal protection" at all—only the realpolitik end of putting the Republican in the White House and ensuring that he'd be naming new justices for the next four years. This, in effect, was the conservatives choosing their potential successors.

It didn't take a cynic to believe the Court majority *had* actually thought through the consequences of its ruling, didn't like what it saw, so issued a this-train-only doctrinal ticket. More than quelling chaos, this would be result-oriented judging at its naked worst. It was ludicrous for Kennedy to conclude his opinion with the statement that "none" stood "more in admiration" than the justices of "the Constitution's design to leave the selection of the president" to "the people."

What if Gore had led by 537 votes and Bush sought a recount? What would the U.S. Supreme Court have done in that case? To play out the hypothetical fairly, you have to go back to the Florida Supreme Court. What would the justices there have done if confronted with reverse political facts? Assume they, too, unavoidably, were partisans, however much they tried not to be. Their ruling, then, would've been to thwart any recounting—Gore would have his victory. Bush would then appeal to the U.S. Supreme Court, petitioning to "count all the votes."

While there's no way to know for sure, does anybody really doubt that the High Court would still have come out 5–4 for Bush? Except that this time, instead of equal-protection prattle, there would be constitutional homilies about the sanctity of votes—precisely the opposite of what the justices said with Bush leading by 537 votes. The only constant with the actual *Bush v. Gore* would be bashing the Florida Supreme Court. Maybe the five conservative justices would have set a uniform chad standard themselves or maybe they would've ordered the Florida justices to do so, but they would have found a way to give Bush a shot. And the December 12 deadline would've given way to December 18 or beyond. In the final analysis, the Court would have exercised its power as it pleased.

Given the inescapable partisanship of the decision, the amazing aspect of *Bush v. Gore* is that it just might have gone the other way. Kennedy wavered, enough that Souter thought until the very end that he'd get him, and that the 5-to-4 ruling for Bush would become a 5-to-4 verdict for Gore. They'd find an equal-protection violation, send the case back to the Florida justices to fix standards and administer the best recount they could under the circumstances and before December 18, and then leave it to the political branches—the Florida legislature and, if need be, the U.S. Congress—to settle it for good.

A month after the decision, Souter met at the Court with a group of prep-school students from Choate. He told them how frustrated he was that he couldn't broker a deal to bring in one more justice—Kennedy being the obvious candidate. Souter explained that he had put together a coalition back in 1992, in *Planned Parenthood v. Casey*, the landmark abortion case in which the Court declined by a 5-to-4 vote to overturn *Roe v. Wade*; Souter, along with O'Connor and Kennedy, made the unusual gesture of writing a joint opinion for the majority.

If he'd had "one more day—*one more day*," Souter now told the Choate students, he believed he would have prevailed. Rehnquist, Thomas, and Scalia had long ago become part of the Dark Side. O'Connor seemed beyond compromise. But Kennedy seemed within reach. *Just give me twenty-four more hours on the clock*. While a political resolution to the election—in the Florida legislature or in the Congress—might not be quick and it might be a brawl, Souter argued that the nation would still accept it. "It should be a political branch that issues political decisions," he said to the students. Kennedy, though, wouldn't flip. He thought the trauma of more recounts, more fighting—more *politics*, as it were—was too much for the country to endure.

In the end, the margin of victory for George W. Bush wasn't 154, 165, 193, or 204 votes (depending on what numbers you believe from the abbreviated recounts). Nor was the operative margin Katherine Harris's initial number, 930. The sands of history will show Bush won by a single vote, cast in a 5-to-4 ruling of the U.S. Supreme Court. The vote was Tony Kennedy's. One justice had picked the president.

In a hotel in suburban Virginia, near the makeshift Bush transition office, Karl Rove, the campaign's political guru, was watching MSNBC at 10 P.M. when the Court ruling was first announced. He called Bush in Texas; the governor was watching CNN, which took longer to decipher the opinions. "This is good news," Rove told Bush. "This is *great* news."

"No, no, this is bad news," Bush replied. Rove was the first person Bush talked to as the verdict came in—Bush had no sense initially that he'd just been declared the winner by the stroke of the Court's pen. It was very confusing. "Where are you now?" he asked Rove.

"In the McLean Hilton—standing in my pajamas."

"Well, I'm in my pajamas, too," said the new president-elect.

Rove laughed at the vision of them both, at this historic moment, in their PJs.

Soon enough, Bush talked to Baker, who talked to Ted Olson and the other lawyers on the team. Within half an hour, Bush was convinced Gore had finally run out of tricks.

At the vice presidential residence, Gore took the night to consider his options. He worked the phones, and read and reread the Court opinions. Among his top advisers, Ron Klain took the hardest line and said the campaign could still go back to the Florida Supreme Court one more time; as a contingency, legal briefs had been in the works since the weekend. Maybe the justices could be convinced to disavow any prior ruling that had suggested December 12 was a real deadline—that is, if the Florida justices were even willing to go near this train wreck again. Klain also raised the possibility of a lawsuit to block the Florida legislature from declaring a Bush slate of electors.

Nobody else in the legal command—Bill Daley, Warren Christopher,

David Boies, Larry Tribe, Walter Dellinger, or Frank Hunger—held out the slightest hope. To carry on at this point would only hurt Gore's chances in 2004, should he decide he wanted to subject himself to this torment again.

On Wednesday night, December 13, Al Gore conceded the election for good. From inside the Old Executive Office Building, adjacent to the White House, he registered his "strong" disagreement with the Supreme Court, paid tribute to his late father, and offered congratulations to the president-elect. "I promised him that I wouldn't call him back this time," Gore said, with the self-deprecation he'd seldom shown since Election Day.

He even used the "concession" word. A few congressmen and senators—"the real Shiites," as Gore's speechwriter, Eli Attie, dubbed them—had urged the vice president to defiantly avoid the C-word.

An hour after Gore's concession, Bush spoke to the nation and, after graciously acknowledging "how difficult this moment must be for Vice President Gore and his family," he claimed the victory he thought he'd won thirty-seven days earlier.

Three days before Christmas, the Florida Supreme Court closed the books on *Bush v. Gore*, formally dealing with the order that the U.S. Supreme Court had issued on December 12. This final ruling went virtually unnoticed in the media.

Because "the Florida election code did not provide the elements necessary for a resolution of the disputed issues, based on the constitutional parameters expressed" by the U.S. Supreme Court, the Florida justices unanimously dismissed the contests. It sounded as if everybody was to blame for what had happened—or, more accurately, had not happened—except the justices themselves. They also seemed to suggest they never would've considered another round of appeals by Gore. For now, they'd found religion. "Upon reflection," the justices stated, "we conclude that the development of a specific, uniform standard necessary to ensure equal application" should be left to the Florida legislature, "the body we believe best equipped to study and address it."

Two Florida justices wrote at length, getting to have the last judicial word on *Bush v. Gore.* They wanted desperately to defend their institution. Justice Leander Shaw, who had dissented from his court's ordering of a statewide recount, nonetheless took issue with the U.S. Supreme Court. He said December 12 "was not a 'drop-dead' date under Florida law" and the emphasis on a safe-harbor deadline was misplaced. He had a point: Under the Electoral Count Act, Congress had to accept a state's electoral slate on January 6, unless there were competing slates. If Bush were to win the manual recounts, he'd be the next president anyway, period.

Shaw's disagreement with the recounts was based only on his belief that the equal-protection problems were insurmountable. In that, he was sorrowful. "The present case posed a simple question: Who won the presidential election in Florida?" he wrote. "The truth lies in the vaults and storage rooms throughout the state where the untabulated ballots of thousands of Floridians are sequestered. . . . All the king's horses and all the king's men could not get a few thousand ballots counted. . . . We still—to this day—cannot agree on how to count those ballots fairly and accurately. In fact, we cannot even agree on *if* they should be counted."

Justice Barbara Pariente, who had enthusiastically supported the statewide recount, tried to be upbeat and offer suggestions to the legislature on reforming the election code. Including the only poem cited in the presidential litigation—John Greenleaf Whittier's nineteenth-century "The Poor Voter on Election Day" ("To-day, of all the weary year, A king of men am I . . . My palace is the people's hall, The ballot-box my throne!")—she lamented the "vulnerability" of American elections, given the defects in voting machines and technology. If countries like Canada, Mexico, and India had "more modern, uniform and efficient methods of making sure that every vote is counted," couldn't Florida and the rest of the nation? She could've noted as well that the United States is one of the few places that allowed partisans to run elections; in most countries, neutral officials are in charge, even at the local level. Pariente also urged Congress to revisit the safe-harbor deadlines it had established 113 years earlier—"in a far different time," when the country had far fewer people.

And that was the end of it for the Florida Supreme Court. By the autumn of 2001, the justices were back to the more mundane business of reviewing death penalties, corporate disputes, and referendum initiatives that the public was proposing for Election Day 2002. It had been a long, unfantastic journey. The court that had been involved in selecting a president now would have to decide whether Florida could have a referendum on a constitutional amendment declaring that pregnant pigs in captivity had legal rights.

When Ron Klain came home to Washington after Gore's concession, his seven-year-old, Michael, was infuriated with him. "So, Daddy, what did you do in the recount wars?" wasn't one of his questions. It was bad enough Dad went missing so much of the fall, but he'd promised to come home the day after Election Day; instead, he stayed gone for five more weeks. On the third or fourth night after Klain returned, Mike lit into him with a litany of Events Dad Had Missed. "It was a very impressive five-minute monologue," Klain recalls.

"Mike," Klain asked his son, the middle child, "isn't Rob your best friend?"

"Yeah, Rob's my best friend."

"What would you do if someone took something that belonged to Rob—what would you do?"

Mike thought about it a little. "I'd try to help him get it back," he said.

"Well, Mike, Al Gore is my friend and somebody took something that belonged to him, and I had to go help him to get it back."

"But Al Gore's not your friend. When you left working for him, he was mean to you. And George Bush didn't take anything that belonged to him. George Bush got more votes—that's why he's our president."

Klain figured out that he wasn't going to debate his way out of this. The son despised all things Florida. If there were a game on TV and a team was from Florida, Mike would root against it; he voted against a family excursion to Disney World planned for spring break. But when Klain managed to get two tickets for the Super Bowl, which was to be played in Tampa in January 2001, they both went. "That," noted the father, "ended Mike's anti-Florida-itis."

The fact that Mike was seven was something Klain ruminated about that winter. When he was that age, growing up in Indianapolis in 1968, a presidential candidate named Robert F. Kennedy visited his dad's plumbing-supply house. A black-and-white photo of little Ronnie and RFK that day hangs in Klain's office now. "My first taste of politics got me interested in it," Klain says. Mike's first taste was another story.

■ ■ ■

A few weeks after *Bush v. Gore* was issued, the basement gift shop at the U.S. Supreme Court—which offers souvenir portraits of the justices, the "Equal Justice Coffee Mug," "Due Process" erasers, "Supreme Court Marble Trinket Boxes" ($48.95, in black or white), *and* Courtney O'Connor's very own book *Meet My Grandmother: She's a Supreme Court Justice* ("find out what Justice O'Connor does when she is at work")—had a special sale item for tourists. It was a fancier version of the pocket Constitution of the United States of America that the late Justice Hugo Black had made famous decades earlier. Black liked to say his job was pretty straightforward: Just look at this here Constitution.

These little blue books are a staple of the gift shop, normally priced at $9.95. However, on this day, a sign above them read, "Special: U.S. Constitutions—Closeout." Maybe it was somebody's idea of a joke.

Deus ex Machina

In *late March* 2001, the 116th annual dinner of the Gridiron Club in Washington promised to be extraspecial, as members of the new administration gathered with the political and media establishment. As was customary, the recently inaugurated president and vice president both attended.

At one of the head tables sat Justice Anthony Kennedy. In contrast to a colleague like David Souter, he loved these kinds of events, which were part of the trappings of office. Seated next to him was supposed to be Joe Lieberman, but the senator didn't show until quite late.

"It was the Sabbath," Lieberman explained to Kennedy, shaking his hand as he arrived.

"I'm glad you're here," kidded Kennedy. "I was afraid you were home drafting a petition for rehearing."

"Maybe I should do that when I get back," retorted the defeated vice presidential candidate.

Kennedy said nothing. He didn't like being upstaged. As always, as the political alignment of the U.S. Supreme Court allowed him to be, he was the center of his own universe.

■ ■ ■

Two months earlier there was a more important gathering in Washington. It was a meeting known only to the participants and their staffs, as well as a few translators and guests. It got no press coverage and the matters discussed during it have remained secret since. Yet in illuminating how *Bush v. Gore* came to be, it was the seminal event. It happened in January as Inauguration Day approached—after the thirty-seven days of Florida, but while emotions were still raging. It was the time when the members of the U.S. Supreme Court let their guards down, without knowing they were providing an X ray into their hearts.

The American justices were playing host to special visitors from Russia. Their guests were six judges, all part of that country's decade-long experiment with freedom after Communism. It was the fifth gathering between the judges and their counterparts at the U.S. Supreme Court—an attempt by the most powerful tribunal in the world to impart some of its accumulated wisdom to a nascent system trying to figure out how constitutional law really works in a democracy. It was by no means obvious, as Alexis de Tocqueville had noted 165 years earlier. To outsiders, the idea that unelected judges who serve for life can ultimately dictate the actions of the other two branches of American government, both popularly elected, was nothing short of unbelievable.

These were always collegial meetings inside the Supreme Court. This time—over the course of two days, January 9 and 10—seven American justices participated, everyone but David Souter and Clarence Thomas. The justices from the Constitutional Court of the Russian Federation were Yuri Rudkin, Nikolai Seleznev, Oleg Tyunov, and Gennady Zhilin; the two other judges were Salman Gadzhimagomedov, chairman of the Constitutional Court of the Republic of Dagestan, and Teimuraz Chedzhemov, chairman of the Constitutional Supervision Committee of the Republic of Northern Ossetia-Alania. They all met in the Court's private ceremonial conference rooms: for an informal reception, the blue-motif West Conference Room; for hours of discussions about law and American heritage, the rose-motif East Conference Room, with a portrait of the legendary nineteenth-century chief justice John Marshall hung over the fireplace.

But this year, the discussions weren't about general topics such as due process or free expression or separation of powers. Some of the Russians wanted to know how *Bush v. Gore* had come to pass—how it was that somebody other than the electorate decided who ran the government. That was the kind of thing that gave Communism a bad name. "In *our* country," a Russian justice said, bemused, "we wouldn't let judges pick the president." The justice added that he knew that, in various nations, judges were in the pocket of executive officials—he just didn't know that was so in the United States. It was a supremely ironic moment.

Bush v. Gore was the elephant in the room. The ruling was on the minds of the Russians, but would it be rude to raise it? Once one of them did, it elicited an extraordinary exchange, played out spontaneously and viscerally among the American justices, according to people in the room. It could have been a partial replay of the *Bush v. Gore* conference itself, where the ruling was cast.

Justices don't typically discuss their decisions with others. That's because all their views are supposed to be within the four corners of their written opinions. Even more so, a good legal opinion isn't supposed to need further explanation. Memorialized in the law books—given a formal case name and citations to a volume and first page—an opinion of the Court speaks for itself for future jurists and generations to see. But *Bush v. Gore*, 531 U.S. 98 (2000), was so lean in its analysis, so unconvincing in its reasoning, that it led all manner of observers to wonder just where the Court had been coming from. That may be why some of the justices so readily engaged their official guests.

Stephen Breyer was angry and launched in with an attack on the decision, right in front of his colleagues. It was "the most outrageous, indefensible thing" the Court had ever done, he told the visiting judges. "We all agree to disagree, but this is different." Breyer was defiant, brimming with confidence that he had been right in his long dissent. "However awkward or difficult" it might have been for Congress to resolve the presidency, Breyer had written, "Congress, being a political body, expresses the people's will far more accurately than does an unelected Court. And the people's will is what elections are about." To have judges do it instead—as the country learned in the Hayes-Tilden stalemate—not only failed to legitimize the outcome, but stained the judiciary. That was "a self-inflicted wound" harming "not just the Court, but the nation," he said.

In contrast to Breyer, Ruth Bader Ginsburg was more baffled than annoyed, attempting to rationalize the legitimacy of the ruling that so ripped away her confidence in the neutrality of the Court. "Are we so highly political, after all?" she said. "We've surely done other things, too, that were activist, but here we're applying the Equal Protection Clause in a way that would delegitimize virtually every election in American history."

"I'm so tired," offered John Paul Stevens. "I am just so exhausted." His weariness may have reflected the fact he was the oldest member of the Court, at eighty—or that he'd been fighting these battles for twenty-four years, and the number he won was decreasing.

Sandra Day O'Connor talked pedantically about the Electoral College, which, of course, had nothing to do with the Russians' curiosity. William Rehnquist and Antonin Scalia—the intellectual firebrands on the Court's right flank—said almost nothing, leaving it up to a floundering Kennedy to try to explain a 5-to-4 ruling in which he was the decisive vote, the justice who gave the presidency to George W. Bush. The virtual silence of Rehnquist and Scalia led some in the room to wonder if the two justices were basically admitting their ruling was intellectually insupportable, all the more in a setting where there might be give-and-take. Maybe they didn't think this was the right forum or audience in which to engage a debate. In any event, Justice Kennedy was left holding the bag.

"Sometimes you have to be *responsible* and step up to the plate," Kennedy told the Russians, adorning himself with the mantle of statesmanship. "You have to take *responsibility*." He prized order and stability. Chaos and commotion were the enemies. This was vintage Kennedy, who loved to thump his chest about the burden of it all. For example, back in the controversial 1989 decision that flag burning was protected by the First Amendment, Kennedy joined the 5-to-4 majority, but dramatized his discomfort. "This case, like others before us from time to time, exacts its personal toll," he wrote. "The hard fact is that sometimes we must make decisions we do not like." A long *New Yorker* profile of him carried the title "The Agonizer." Then there was his opening line in the 1992 Casey opinion on abortion: "Liberty finds no refuge in a jurisprudence of doubt"—minutes before the issuance of which came his self-comparison to Caesar "about to cross the Rubicon."

Everything Kennedy did or thought seemed to him to carry great weight. It had to—he was a justice of the United States Supreme Court. It was as if Kennedy kept telling himself, and us, that—but for him and his role—the Republic might topple. In *Bush v. Gore*, that meant entering the breach to save the Union from an electoral muddle that could go on for many weeks more. The equal-protection stuff? That was the best he could come up with on short notice. It was apparently no big deal that there was another branch of the government right across the street—that was democratically elected, politically accountable, and specifically established by the Constitution, as well as by federal statute, to finally determine a disputed presidential election. "Congress" wasn't even mentioned in the Kennedy opinion, or for that matter in Rehnquist's concurrence. Congress was the appropriate, co-equal branch not because it was wisest or fairest, but because it was legitimate. It was *us*. It is *us*. The Supreme Court's very independence rendered it the worst—and most dangerous—branch to resolve who would be the *political* chief executive of the country.

What was Kennedy's explanation for becoming the deus ex machina? It was George W. Bush and Al Gore who should be blamed for bringing their problems to the Court. "When contending parties invoke the process of the courts," he wrote, "it becomes our unsought responsibility to resolve the federal and constitutional issues the judicial system has been forced to confront." That was theatrical nonsense. The justices refuse to hear 99 percent of the appeals they're asked to take. Since 1925, their discretion has been unbridled—they can decline to take a case because it fails to raise significant issues, because the questions involved are purely state affairs, because they've decided a similar appeal in recent years, or for no reason at all. Accepting jurisdiction in the presidential election of 2000 showed not respect for the rule of law, but the hubris of kings. Any imminent constitutional "crisis" was only in the imaginations of the justices.

Three months later, before a House of Representatives appropriations subcommittee considering the Court's proposed budget, Kennedy mocked the entire notion of judicial self-restraint. "Sometimes it is easy to enhance your prestige by not exercising your responsibility," he testi-

fied. "But that has not been the tradition of our Court." In that observation he was correct, obviously. It might have occurred to him, however,
that he was describing a failing rather than a virtue.

Nobody "forced" Kennedy or four of his brethren to hear *Bush v.
Gore*. In the very first instance, they had to choose who chose—whether
the Court or Congress was the proper branch of the government to settle the presidential dispute. The justices chose themselves.

Is this the message the justices intended for their countrymen—that it
is the Court that governs the nation? It's a profound question that didn't
appear to dawn on them, even with a 5-to-4 split. Indeed, they seemed
oblivious to how their ruling would play in the body politic—which, in
retrospect, wasn't surprising, since they were so isolated from it, just as
the constitutional structure planned it. For weeks after *Bush v. Gore*,
O'Connor privately expressed bafflement at the letters that justices
were receiving that excoriated the decision. That was just more evidence
of how far removed the justices were from the real world of politics they
reigned over. Whatever deficiencies a congressman from Nowhereville
might have, he understood he was answerable. Wasn't that a good thing
when the presidency was at stake?

To the extent that one wants to ascribe the worst partisan motives to
the justices, it wasn't as if they had to choose themselves in order to
ensure a Bush victory. Under any plausible scenario, Bush would ultimately have triumphed if Congress had to decide the election.

Either the House of Representatives and the Senate both would have
chosen the Bush slate of electors from Florida and that would've been
the end of it. (This was how the Electoral Count Act of 1887 set it up
when there were competing slates of electors.) Or if those bodies disagreed on competing slates, they would've decided that, since neither
candidate received an absolute majority of electoral votes, the Twelfth
Amendment kicked in. That amendment requires the House to choose
the president, and the House was controlled by the GOP—Bush
would've won. The best the Democrats could have hoped for was Joe
Lieberman becoming vice president. That might've happened because,
under the Twelfth Amendment, the choice of vice president falls to the
Senate, which was divided 50–50 between parties. In that situation,

Gore—still the vice president and, as such, the presiding officer of the Senate—would get to cast the deciding vote.

What if Congress decided the Twelfth Amendment didn't apply at all, and then the House and Senate each chose a different presidential slate of electors—and both refused to budge? This was the Doomsday Scenario, in which Inauguration Day approached with no president-elect. Bill Clinton wasn't very well going to be asked to stay on as "acting" president under the Twentieth Amendment. So, without a president- or vice president–elect, the regular course of presidential succession would happen. That meant Dennis Hastert, the Speaker of the House, would become president. But he'd said he wouldn't take it—he didn't want to relinquish his congressional seat. The next person on the list was the president pro tem of the Senate, traditionally its most senior member. President Strom Thurmond? There's no evidence Tony Kennedy had thought things this far through and was in fact worried about a ninety-eight-year-old man with orange hair running the nation.

For American liberals, December 12, 2000, is a date that will live in infamy. Conservatives mark their history calendars with their own date of disgrace: January 22, 1973, when *Roe v. Wade* was announced and the U.S. Supreme Court proclaimed, 7–2, that a woman has a constitutional right to an abortion. The Bush and Roe decisions are bookends to our modern jurisprudence—the doctrinal chickens of one coming home to roost in the other.

Roe was the culmination, if not the logical conclusion, of forty years of Court decisions on "reproductive rights." On matters of marriage, sex, and procreation, the justices first asserted themselves in 1942. In an Oklahoma case, the Court unanimously threw out a law compelling sterilization for felons with two or more convictions "involving moral turpitude." While Justice William O. Douglas described the right to reproduce as "one of the basic civil rights of man," he knew the Constitution didn't have a clause on that. Instead, he said that because a three-time larcenist was subject to sterilization, while a three-time embezzler was not, the law was unfair. It wasn't much of an explanation, since criminal law treats similar acts differently all the time—homicides can range from murder to manslaughter to self-defense—but it was now constitutional law.

Two decades later, in 1965, the issue moved closer to the home. The justices were asked whether there was, in effect, a right *not* to reproduce. *Griswold v. Connecticut* concerned a statute that banned the use of contraceptives. By a 7-to-2 vote, the Warren Court found the law unconstitutional. This time, Douglas was more honest than in the sterilization case. Candidly admitting the absence of any textual mandate, he found a right of marital privacy implicit in the Constitution as a whole. In a flourish, he declared that "specific guarantees in the Bill of Rights have penumbras, formed by emanations . . . that give them life and substance." How an enforceable penumbra differed from the mere predilection of five justices wasn't something Douglas troubled himself with.

Seven years after that, the High Court extended Griswold to unmarried individuals. The analysis in *Eisenstadt v. Baird* seemed even more wobbly. "If the right of privacy means anything," wrote Justice William Brennan for a 6-to-1 majority, "it is the right of the individual, married or single, to be free from unwarranted governmental intrusions into matters so fundamentally affecting a person as the decision whether to bear or beget a child." It was an astonishing sentence. The Massachusetts law didn't eliminate a person's freedom to forgo having children— abstinence could accomplish that. Rather, it embraced the more limited freedom to have sex without having children. Did Brennan truly believe that "if the right of privacy means *anything,*" it was that latter freedom? This was hyperbole. To most folks, privacy means not having the police barge into your home in the middle of the night without a warrant.

Despite their rhetorical excesses, Griswold and Eisenstadt could be rationalized as decisions more about outrageous government "snooping" and thus within the reach of the Fourth Amendment's proscription "against unreasonable searches." How else could the state enforce the law on private sexual activity? "Would we allow," Douglas asked, "the police to search the sacred precincts of marital bedrooms for telltale signs" of contraceptives? The same logic is present in Eisenstadt, if the word "marital" is removed. Nonetheless, the two rulings, as written, were not so confined to constitutional text. And the next privacy case— *Roe v. Wade*—would expose the perils of that gap.

On that Monday morning in early 1973, Justice Harry Blackmun knew he was about to make history. He'd even invited his wife to the big courtroom to hear him announce the Roe ruling. Reading a summary from the bench, Blackmun said: "We forthwith acknowledge our aware-ness of the sensitive and emotional nature of the abortion contro-versy . . . of the deep and seemingly absolute convictions that the subject inspires. One's philosophy, one's experiences, one's exposure to the raw edges of human existence, one's religious training . . . are all likely to influence and to color one's thinking." It was a remarkably revealing appraisal from a judge. Yet it never mentioned what place *law* might have in reaching a decision.

Neither did Blackmun's fifty-two-page opinion. First, he reviewed the history of attitudes toward abortion since the Persian Empire, point-ing out that abortion laws dated only to the nineteenth century. Next, he surveyed the range of cases that seemed to talk about privacy. Even before the sterilization case, he noted Justice Louis Brandeis's dictum in 1928 about the "right to be let alone." Blackmun then listed Griswold and Eisenstadt, as well as decisions upholding parents' rights to educate their children. From these cases, Blackmun asserted without explana-tion, emerged a "right of privacy" that was "broad enough to encompass a woman's decision whether or not to terminate the pregnancy." The right, he said, was traceable to the Fourteenth Amendment, which pro-hibited states from denying "liberty" to anyone without "due process." And presto!—that was it. With a wave of the judicial wand, abortion had become a constitutional right, without an accounting of why. Now it was merely left to map out an abortion regime that the Court believed would balance the irreconcilable interests of the woman and the fetus.

Blackmun, former counsel to the Mayo Clinic, borrowed from med-icine. He adopted a trimester approach. During the first trimester, the abortion decision would be left to the woman and her physician. In roughly the next three months, up until the point of fetal viability, the state could regulate abortion to keep it safe for the woman. After that, the government—in order to protect the unborn—could prohibit abor-tion, except where necessary to preserve the mother's life or health. In political terms, this was an entirely sensible solution—the kind of pro-posal best delivered from the well of the Senate—even if medical tech-nology would make viability a changing line of demarcation. But as a constitutional matter, it was preposterous. Why did the government's interest in the fetus prevail only after viability? Blackmun's answer: "The fetus then presumably has the capability of meaningful life outside the mother's womb." But as one legal scholar put it, that seemed "to mistake a definition for a syllogism."

The larger problem with Roe was its careless use of legal doctrine. Unlike in Griswold and Eisenstadt, the Court didn't even try to ground its ruling in specific provisions of the Bill of Rights, penumbral or otherwise. And Roe certainly couldn't be rationalized as a decision about "snooping." The doctor's office, regulated by the very grant of a license, may be a private place, but not remotely similar to the bedroom. Instead, the justices said simply that Fourteenth Amendment "liberty" included more than the freedoms cataloged in the Bill of Rights—and privacy was now one of them.

Liberty, of course, can't be so narrowly defined. The fixed constitutional menu, if ever it existed, was suddenly a judicial smorgasbord. Carried to its end point, this seemed to give the justices free rein to obliterate any laws. A generation earlier, the Court had learned the risks of an expansive "liberty" clause; back then, the focus was "economic" rather than "reproductive" liberty. From 1905 to 1937, the Court struck down laws on minimum wages, maximum hours, and other reforms intended to benefit workers—all as unconstitutional restraints on capitalism. Much of the early New Deal met a similar fate. In time, the justices did an about-face.

The dissenters in Roe, and its academic critics over the years, feasted on the Court's hypocrisy in resuscitating the "liberty" clause to suit its agenda. Yet listen to Rehnquist in Roe. "If the Texas statute were to prohibit an abortion even where a mother's life is in jeopardy," he wrote, there would be "little doubt" the law would fall. Says who? Why couldn't a legislature conclude that a healthy fetus overrides the interests of a feeble mother? What if she were carrying twins? The point is that even Rehnquist couldn't avoid inserting his own values. His disagreement with Blackmun seemed to have been only about result.

The core of *Roe v. Wade* wasn't about "a woman's right to choose" or gender equality, or whatever other good intentions Blackmun might have had. Its essence was about mistrust of legislatures and, thereby, the people. At the time Roe was decided, most state legislatures were wrestling with the tragic choice that abortion reflected, between fetal life

and personal freedom. Some legislatures opted for keeping the procedure illegal, others greatly liberalized regulations. The political struggle
was ongoing—the "pro-choice" lobby won some, the "pro-life" move-
ment won others. What a legislature did or didn't do this session could
always be revisited next time. Such was politics at work, and what happened smoothly in many countries of the world as consensus of sorts
was reached. If the United States survived slavery and segregation, it,
too, would have endured political strife over abortion, whichever way it
came out. For women, for the unborn, for society—the outcome was
important. But so also was the way we reached it.

By issuing Roe, the Court removed the impassioned moral debate
from the political forum, where it was best ventilated and where even
the loser could rest assured that tomorrow was another day. That safety
valve was turned shut after abortion became constitutionalized and
therefore no longer fair game for legislative experimentation and democratic compromise. Roe jump-started the conservative judicial revolution, whose M.O. was to use the courts just as the liberals had—except
for opposite ends. The GOP's objection wasn't to judicial activism, but
to *liberal* judicial activism. The way to counter it wasn't institutional
restraint, but *conservative* judicial activism ushered in by a new roster of
justices. In the modern judicial culture, turnabout was fair play. *Roe v.
Wade* galvanized and radicalized the Republican party, helping Ronald
Reagan's rise to power. Abortion became central in every presidential
election after 1973 and it is why, under Republican administrations, the
Supreme Court veered to the right, even if Roe never was overturned.

One justice of the Court had eloquently warned of the dangers of
"the Imperial Judiciary." Quoting Lincoln, he wrote: "The candid citizen must confess that, if the policy of the government upon vital questions affecting the whole people is to be irrevocably fixed by decisions
of the Supreme Court . . . the people will have ceased to be their own
rulers, having to that extent practically resigned their government into
the hands of that eminent tribunal." The justice was Antonin Scalia, dissenting in *Planned Parenthood v. Casey* in 1992, when the Court
refused to throw out Roe. What had Roe done? It "fanned into life an
issue that has inflamed our national politics in general," Scalia grieved,
"and has obscured with its smoke the selection of justices to this Court,
in particular, ever since."

Did Scalia have such a short memory by the time *Bush v. Gore* arrived at his "eminent tribunal"? *Bush v. Gore* continues to "inflame our national politics" and is certain to infect the appointments process for new justices throughout George W. Bush's administration.

It is a weak society, afraid of its own representative democracy, that countenances the Court to resolve its hardest choices—whether they be about abortion or the presidency. It is a sign of laziness, not creativity, that justices blessed with absolute power allow themselves to short-circuit the political process instead of sending disputes right back whence they came. While politics may be messy, it is a mess born of the people and the choices they make. Democracy can defend itself. In a republic, under a constitution, we should rarely need to be saved from ourselves.

George W. Bush may be forgotten soon enough. His presidency is accidental and the tranquil times don't cry out for great leadership. Al Gore may wind up no more than a historical footnote. But Bush and Gore are not what count. In the end, the legacy of the thirty-seven days is what the Supreme Court wrought; that is what will be debated years from now. And the legacy of *Bush v. Gore* is just the same as it was with *Roe v. Wade*: One is about morality, the other about voting rights, but together, they are of a piece. The one is the other come full circle. Once upon a time, it was the liberals who basked in the glow of judicial salvation. Today, the tables have turned and the conservatives get to gloat. *Bush v. Gore* avenged *Roe v. Wade*. But one day, if the dynamic doesn't change, the liberals will reign again—and they will reap what the conservatives now sow. It's tough to be sympathetic with any of them. What matters to them all is the result—the reasoning and principles be damned.

The American system has forever boasted that it is "a government of laws and not of men." It is not so. In the ideological pitch and roll represented by the Supreme Court's journey from *Roe v. Wade* to *Bush v. Gore*, there is a kind of poetic justice: He who lives by the judicial sword dies by the judicial sword. The symmetry seems in the nature of things, the balance quite right. But the Constitution weeps.

acknowledgments

I watched Election Night 2000 with the same fascination and horror as the next person. In the five weeks that followed, I kept coming up with more questions than anyone was providing answers. This book is the result. It allowed me to return to my days as a legal affairs journalist, and gave me the chance to explore political currents that made the thirty-seven days of Florida unique.

I am grateful, as always, to work for a magazine that lets its writers pursue outside projects—all the more when it does so repeatedly. I'm fortunate to have the support of Mark Whitaker and the other *Newsweek* editors. I owe special thanks to Ken Auchincloss and Peter McGrath. Ken is not only an editor nonpareil but a Mets fan. Peter shares my interests in high-tech culture and has a sense of humor. I'm lucky to have both as colleagues.

Thanks to other friends and co-workers for indulging my queries, pleas, and complaints: Jonathan Alter, Adam Bryant, Tommy DeFrank, Norman Dorsen, Dave Friedman, Stephen Gillers, Tita Gillespie, Dana Gordon, Rose Goulbourne, Shirley Gray, Gerry Gunther, Michael Isikoff, Joe LaBracio, Lucy Morgan, Tim Nickens, Keith Olbermann, David Pike, Peter Richmond, Adam Rogers, Paul Saffo, John Schwartz,

John Sexton, Steve Shabad, Gary Simon, Neil Skene, Mark Vamos, Stephanie Vardavas, Mike Wilson, and Publius, who knows who he is.

E-mail is a wonderful device for getting "just a few more details," but only if folks are generous enough to respond. (Mea culpa: I managed to ask more than a thousand times.) In both the Bush and Gore campaigns, a group of individuals—some of whom are included in the list of interviewees at the end of the book—extended me courtesies above and beyond the call: Nick Baldick, Josh Bolten, Walter Dellinger, Michael Feldman, Ben Ginsberg, Tommy Goldstein, Ron Klain, Chris Lehane, Terry Lewis, David Morehouse, Barry Richard, Christina Roberts, Mac Stipanovich, Larry Tribe, Margaret Tutwiler, and Craig Waters.

Thanks also to: Gil Sperling and his family, for their Washington hospitality (but no thanks to their cat); Marty Sklar, for giving up tennis in order to read and read; Joel Gilbertson-White, senior engineer at Sonic Foundry, for rescuing audiotapes; and Jean Brown, who remains the master of transcription.

I am indebted to my research assistant, Richard Rubin, Duke University, class of 2000. His organizational skills and observations were invaluable. Despite his lack of appreciation for puns, I want to especially acknowledge his careful reading of the manuscript under intense time pressure.

This is my second time being published by William Morrow/ HarperCollins. Henry Ferris is a good egg, a wise counselor, and the champion this book needed. I'd say more, but he wants the final version of this page *right now*. At ICM, Kris Dahl and her assistant, Jud Laghi, put up with me. They are patient people and I thank them, along with the inestimable Esther Newberg, the Pedro Martinez of literary agents.

My wife, Audrey Feinberg, is my best friend and my best editor. I can't think of a better combination. Without her, for so many reasons, I could not possibly have gotten through this project.

The advantage of working at home is getting to see your children a lot more. The disadvantage is having to tell them too often you don't have time to play. Yes, Joshua and Nathaniel, the book is done. Let's have a catch today.

Sources and Bibliography

The principal sources for this book are my own interviews and observations of the election proceedings, as well as court records and contemporaneous journalistic accounts of others.

Between early December 2000 and late July 2001, I interviewed the following individuals:

John Attanasio
Eli Attie
Jenny Backus
Charlie Baker
Jim Baker III
Jackie Baldick
Nick Baldick
Joe Bizzaro
David Boies
Mary Boies
Josh Bolten
Bob Butterworth
Nikki Ann Clark

Hillary Rodham Clinton
Bill Daley
Jack Danforth
Tommy DeFrank
Walter Dellinger
Marie Therese Dominguez
Dexter Douglass
Gerald Ensley
Randy Enwright
Mark Fabiani
Michael Feldman
Ed Fleming
Elizabeth Gianini

Ben Ginsberg
Tommy Goldstein
Gerry Hammond
Paul Hancock
Jane Harding
Katherine Harris
Mark Herron
Banner Higgins
Jen Howard
Frank Hunger
Ron Klain
Gerald Kogan
Ted Koppel
Larry Kramer
Kendra Krause
Chris Lehane
Fran Lewis
Terry Lewis
Joe Lieberman
Goody Marshall
Ben McKay
Kiki McLean
David Morehouse
Gillie Muller

Tim Nickens
Ted Olson
Vanessa Opperman
Rick Pildes
Jonathan Prince
Barry Richard
Clay Roberts
Karl Rove
Joe Sandler
Charles Schumer
Neil Skene
Chesterfield Smith
Mac Stipanovich
Graham Streett
George Terwilliger III
Larry Tribe
Margaret Tutwiler
Steve Uhlfelder
Jason Unger
Craig Waters
Bobby White
Michael Whouley
Natalie Zellner
Bob Zoellick

Both George W. Bush and Al Gore declined to be interviewed on the record.

Except for Terry Lewis and Nikki Ann Clark, cited above, no judges (or justices, from either the U.S. Supreme Court or the Florida Supreme Court) agreed to be interviewed on the record. Those who did agree to talk did so on a not-for-attribution basis. According to the conventions of reporting, as I agreed to with these sources, I do not indicate here by name that I spoke to them. Nor do I attribute any of their remarks to them. But I did use their accounts of conversations or facts they disclosed. I recognize this doesn't let the reader know whether the source of a specific quotation is the speaker himself or herself, or instead is someone else—clerk, colleague, or friend—who heard the remark and recounted it to me. There is no perfect way to deal with unattributed material, but it is a compromise I reached in order to provide information to the reader that I deem reliable.

Aside from members of the judiciary, I interviewed fourteen other people who talked on the condition that they would not be identified as sources. Most of them weren't critical to the narrative, with the exception of some material in chapter 10 and the epilogue concerning the U.S. Supreme Court. In all but a few places, however, I have not used unattributed quotations.

In addition to my interviews, I had to wade through the court records that form the core of the state and federal litigations. Almost all these opinions, briefs, transcripts, motions, and exhibits are available at three excellent archival Web sites. They are maintained by the U.S. Supreme Court, www.supremecourtus.gov/florida.html; the Florida Supreme Court, www.flcourts.org/pubinfo/election; and Stanford University, http://election2000.stanford.edu.

Beyond my interviews and the court records, I immersed myself in the journalistic coverage of the thirty-seven days of Florida, provided by newspapers, magazines, the networks, and, in a few instances, the Web. Where pertinent, I have cited sources directly in the text, especially those Florida publications that on occasion had exclusive information. In particular, among newspapers, I relied on the superb reporting of the *Washington Post,* the *New York Times,* the *Los Angeles Times, USA Today,* the *St. Petersburg Times,* and the *Palm Beach Post.* The *Washington Post*'s eight-part series on the election, which ran between January 28 and February 4, 2001, was invaluable in providing initial leads and filling in pieces of the narrative. Among magazines, I acknowledge my preference for *Newsweek*—I work for it and know my colleagues; some of the material about the U.S. Supreme Court is based on my journalistic efforts for *Newsweek.* On the Web, the postings on slate.com and kausfiles.com were notably smart and provocative.

Books were of most use to me in thinking about the institutional role of the U.S. Supreme Court. There are also several worthwhile books already published on the 2000 election. This is a complete list of the books I used in this project:

Abraham, Henry L. *Justices and Presidents: A Political History of Appointments to the Supreme Court* (2d ed.). New York: Oxford University Press, 1985.

Baum, Lawrence. *The Supreme Court* (4th ed.). Washington D.C.: Congressional Quarterly Press, 1992.

Bickel, Alexander M. *The Least Dangerous Branch: The Supreme Court at the Bar of Politics* (2d ed.). New Haven, Conn.: Yale University Press, 1962.

Blaustein, Albert P., and Roy M. Mersky. *The First Hundred Justices: Statistical Studies on the Supreme Court of the United States*. Hamden, Conn.: Shoe String Press, 1978.

Bok, Derek. *The Trouble with Government*. Cambridge, Mass.: Harvard University Press, 2001.

Bork, Robert H. *The Tempting of America: The Political Seduction of the Law*. New York: Free Press, 1990.

Bridger, David, ed. *The New Jewish Encyclopedia*. New York: Behrman House, 1962.

Brock, William R. *Conflict and Transformation: The United States, 1844–1877*. Harmondsworth, England: Penguin Books, 1973.

Bronner, Ethan. *Battle for Justice: How the Bork Nomination Shook America*. New York: W. W. Norton, 1989.

Dershowitz, Alan M. *Supreme Injustice: How the High Court Hijacked Election 2000*. New York: Oxford University Press, 2001.

Dionne, E.J., Jr., and William Kristol, ed. *Bush v. Gore: The Court Cases and the Commentary*. Washington, D.C.: Brookings Institution Press, 2001.

Ely, John Hart. *Democracy and Distrust: A Theory of Judicial Review.* Cambridge, Mass.: Harvard University Press, 1980.

Glendon, Mary Ann. *Rights Talk: The Impoverishment of Political Discourse.* New York: Free Press, 1991.

Gunther, Gerald. *Learned Hand: The Man and the Judge.* New York: Alfred A. Knopf, 1994.

Issacharoff, Samuel, Pamela S. Karlan, and Richard H. Pildes. *When Elections Go Bad: The Law of Democracy and the Presidential Election of 2000.* New York: Foundation Press, 2001.

Mayer, Jane, and Jill Abramson. *Strange Justice: The Selling of Clarence Thomas.* Boston: Houghton Mifflin, 1994.

Political Staff of *The Washington Post. Deadlock: The Inside Story of America's Closest Election.* New York: Public Affairs, 2001.

Posner, Richard A. *Breaking the Deadlock: The 2000 Election, the Constitution, and the Courts.* Princeton, N.J.: Princeton University Press, 2001.

Potter, David M. *The Impending Crisis: 1848–1861.* New York: Harper & Row, 1976.

Rodell, Fred. *Nine Men: A Political History of the Supreme Court from 1790 to 1955.* New York: Random House, 1955.

Rosenblatt, Roger. *Life Itself: Abortion in the American Mind.* New York: Random House, 1992.

Savage, David G. *Turning Right: The Making of the Rehnquist Supreme Court.* New York: John Wiley & Sons, 1992.

Scalia, Antonin. *A Matter of Interpretation: Federal Courts and the Law.* Princeton, N.J.: Princeton University Press, 1997.

Silverstein, Mark. *Judicious Choices: The New Politics of Supreme Court Confirmations*. New York: W. W. Norton, 1994.

Sinclair, Mick. *Florida: The Rough Guide*. London: Penguin Books, 1993.

Specter, Arlen. *Passion for Truth: From Finding JFK's Single Bullet to Questioning Anita Hill to Impeaching Clinton*. New York: William Morrow, 2000.

Sunstein, Cass R. *One Case at a Time: Judicial Minimalism on the Supreme Court*. Cambridge, Mass.: Harvard University Press, 1999.

Tapper, Jake. *Down and Dirty: The Plot to Steal the Presidency*. Boston: Little, Brown, 2001.

Tribe, Laurence H. *American Constitutional Law* (2d ed.). Mineola, N.Y.: Foundation Press, 1988.

——. *Abortion: The Clash of Absolutes*. New York: W. W. Norton, 1990.

Woodward, Bob, and Scott Armstrong. *The Brethren: Inside the Supreme Court*. New York: Simon & Schuster, 1979.

index